Knowing
Your
Place

Knowing Your Place

Rural Identity and Cultural Hierarchy

Edited by
Barbara Ching
and
Gerald W. Creed

Routledge
New York & London

Published in 1997 by
Routledge
29 West 35th Street
New York, NY 10001

Published in Great Britain by
Routledge
11 New Fetter Lane
London EC4P 4EE

Library of Congress Cataloging-in-Publication Data

    Knowing your place: rural identity and cultural hierarchy / edited by
Barbara Ching and Gerald Creed
      p.   cm.
    Includes bibliographical references and index.
    ISBN 0-415-91544-9 (hc). — ISBN 0-415-91545-7 (pbk).
    1. Sociology, Rural. 2. Rural conditions I. Ching, Barbara, 1958–.
II. Creed, Gerald, 1958–.
HT421.K549   1996
307.72—dc20
                                             96-28866
                                              CIP

CONTENTS

PREFACE

In the midst of their stirring manifesto against the bourgeoisie, Marx
and Engels begrudge this class one accomplishment: "It has created
enormous cities, has greatly increased the urban population as compared with the rural, and has thus rescued a considerable part of the
population from the idiocy of rural life." In spite of the vicissitudinous
fortunes of Marxist theory, this perspective on place pervades contemporary social thought. We will argue, instead, that the bourgeoisie is
getting credit where none is due. The essays in this volume show how
rural places and the people who identify with them retain their vitality despite repeated claims to the contrary. We thus focus on rural
places to challenge the urban gaze and its constant sightings of rural
idiocy. But just as there is more than one place to know, there is more
than one way to know places, and there are many ways to construct
identities that are tied to place. An interdisciplinary collection of
essays thus seems to us the best way to open a new approach to the
subject of rural and urban places in the politics of identity. As Richard
Handler noted in his review of Lawrence Levine's *Highbrow/Lowbrow*
(see *American Ethnologist* 19: 818–24), anthropologists have paid
almost no attention to cultural hierarchies. Thus, even though many
have studied rural people and places, they have generaly failed to recognize the systematic *devaluation* of the rustic as a source of identity.
While the disciplines of cultural studies and literary criticism have
enthusiastically taken up the issue of cultural hierarchies and identity-
construction, they focus primarily on urban contexts, ignoring rural
culture altogether. Bringing together these approaches, then, forces us
to *recognize rusticity*.

The idea for this book grew out of a conversation between the edi-
tors; it first took the form of a panel at the 1993 meeting of the American
Anthropological Association in Washington D.C. The panel, entitled
"Constructing Cultural Hierarchies: Rural and Popular Distinctions,"
also included papers by Karen Frojen, Richard Handler, and Donna
Kerner which could not be included in this book. Their analyses, how-

ever, were crucial to our evolving understanding of the issues discussed here, so we thank them for their inspiration. Additional papers were solicited from Marc Edelman, Aaron Fox, and William Maxwell. We are grateful to all the contributors for their encouragement, suggestions, and criticisms; we couldn't have done it without them. Kay Easson, Lesley Ferris, Allison Graham, Kevin Hagopian, Aisha Khan, Susan Lees, William O'Donnell, Susan Scheckel, and Elizabeth Sheehan provided excellent advice, as did our anonymous readers for Routledge. We know they saved us from various idiocies, rural and urban, although no doubt we persisted in some. We thank Marlie Wasserman for seeing the value of this book in its early stages, and Christine Cipriani for seeing it through the final stages. The English Department of The University of Memphis and the Anthropology Department of Hunter College provided much material support. The Eugene Lang Junior Faculty Awards Program at Hunter also provided financial assistance. Michael Ching and Gene Oyler deserve a special place for their enthusiasm, patience, and encouragement.

INTRODUCTION ~ GERALD W. CREED
AND BARBARA CHING

Recognizing Rusticity

Identity and the Power of Place

ESSENTIAL secrets of power often lurk in the last *place* where you would think to look. Finding them is inevitably difficult, but the value of seeking lies in the possibilities for self-determination that these secrets promise. We thus propose looking in the places that are culturally the most remote: in the sticks, in the middle of nowhere, in the backwaters of this country and many others, in a word, in the countryside. While the forces of (post)modernity insistently direct our attention to city life, no degree of "development" can obliterate the continuing economic importance and cultural distinctiveness of the countryside, where food is produced and human life sustained. As Raymond Williams wrote in *The Country and the City*,

> If we are to survive at all, we shall have to develop and extend our
> working agricultures. The common idea of a lost rural world is then not

only an abstraction of this or that stage in a continuing history. . . . It is
in direct contradiction to any effective shape of our future. . . . It is one
of the most striking deformations of industrial capitalism that one of our
most central and urgent and necessary activities could have been so
displaced . . . that it can be plausibly associated only with the past or
with distant lands. (1973: 300)

Williams was inspired to write his book because he knew the coun-
try/city distinction from personal experience, and he believed that the
attendant tension was "for many millions of people a direct and
intense preoccupation" (1973: 3). Indeed, more than twenty years after
Williams made this observation, the experiential significance of the
rural/urban distinction still holds. In 1995, urban America took a new
look at the "heartland" through the ruins of the Oklahoma City bomb-
ing and found it more threatening than threatened—the home of des-
perate rural militia with expansionist agenda. Two years earlier in
China, the ranking Communist Party official told participants in an
"Agricultural Work Conference" that increasing rural/urban differentiation was threatening the country's political and social stability (BBC
World Service, October 19, 1993). Political events in eastern Europe
seem to bear out the Chinese leader's warnings: post-communist elections throughout the region reveal uncompromising rural/urban
polarities (Creed 1993; 1995). In the former Yugoslavia, Misha Glenny
suggests that the battle for Sarajevo was not a nationalist conflict, but
rather "a struggle between the rural and the urban, the primitive and
the cosmopolitan, and above all, between chaos and reason" (1992: 38).

As these examples suggest, the rural/urban distinction underlies
many of the power relations that shape the experiences of people in
nearly every culture. Not surprisingly, then, many cultural activities
operate to keep people in their places even in the face of global demographic and economic dislocations such as rural to urban migration
and industrialization. Consequently, the rural/urban distinction signifies far more powerfully than physical appearances suggest; inhabitants of areas where town and country seem nearly indistinguishable
may nevertheless elaborate a difference through extensive cultural

discourse. Where visible differences do exist, cultural oppositions may exaggerate them and erase countervailing similarities (e.g., Caro Baroja 1963: 38). Indeed, people live the rural/urban distinction through mundane cultural activities such as their selection of music (country versus rap) and their choice of clothing (cowboy boots versus wing tips)—means through which identity is commonly expressed. Hank Williams fans and chic Parisians eating "peasant food" in three-star restaurants make statements about who they are and where they belong with these choices. Recreational hunters and avid gardeners sustain an identification with the countryside long after their address-es and incomes divorce these activities from economic necessity (Marks 1991). Such choices shape identity in concert with less flexible markers of place such as regional accents and hometown origins. In other words, the rural/urban opposition generates not only political and economic conflict but social identification as well.

Given the pervasiveness of the rural/urban opposition and its related significance in the construction of identity, it is remarkable that the explosion of scholarly interest in identity politics has general-ly failed to address the rural/urban axis. The resulting representation of social distinctions primarily in terms of race, class, and gender thus masks the extent to which these categories are inflected by place iden-tification. For example, social theorists generally fail to acknowledge that a rural woman's experience of gender inequality may be quite dif-ferent from that of an urban woman, or that racial oppression in the city can take a different form from that in the countryside. As we will argue in detail, contemporary discussions of the fragmentation and recombination of identities locate this process almost exclusively in the city. Conversely, the few scholars who explicitly discuss rural identity have generally failed to connect it to these larger theoretical debates; instead they have positioned their work in other specialties such as community ideology (Hummon 1990) and rural development (Fitchen 1991).

Such blindness reflects other political and economic processes that have globally "marked" the rural end of the place spectrum. In many spheres, the urban has come to be the assumed reference when terms are used that could in theory refer to both rural and urban subjects. For example, *The New York Times Magazine* recently published a photographic essay on farm animals with the subtitle "The barnyard animals live at a distance from us now" (Weil and Klinkenborg 1995). Even though the magazine is read throughout the world, the authors and editors felt no need to specify that "us" refers only to urban readers. Even where rural residents outnumber urbanites, they can become the culturally marked category (Pigg 1992). The fact that we must make a point of clearly marking the rural reveals the cultural hierarchies that make place such a politically and personally charged category. As with other dimensions of identity, it is the marked/marginalized group that experiences the distinction more intimately and for whom it becomes a more significant element of identity. In this case, the urban-identified can confidently assume the cultural value of their situation while the rural-identified must struggle to gain recognition. Ironically, the rural-identified may experience their marginalization as both invisibility and as a spectacularly exaggerated denigration. At either extreme, though, they are placed as "low others" (Stallybrass and White 1986: 5–6). Thus we argue that neither an apparent decline in the demographic and economic salience of the contemporary rural sector nor any convergence of rural and urban lifestyles should be allowed to overshadow the continuing significance of rural-based identities. In order to signal both the importance of these places and the power relations concealed there, we propose familiar terms which jarringly remind us of the potential for imbuing the apparently hard facts of demography and geography with cultural meaning and value: identities based in the country can be considered *rustic* while those associated with the city are *urbane*, or, more vernacularly, *sophisticated*. Presented in these antithetical terms, the possibility of a culturally valuable *rusticity* becomes difficult to imagine in spite of the *rurality* we often sentimentally associate with a sublimely unpeopled wilderness or a severe agrarian past.

This collection, then, fruitfully returns to places which contemporary thought has rendered almost unthinkable. The essays confirm that people concretely live the distinction between the country and the city. Thus, we insist on the need to maintain the visibility and vitality of the rustic and the rural, not only for the sake of the food supply, but also for the analytical possibilities opened up by attention to life at the rustic margin. We focus on three interrelated issues: the nearly omnipresent cultural hierarchies, often buttressed by political and economic stratification, in which rustic people (wherever they reside) are marginalized and their culture devalued vis à vis urban(e) culture; the radical embracing of that marginality by many people in order to contest the late twentieth century's hegemonic urbanity and its associated socio-political structures; and the inability of many scholars and social commentators to see rural and urban places within the model of identity politics so central to postmodern theory. Since this threefold focus raises questions that touch several academic disciplines, we have taken a broad, interdisciplinary approach to "knowing" place. This collaboration reveals the interaction between processes that signify rusticity and conditions that shape rural life, but it violates many disciplinary conventions: in seeking to locate place identities in cultural hierarchies, we move without qualification from personal experience to ethnographic accounts, literary traditions, and popular culture. Still, we make no claim to an exhaustive survey. Rather than reciting all the evidence for rustic identification, we focus instead on why it has been overlooked and how such avoidance can be overcome. In so doing we are able to suggest how such identities are created and change in relation to historical, political, and economic processes, thereby acknowledging a difference that cultural studies and the more established disciplines are in danger of eliding.

We begin by discussing intellectual traditions that hinder discussion of place. We then explore the forces that so often place the rustic at the bottom of cultural hierarchies, first analyzing the relativity of the place categories involved and then interrogating familiar discourses that vilify the city and glorify the country. We conclude by probing potential interactions between rusticity and other dimensions of identity, widening the possibilities for a unified challenge to diverse systems of stratification.

THE DISPLACED COUNTRY

Despite the significance of the rural/urban distinction, contemporary cultural research and theory have focused little attention on it. One reason for this neglect is the lack of a conceptual vocabulary for articulating the blend of psychic, cultural, and "real" geography that concerns us here. While many social scientific studies of rural societies and many artistic works take the rural as their theme, the very attempt to distinguish identity from theme, rusticity from rurality, exposes not only our limited intellectual framework but also the extent to which this element of identity has been naturalized. While terms such as gender have particulars—masculine and feminine—the over-arching term "gender" allows us to see that both are socially constructed and culturally flexible variants. Likewise, individuals who speak of themselves as middle-class speak simultaneously and implicitly of the class system which conveys the meanings of their own situation. However, without an over-arching term to speak of place-based identity, the dialectical construction of such affiliations becomes obscure and inscrutable; we can speak only of specifics such as rural and urban, and, as we have already argued, speaking of the rural is increasingly difficult. To fill this gap, we are pointedly calling these categories (distinctions) "place" although it must be stressed that physical location is not a necessary component of an identification with the rural or the urban. Well-grounded farmers and uprooted urban cowboys can both be considered rustics. The point, after all, is the social construction of identity.

At the same time, our insistence on geographically rooted places distinguishes our use of the term from the plethora of current "place" and "space" studies, even those focused directly on identity. Many recent books and articles which purport to be about "place" simply conflate the term with the more fashionable components of identity, using it to argue that one must situate oneself in a nexus of class, race, gender and ethnic possibilities. For example, in *Place and the Politics of Identity*, editors Michael Keith and Steve Pile use the terms "space" and "place" nearly interchangeably in their exploration of identity formation, and while they argue that "the spatial" can comprise "real spaces, imaginary spaces, or symbolic spaces" (1993: 35), they never explicitly discuss traditional place designations such as the country and the city. Similarly, while James Duncan and David Ley's collection *Place/Culture/Representation* argues that "any interpretation of landscape" is colored by "cultural, economic and political processes" (1993: 12), they, too, mention only the nearly canonical identity components as aspects of the symbolically charged landscape. Such use of the term "place" to encapsulate various identity components further erases the role of "real" places in identity formation. We argue instead for a theoretical middle ground in which "place" can be metaphoric yet still refer to a particular physical environment and its associated socio-cultural qualities. In this view, place becomes a *grounded* metaphor. Our collection, then, insists on marking the conceptual and experiential difference between the country and the city by uncovering and extending the longstanding discourse which constructs these differences.

A purely metaphoric place emerges from postmodern social theory, and this intellectual trend blocks the country from view in still other ways. Postmodern social theory's stable reference point has been the city; it unquestioningly posits an urbanized subject without considering the extent to which such a subject is constructed by its conceptual opposition to the rustic (Ching 1993). In much postmodern social theory, the country as a vital place simply doesn't exist. The influential French philosopher Henri Lefebvre (1970: 7), for example, simply asserts that the contemporary situation is one of "complete urbanization."[1] This placement is tacitly assumed in more recent studies of the postmodern: Marxist theorist Fredric Jameson (1991) feels no need to justify his equation of the postmodern with the urban, and although cultural geographers have argued that the postmodern condition demands more attention to space, in practice their focus has been almost entirely urban. In his *Postmodern Geographies: The Reassertion of Space in Critical Social Theory*, Edward W. Soja claims that his discipline must assert the primacy of space over history and recognize the role of "formative geography" in human experience (1989: 2). Yet when Soja turns his attention to such "formative geography," he simply reaffirms the traditional terms of development and underdevelopment, tacitly assuming that the city will eventually engulf the country:

> To be urbanized still means to adhere, to be made an adherent, a believer in a specified collective ideology rooted in extensions of *polis* (politics, policy, polity, police) and *civitas* (civil, civic, citizen, civilian, civilization). In contrast, the population beyond the reach of the urban is comprised of *idiotes*, from the Greek root *idios*, meaning `one's own, a private person', unlearned in the ways of the *polis*. . . . Thus to speak of the `idiocy' of rural life or the urbanity of its opposition is primarily a statement of relative political socialization and spatialization, of the degree of adherence/separation in the collective social order. (1989: 234–35)

In spite of Soja's careful qualification, he argues that only the urban is worthy of critical attention; in his eyes, rusticity is not only idiotic but justifiably marginal and vestigial.

Similar assumptions have animated much of the new discipline of cultural studies and explain why its subject matter has been predominantly urban. While visions like Andreas Huyssen's *After the Great Divide* (1986) and Jim Collins' *Uncommon Cultures* (1989) posit a breakdown of cultural hierarchies into a diverse range of unranked cultural choices, they do not obliterate hierarchy to the extent that they promise. For instance, Collins' examples of diversity—detective fiction, performance art, cult films, etc.—simply inaugurate a new canon of sophisticated entertainments which, no matter how diverse, can still operate as high cultures to mark rustic lowness. In other words, one of the things that these so-called "uncommon cultures" do have in common is their reliance on a relatively affluent, educated, and mobile consumer. The class biases of this perspective hardly need to be pointed out, and its place biases should be equally clear. Indeed, the very silence surrounding non-urban forms of popular culture provides evidence of a persistent cultural hierarchy that devalues, even erases, the rustic. In the near explosion of work exploring popular culture and identity, studies of rap and fashion display abound while moonshining and harvest rituals have yet to find their analyst.[2] Primers introducing students to this new discipline systematically neglect place. Brantlinger's *Crusoe's Footprints* (1990), for example, features a chapter on race, class, and gender, and the landmark Routledge *Cultural Studies* anthology reinforces the emphasis on this trinity with the addition of ethnicity (Grossberg et al. 1992); no essays propose concomitant attention to place. The neglect of rural places in particular is most explicitly captured by the titles of several prominent works in cultural studies: Celeste Olalquiaga's *Megalopolis: Contemporary Cultural Sensibilities* (1992), Iain Chambers' *Popular Culture: The Metropolitan Experience* (1986), and *The Journal of Urban and Cultural Studies* (founded 1990). In their fascination with the urban "low," then, the most prominent forms of cultural studies overlook the rural low*er* and thus fail to recognize how place may shape identities and cultural hierarchies. In hopes of crossing the "great divide," cultural studies may actually replace traditional high culture with a popular culture that is primarily urban and still relatively privileged.

At the same time, there is no inherent reason that place as a grounded metaphor could not be incorporated into contemporary cultural studies. Indeed, Raymond Williams is often considered a founder of the field, and *The Country and the City* clearly included this kind of attention to place. John Storey (1993), in his *Introductory Guide to Cultural Theory and Popular Culture*, and Graeme Turner (1990), in his *Introduction to British Cultural Studies*, both include sections on Williams' works in their accounts of the origins of their subject, yet oddly enough, neither Turner nor Storey discuss *The Country and the City* in their pages devoted to Williams. Likewise, the silence of postmodern theorists such as Harvey and Jameson nevertheless leaves room for an engagement with place, identity, and cultural hierarchies. Harvey, in particular, argues for attention to social and material geography and suspects that postmodernism is a high-culture fad (1989: 7). Jameson, too, argues that resistance to postmodernism, or the "cultural logic of late capitalism," will require some new ability to situate oneself (1991: 51–54). The point, then, is not that cultural studies cannot consider rural places as a component of identity, but rather that it has yet to do so. Indeed, when read with place in mind, existing work in cultural studies and postmodern theory suggests that the very attention to place that this collection pays can be a crucial form of cultural awareness and resistance.

Reinforcing the urban bias of postmodern theory is another barrier that shields places from academic sight: the identity politics of being and becoming an intellectual. In the West, few intellectuals have deep rural roots, and for those who do, education often severs these connections. The traditional pedagogical agenda, with its emphasis on enlightenment through the liberal arts, has long been opposed to the supposed essence of rusticity—lack of cultural sophistication and a preference for practical know-how over erudition. Indeed in Soja's variation on the Marxist distaste for rural idiocy, knowledge itself is urban. It is not surprising, then, that writers on the rural situation, from academics to essayists, have described education as tantamount to an urbanization of the mind (Kohn 1988; Nagengast 1991: 123; Weber 1976). Novelist Wallace Stegner, describing his rather traditional education in the Saskatchewan prairie, puts it bluntly: "I was educated for the wrong place" (1962: 24).

When intellectuals steeped in years of educational displacement do consider rural issues, they often turn to schemes of "development" and "improvement" which validate their own culture or place. For example, Romanian intellectuals in the interwar period who claimed to speak on behalf of the peasants actually distanced and silenced them:

> The forms of distancing varied from one group to another, but nearly all had the effect of inviting the state in and giving it work to do, and of widening the chasm between the peasants and those who claimed to speak in their defense. . . . Behind the celebrations of peasant innocence, the many proposals for reform of the countryside, and the rhetoric of disinterested concern, then, lies a celebration of the peasantry's elite patrons, set firmly apart on the far side of a class barrier. (Verdery 1991: 57–58)[3]

Indeed, what peasants learn from intellectuals tends to reinforce the hegemony of the urbane—they accept the central value of erudition and begin to see themselves in dire need of what intellectuals can provide (Baumann 1987: 18). Even when intellectuals champion rural causes, they are usually not motivated to explore the cultural hierarchy that prefers their erudition to "rural idiocy." To do so would undermine their authority and their laudable role as spokespeople for the disadvantaged rustic. Yet to speak *for* rustics without questioning the forces that make this ventriloquism necessary ultimately reinforces the very cultural hierarchies it ostensibly challenges.

Given the thinly-veiled self-congratulation and condescension that informs such intellectual efforts, it is not surprising that self-consciously rustic people often become emphatically anti-intellectual. Rural Bulgarians, for example, often complained more vehemently about urban intellectuals than about the Communist Party bosses who actually made the policies that disadvantaged them. Likewise, American country music songs often target intellectuals rather than corporate executives or politicians as the primary oppositional "other." Charlie Daniels (1990) follows a lyrical call for "a few more rednecks" with the threat that "you intellectuals might not like it but there's nothing you can do," while Aaron Tippin (1993) glorifies the "*pride, honor, and dignity*" of the "working man's Ph.D." It is tempting for intellectuals to dismiss such criticism as "rural idiocy," but once we recognize anti-intellectualism as an aspect of identity politics, we need not take it personally. Instead, we can see it as a part of urban hegemony: as long as rustic discontent is directed exclusively at intellectuals, it poses no great political threat. Nevertheless, when rustics target intellectuals or champion conservative causes, they render their identities less interesting to scholars fascinated by the resistance potential of identity politics. These intellectuals thereby collude with "liberal" urbanites in casting rustics as homogeneous oppressors of other marginalized groups. Thus demonized, rustics seem to merit whatever degradation and neglect they may experience.

Finally, many intellectuals seem hesitant to pursue identities grounded in the rural/urban distinction because "real" places seem so antithetical to constructionist thought. Linked to something as seemingly fixed as land, rural identities appear more immutable and "essential" than radical constructionism would allow. Thus, even when such intellectuals make a conscious effort to discuss actual places, they may ignore the material realities that separate the country from the city. Like many pathologists of the postmodern condition, Albert Borgmann condemns passivity and consumerism. To counter these malaises, he advocates a simple "ground[ing] and center[ing] in reality," which, he claims, "comes most vigorously to the fore in the provinces" because "the dominant contemporary culture . . . is inescapably urban and indeed megalopolitan" (1992: 128). Yet, it is not clear what Borgmann considers "real" about the provinces. Unlike Williams' compelling awareness of the material basis of most country life, Borgmann's sense of "reality" never obliges him to say where food and fuel come from. Indeed, as his prescription continues, he implies that he expects country "reality" to be swallowed by the city. In its place he advocates remodeling cities to allow for trails into the country (133). In Borgmann's dream of the postmodern future, then, the countryside disappears from productive labor and lived experience except as a place for a diverting stroll. In his phenomenological account of how humans experience place, Edward Casey (1993) similarly collapses all places into an immaterial postmodern urbanism. In spite of his recognition of the importance of place in the creation of human identity, Casey recognizes neither a hierarchy of places nor any tension among them. He names "five forms of implacement . . . : houses, gardens, nature, cities, and regions" (181) without imagining the country as either a meaning-saturated form of "implacement" or a necessary resource for the support of cities.[4] In this avoidance of essentialism, then, intellectuals misunderstand both the metaphoric and the material aspects of place.[5] We propose neither an essentialist nor a metaphoric alternative to the nature of place, but rather a grounded concept; place identities are clearly linked to a particular kind of place, but even identities built upon the land are social constructions.

THE RELATIVITY OF PLACE

We argue that almost any inhabited place can be experienced as either rural or urban. Memphis, for example, looms in the Faulknerian imagination as *the* metropolis, yet a Parisian we know experienced life in Memphis as a painful rustication. Of course, the United States was founded on an insistent rusticity.[6] Thomas Jefferson envisioned the country's stability and prosperity growing out of the labor of yeoman farmers. He actively feared the population density and proletarianization that he associated with European metropolises and thus hoped that nearly all Americans would stay up on the farm.[7] While obviously no longer a possibility, the Jeffersonian vision of an uncorrupted rural America still has a certain resonance. When the emphasis of this cultural logic shifts slightly, it renders the United States a vast and vulgar province while Europe or France or Paris is figured as a status-conferring cosmopolis. Henry James insists on this problematic emplacement by calling his novel on this theme *The American* (1877). James' representative American is Christopher Newman, a wildly successful businessman born in San Francisco who goes to the *old* world in search of elevating experience. But Newman in Paris is like a newborn, an easy mark for high-class prostitutes and otherwise powerless aristocrats. That these forms of evil are not only European but also urban is indicated most forcefully by the name of one of the most scheming nobles, *Urbain* de Bellegarde. Ultimately, Newman must renounce his European dreams. But the novel, which opens as a comedy of manners, ends unhappily since Newman's rejection of old world urbanity entails no counterbalancing rustic solace. Sinclair Lewis' work provides another example of this dynamic, especially *Dodsworth* (1929). In this book, American life seems problematically rustic for all the main characters. The hero, Sam Dodsworth, is another restless, self-made millionaire, but when he succumbs to his wife's longing for European polish, he ends up cast in the role of "undependable hick" (1929: 292). Once he becomes disgusted with what he perceives as the corrupting sophistication of the continent, he loses his wife but acquires a goal: exploring or even building a new kind of space where the cultural hierarchies that denigrate his success no longer prevail. The truly happy ending, however, is postponed to an unspecified time and place. These unsettling, typically American novels seem to say that the new world isn't new enough to escape longstanding hierarchies of place.

The vocabulary of Americana provides further evidence for the simultaneous permanence and relativity of the rural/urban distinction. The term "heartland," for example, can conjure up images of charming patchwork farms in the Midwest or the bustle of Sandburg's rough-hewn Chicago, or most recently, the devastation of Oklahoma City. But the fact that the "heartland" encompasses urban areas does not alter the hierarchy that confers status on the urban. One point of invoking the "heartland" is to contrast it with what are somehow seen as the cultural and financial capitals of the United States—the East Coast megalopolis and increasingly the West Coast cities as well.[8] While the decay of heartland values is often mourned, many of our most visible articulations of this contrast allude to the cultural prestige of the coastal cities. *The New Yorker's* map of the country is one widely recognized example of this dynamic. In it New York City looms large while places to the west, even urban areas, are depicted as dreary frontiers.[9] Country music superstar Waylon Jennings abjectly (and ironically) claims a rustic identity within this logic in his "Too Dumb for New York City, Too Ugly for L.A." (1992). Rather than glorifying life on the farm, the singer's only preference is "somewhere in the middle." Similarly, popular images of the rapidly urbanizing American South still represent it as a rural outpost of backward rubes. Being *down* south is being at the bottom of the cultural heap; such cultural logic has thus been the catalyst for social movements led both by white supremacists and, as William Maxwell's essay in this volume demonstrates, by African-Americans.

Reading the discourse of colonialism in light of place can likewise reveal the relativity of the rural/urban distinction. For example, Aisha Khan's contribution to this volume shows how powerful northern Trinidadians assert superiority over symbolically rustic southerners, thereby maintaining a ranking created by colonialism. Elizabeth Sheehan shows in her contribution on Ireland how a similar cultural geography shifted to an east-west axis while leaving the cultural hierarchy intact, albeit more contested, as a result of colonial relations with Britain. Most telling is the term used to refer to *any* inhabitant of the European colonizing country: even a field hand living in the most remote sticks of France is "metropolitan" in contrast to a native of the colonies. Moreover, rural/urban distinctions may take on a greater weight within the colonies once European ideas about the opposition between the country and the city are imported. Colonial administrations often installed "city life" and divisive modes of production in places where cultural and economic activities were once organized along other axes. The Senegalese writer Sembene Ousmane evokes this mode of urbanization as he narrates his traditional Muslim hero's failed attempt to negotiate Dakar's Frenchified bureaucracy. As one appalled witness to his defeat proclaims, "I have never left Ndakaru [Dakar], but . . . I do not recognize this country" (1972: 120). Indeed, as some of our contributors show, physical distinctions between the country and city need not be remarkable for this opposition to structure the experiences and identities of the colonized—what Beatrice Guenther presents in her contribution as psychic colonization.

Of course, "purely rural" or "purely urban" spaces make up only a portion of the various places in which people live and form their identities. In developed countries in particular, cities merge into megalopolises which in turn bleed into the countryside through rings of suburbs and exurbs. The country, too, can be interpreted through a grid of population density and development, particularly as environmentalists mark off supposedly pristine wilderness areas from sites of rural work and production (an issue examined by Michèle Dominy in her contribution). Within the productive countryside of Kentucky anthropologist Rhoda Halperin (1990: 4) distinguishes "'shallow rural' —a term referring to the middle ground between country and city" from the more stereotypical "deep rural." While her distinction is "designed to overcome the traditional and well-entrenched dichotomy between rural and urban," such new configurations make sense only in reference to the persistent polarity of city and country.[10] As Raymond Williams puts it,

> our real social experience is not only of the country and the city, in their most singular forms, but of many kinds of intermediate and new kinds of social and physical organization. Yet the ideas and the images of country and city retain their great force. . . . Clearly the contrast of country and city is one of the major forms in which we become conscious of a central part of our experience and of the crises of our society. (1973: 289)

Joel Garreau (1991) introduces his study of the newest American urban developments by expressing a similar belief:

> My first reaction to the phenomenon I would later dub Edge City was to feel threatened. I had always believed that there were only two sensible ways to live—in a yeasty urban neighborhood . . . or a remote, leafy glade. . . . I could never understand why anyone would want anything in between. (xxi)

Although Garreau doesn't tell how he resolved the discomfort he felt, his book's title and introductory rhetoric clearly indicate that he simply placed the phenomenon he is describing, the booming growth of certain American residential areas, at the urban extreme of the place continuum. The first pages of his first chapter refer constantly to "new urban center" (3), "new urbs," "new city centers," and "new urban areas" (4).

Ethnographic fieldwork also supports Williams' theory of the omnipresence of the rural/urban distinction in the face of more ambiguous forms of settlement. Robert Redfield's seminal work on *The Folk Culture of the Yucatan* (1941) conceptualized a rural/urban continuum in which various types of settlement acquired character as much through the polar oppositions as through their own demographic particularities. Likewise, Michael Bell, in his study of the London exurb Childerley, notes that the residents of this enclave don't willingly embrace their locational liminality but instead turn it into "constant topics of discussion" in order to maintain their sense of themselves as country people who resist the lures and snares of the urban (1994: 8).[11] Similarly, Aaron Fox's contribution to this collection describes how a group of Texas "rednecks" maintain their affiliation with the country by deliberately situating their lives on the edges of the city where they find work.

CONTRARY PLACES

When we suggest to our students or colleagues that rusticity is chronically devalued, they often object by citing opposing views: the pervasive fear and loathing of big cities, the peace of the countryside, and the charm of rural artifacts. In some sense, it is the reversibility of the rural/urban hierarchy that makes the distinction so culturally useful. We are all familiar with images of decaying ghettos and corrupt corporate headquarters sharing an urban landscape perpetually threatened with random violence. Still, we believe this gothic trope of urban danger can be interrogated to reveal a continuing validation of the urbane even as it openly attacks city life. After all, the city remains the locus of political, economic and cultural power. In fact, the presence of this power is one reason for high urban crime rates: there are simply more resources to contest, legally or illegally, than in the country. Nor does urban crime generally drive the fearful into the countryside. Instead, wealthy urbanites create carefully guarded sanctuaries inside the city limits or push urban amenities into the suburbs which, whatever else they may be, are decidedly not rural. Moreover, while cities may include drug dealers and "city slickers" *among* their inhabitants, it is linguistically difficult to denigrate urbanites *as a group*, whereas the opportunities for criticizing the rustic are vast: crackers, rubes, hayseeds, hicks, hillbillies, bumpkins, peasants, rednecks, yokels and white trash.[12] If we turn to the cultural adjectives derived from the two places the difference is even more obvious: "rustic" is predominantly pejorative, while "urbane" is decidedly positive. As Marc Edelman's contribution confirms, the story is similar in other languages—far more negative connotations attach to words describing country affiliated people than to those describing city folk.[13] Such analysis exposes criticism of the city as ideological in the strictest sense: a force that masks and thereby protects urban cultural and economic superiority.

When rustics denounce city life they may be deploying an identity politics that challenges this urban hegemony and asserts their own value. Lest we be completely seduced by the "romance of resistance" (Handler 1994), however, we must also recognize elements of what Bourdieu (1984: 372) calls the "choice of the necessary," an attempt to present one's way of life, about which one may have few choices, as a conscious preference. In fact, advocates of rural life are often quick to reveal their belief that mobility and "improvement" are somehow linked to leaving the country. The same Bulgarian villagers who criticize city life push their children to get educations and jobs in town; they see their children's security, and by extension their own, as tied to eventual urbanization. The rock classic about Johnny B. Goode teaches a similar lesson. As a child, Johnny is hidden in the backwoods, which he must leave in order to fulfill the optimistic potential of his name. The song that narrates his success thus urges him at every interval to "go."

Many rural people do go, but once in the city they are often blamed for eroding the quality of life there. This kind of criticism can be seen as yet another veiled defense of urbanity since it denounces not the city per se but rather "matter out of place." As Mary Douglas (1966) suggests, danger and impurity are often associated with experiences that seem to violate the culturally developed categories by which societies order the world. According to this logic, if the city is undesirable it is not necessarily because urbanity and sophistication should be abandoned in favor of rusticity, but rather because there are too many unsophisticated people there, turning the city into something that is neither urban nor rural, but rather a terrible hybrid, polluted and dangerous. Those who lack the requisite qualities then become the scapegoats for all that is not urbane about the city. For example, an explanation of urban deficiencies which we have heard both on the streets of Sofia, Bulgaria and in upper-middle class homes in Memphis, Tennessee, is that there are too many "peasants" there. This condition, intimated by the titles of such urban analyses as *Cities of Peasants* (Roberts 1978), *The Peasant Urbanites* (Simic 1973), and *Peasant Metropolis* (Hoffmann 1994), finds an explicit formulation in Slavenka Drakulić's attempt to account for the sorry state of public toilets in Bucharest:

> After the "glorious victory of communism," the masses migrated to the cities. . . . The fact that they flocked to urban areas, however, does not mean that they changed their ways . . . the communist crash course in turning these peasant newcomers into urbanites did not help them to change. They were forced to jump from a village into a city, from feudalism into communism, without an opportunity to develop a civil society with all its values and habits, from private property to human rights, from democracy to toilet paper. (1994: 12)

American urbanites likewise call attention to unsuccessful transitions from the country with snide jokes about the aesthetic failings of trailer parks and low-income neighborhoods where front yards serve as storage spots for decrepit cars. While such places are often located on the margins of cities, they have an analogue downtown—the marked areas of the "inner" city. Qualified as "inner," however, this menace to urbanity does not threaten the "true" city. Discursively protected between the "inner" city and the "outskirts of town," the city itself retains its cultural value and significance as an ideal. Unfortunately defenders of the city who employ this logic implicitly denigrate the rustic (and the African-American).[14] It is not surprising, then, that many of the negative English terms associated with the trope of urban danger and decay actually evoke distinctively rural or unsettled imagery: wastelands, urban blight, and the urban jungle.

The gothic trope of urban danger is complemented by a romantic trope of the countryside as an idyllic retreat (Bunce 1994), yet even this image subtly perpetuates urban superiority. Rather than valorizing the rustic, positive images of rural life often provide ways to talk about improving the city. In his discussion of Zambia, for example, James Ferguson (1992) shows how cosmopolitan urbanites used rural themes, first to reform or replace the colonial system, and then to purge the postcolonial order of its white colonial cast. The village was invoked not as an alternative to the city, but as a moral image to inspire or discipline urban behavior. Similarly Mark Shutes (1993: 133) finds that urban classes in Ireland widely accept the idea that rural people somehow retain a core of crucial values. This romantic trope often values rural places because of their nostalgic evocation of simpler times— an idealization that simultaneously evokes rustic backwardness while it evades the pervasive desperation of rural poverty.

The ideal country is the place urbanites visit, not the place where poor people eke out a living. Urban dwellers who are free from the stigma of rusticity can wax eloquently about the countryside or embrace it as a retreat without undermining their own cultural superiority—*going to* the country with a fully formed urban identity is not the same as *being from* the country. The very concept of a "country" home, for example, reinforces the fact that its owner is urban(e) and has an unqualified/unmarked home in the city. Any urban resident who decides to fully adopt a rustic lifestyle is seen as *counter*-cultural. If these protestants are eccentric geniuses like Thoreau or Rousseau, the worst that can be said about them is that they march to the beat of a different drummer; more current in our imaginations, though, are the fools of popular fictions such as *Green Acres* and *City Slickers*. In any case, such transitions rarely take place. In Bulgaria, the postcommunist restitution of property rights presented many urban residents with the possibility of returning to work their village land. Villagers, however, universally and accurately doubted that any town folk would do so, and in one case when a doctor actually did, there was widespread gossip about what scandal had forced his return.

Even when economic advantages and cultural cachet keep people close to the city, the countryside holds the promise of natural beauty. Unfortunately, nature lovers effect only a slight variation in the rural idyll since they often valorize an abstract environment at the expense of the productive countryside. Real farmers and their labor nearly vanish as their products and activities are either aestheticized into "scenery," such as "quaint" barns and "amber waves of grain," or frozen into "living history" for tourist consumption. As Michèle Dominy demonstrates in her contribution, rustics can be incorporated into this urban imaginary, and even profit from urbane interest in their surroundings, but only on terms defined by urban consumers. They lack the power to define what is attractive or valuable about the places where they live, and if they insist on such privilege, they may be excluded completely. For example, the pastoral Masai and their cattle have been expelled from Tanzanian game preserves to make park lands safer for wildlife and more appealing to tourists (Perlez 1989). Similarly, a senior fellow of the Cato Institute links federal environmental regulations in the American West to the demands of non-resident nature lovers: "The public wants access. They want to see wild country that looks wild; they want to see wildlife—and a lot of it; they want to see clear water, not muddy; and they don't want to see cow turds everywhere" (Larson 1995: 64). When rural people respond aggressively to such attempts to curtail their economic activities, they inadvertently supply urbanites with further evidence of their apparently well-deserved degradation. In fact, well before loggers in the American northwest started tying dead spotted owls to their trucks, the urbane believed rustics incapable of appreciating nature. "[A]s the art critic C. G. Laurin put it in 1909: 'A shepherd boy usually has no eye for the sunset over the sea or the beauty of the white swans flying over dark blue waters'"(Frykman and Löfgren 1987: 72–74). Of course, direct economic dependence on natural resources does not preclude an appreciation of nature; farmers often defend their choice of career by citing the closeness to nature that agriculture affords. By overlooking such motives, environmental rhetoric affirms the dominance of the urban perspective.

Finally, it can be argued that the popularity of folk art and rural "style" reveals a cultural value attached to rural places and people. Yet, whether the object in question is a priceless icon or a stylish cowboy hat, its value comes not from rustic appreciation, but from the judgements of highly visible urban consumers who use such objects to signal their class and cultural superiority. For example, Andrew Lass (1989) argues that in Czechoslovakia, the purchase of folk products distinguished and legitimated not the folk, but the high culture consumers of the commodity, making them in effect distinct from the rural and lower classes who made the products. Similarly, in the short story "Everyday Use," Alice Walker (1973) sympathetically recounts a rural black woman's refusal to allow her status-seeking daughter to turn the family's butter churn into a decoration for her urban apartment. Conversely, when rural people attempt to aestheticize elements of everyday life and labor for themselves—such as using a tractor tire as a flower bed in the front yard—they unwittingly provide further evidence of their laughable lack of taste. Apparently, only urban consumption or authorization can transform rusticity into high culture. Rustic people simply lack the cultural capital to enforce their aesthetic judgments, and they usually lack the monetary capital to reappropriate the images sanctioned by urban commodification. One need only think about the price of Tony Lama boots or a Grandma Moses painting to get the point. Cross-examined in this way, the value of folk artistry and craftsmanship, like the romantic countryside and the gothic city, reveals the same "flexible, positional superiority" for urbanity that Said (1979: 3) finds in western models of "orientalism." In all of these discourses on place, the urbane has the last word.

EMPLACING RACE, CLASS, AND GENDER

While we have been asserting the significance of place-based distinctions in the formation and interpretation of identities, we recognize that place is rarely, if ever, the sole dimension of identification. Rather, place inflects other dimensions such as race, class, gender, and ethnicity. However, since researchers often assume an urban setting, they fail to recognize the interaction of place with other identity elements. Just as these other factors take on a variety of meanings cross-culturally, their interaction with place creates a staggering and fascinating range of images. The rustic male in American culture, for example, works heroically on his farm or in his logging camp, but he is no Lady Chatterley's lover; instead he is often depicted as an almost asexual child more interested in hunting and drinking than women.

Jed and Jethro Clampett in *The Beverly Hillbillies* were comically oblivious to the glamorous gold-digging females who pursued them while the eponymous hero of the *Li'l Abner* comic strip was equally uninterested in the charms of his voluptuous hillbilly counterpart Daisy Mae.[15] The rustic male's apparent inability to master the etiquette of courting also contributes to his association with more taboo sexual activities. To judge from popular American movies like *Deliverance* (1972), *Pulp Fiction* (1994), and *Falling Down* (1992), rustic sexual expression often takes the form of homosexual rape. The latter two movies are particularly revealing since they take place in Los Angeles yet the sexual violators are bizarrely marked as southern rustics.[16] Similarly, the incest implied in countless hillbilly jokes not only reflects the logistical difficulties of finding unrelated women in remote hamlets but also suggests an actual preference for kin: "You know you're a redneck," explains comedian Jeff Foxworthy, "if you go to family reunions to meet girls." These scandalous sexualities fused in the alleged case of fratricide in rural New York documented in the acclaimed film *Brother's Keeper* (1992). Here the fact that two brothers slept in the same bed led investigators to assume homosexual incest was a factor. There is little doubt, at least from the filmmakers' sympathetic perspective, that this accusation was provoked largely by the family's rustic lifestyle. Finally, accusations of bestiality are common in derogatory jokes about rustic males in many cultures. Interestingly, we have never heard such jokes about urban men, who are often quite attached to their pets.

Feminine imagery is strongly inflected by place as well. In contrast to America's voluptuous Daisy Mae and generic "farmer's daughters," rural women can also be cast as no-nonsense earth mothers: we are all familiar with the sturdy grandmothers used to represent east European peasant women. In these countries, the earth mother image is partially authorized by women's disproportionate responsibility for agricultural production (Cernea 1978). This association, however, is not necessarily liberating; it can actually contribute to the cultural devaluation of women as farming declines in economic importance and cultural status. In fact, women sometimes take on more farm work *as a result* of its declining status in industrializing societies. This, of course, is only one scenario;[17] Beatrice Guenther's contribution to this volume describes not only how the rustic earth mother became part of Québécois literary tradition but also how feminist writers altered the tradition. Likewise, by reading James Joyce through this gender/place interface, Elizabeth Sheehan shows how his story "The Dead" troubles the traditional Irish association of women with the unsophisticated countryside. In so doing, Sheehan opens up a range of interpretive possibilities previously unrecognized in Joyce's work.

One of those possibilities is to read "The Dead" as a challenge to the persistent association of Irish nationality with rurality—an association common in the annals of nationalism. As Raymond Williams points out, the word "country" itself has a double valence in the English-speaking world, fundamentally linking nationality with "the land from which directly or indirectly we all get our living" (1973: 1). While this connection can be ignored, it can also be used to promote various nationalist agenda. Around the world nationalist projects invoke rural life as the source of the national essence. While the rural origins of nationalist myths have been widely recognized (Kisbán 1989, Østergård 1992), the interaction between national and rural-based identities has not. For example, Benedict Anderson (1983) has theorized that colonial elites, frustrated by their marginality, spurred the first nationalist movements. This theory gains even more credence, however, when the inevitable rusticity of the colonies is seen as a factor in that marginality.

The articulation of nationality and rurality generates still other possibilities. On the one hand, nationalist myths validating the "folk" may resonate more deeply for rural dwellers. But since these myths often homogenize distinctive regional cultures, they may actually threaten other locally based identities (see Silverman 1983 and Weber 1976). At the same time, when national origins are traced to the primeval countryside, those living there are cast as relics of the nation's past rather than as vital representatives of the contemporary nation. These varied, sometimes contradictory, interpretations indicate that the relationship between national and rural identities is complex and fecund. Not surprisingly, then, several contributors attend specifically to such relationships. By examining folklore exhibits in French museums through the lens of the Breton Movement, David Maynard shows how the complex relationship between rurality and nationality can provide a basis for identities distinct from the nation-state. Susan Lees describes the valorization of the peasantry in the nascent Israeli nation as a means both to unify the disparate cultures of the diaspora and to encourage land settlement. This value was undercut, however, when economic development and political change generated tension between the declining cultural value of rural affiliations and the continuing political importance of national ones. Similarly, Michèle Dominy shows how images of alpine cultural heritage that were once essential to Australian national identity and nationalist discourse lost their prestige as urban perspectives gained power.

The utility of the countryside as a locus of national essence is more complicated in plural societies where rural populations are ethnically or racially marked, hence hardly a national unifier. In these cases rural/urban differences often qualify ethnic and/or racial ones, demanding that all three be examined in tandem. For example, Susan Lees documents how the peasantry's fall from grace in Israel was connected to the shifting of the ethnic profile of agricultural labor from Jewish to Arab.[18] For the leaders of the Breton movement studied by David Maynard, however, rural affiliations were too useful to abandon completely. While as urbane intellectuals they found the rustic connotations of Brittany degrading, they nevertheless needed popular images of rural Breton culture to mobilize support for their movement. Aisha Khan's contribution shows how east Indians in Trinidad solved a similar problem. Historically connected to agricultural production in the rural south, Indo-Trinidadians used rusticity to mark and maintain their ethnic distinctiveness. At the same time, they lost status as the role of agriculture and the countryside declined in national cultural hierarchies. In response, they emphasized the more positive images of rurality and the land. Since they defined themselves primarily against the predominant Afro-Trinidadians, their rural affiliations took on racial connotations, constituting what Khan calls a "racial landscape." While such a landscape would be much more discontinuous in the United States, William Maxwell's contribution demonstrates the value of looking at race with place in mind. Focusing on a debate in African-American literature, he explores the conflicting images that the rural South offers African-Americans in their search for racial justice and racial identity. Using the literary products of the combatants (Richard Wright and Zora Neale Hurston), Maxwell shows how the invidious option between embracing the rural South as the source of African-American culture and rejecting it as the locus of racial oppression is overcome by the very authors most closely associated with the two positions. His discoveries regarding the interaction of race and place in the South demand that we pay closer attention to the racial dimension of rural identification elsewhere in the United States, for both African- and European-Americans.[19]

Any discussion of ethnic and racial categories must also address class, which is the dimension of contemporary identity politics most explicitly connected to rural identities. As we have intimated throughout our discussion, the cultural devaluation of rural people often reflects their economic marginality. One need only think about the dominant images of rusticity in the United States to recognize poverty as a central element: Deep South shacks, Appalachia itself (Batteau 1990), and labels such as "poor white trash." Even economic "success" seems limited in a rural context. Peggy Barlett (1993) points out that American family farmers who want to continue farming must avoid debt and minimize hired labor, strategies that nearly foreclose the possibility of significant profit. The evidence is similar elsewhere; in fact, Michael Lipton (1982) suggests that the principle economic division in developing countries is between a small urban elite on the one hand and all rural people on the other. Such inequality stems in part from the role of agriculture in global capitalism. However, as Harvey (1993) and Davidson (1990) point out, it is not only agriculture that exploits. Rural industries are equally guilty: "For it is here [in rural and small town settings] that the decline of agricultural employment (to say nothing of the rash of farming bankruptcies) over the past decade or so has left behind a relatively isolated industrial reserve army . . . which is far more vulnerable to exploitation than its urban counterpart" (Harvey 1993: 43). At the same time, the bumbling country transplant forced to seek economic opportunity in the city cuts an instantly recognizable figure.

While the cultural devaluation of rural and rustic people may be grounded in economic marginalization, it also exercises its own determinacy. In China Myron Cohen (1993) notes that rapid economic development has blurred the rural/urban gap that inspired the "peasant" designation in the first place, yet "the idea of the peasant as comprising a distinct and backward cultural category shows no sign of losing its force" (1993: 166). This outcome mirrors development experiences elsewhere. Thus, American ranchers who are comparatively better off than struggling New York actors or would-be opera divas cannot expect to be considered culturally superior. Likewise, nothing is more discordant in the Western cultural imagination than rustics striking it rich. Several of our contributors thus look at how class and place identities interact. Significant in Dominy's, Khan's, and Sheehan's analyses, class is at the heart of Fox's discussion of "redneck" sociability in Texas. Recounting a low-tech narrative which affirms "redneck" identities in the face of high-tech lives, Fox sees his informants' identification with explicitly rustic places as an insistence on the significance of class, in this case an insistence that their engagement with technology has not made them like everybody else. Crucially, their distinction *as a class* is embedded in a particular kind of place. Marc Edelman takes up a similar conflict in Central America, where rural technological sophistication could be seen as a challenge to the economic distinction between country and city people. Instead technology is embraced by rural people to facilitate political action around place- *and* class-based identities of the "peasant."

These examples suggest that our failure to aggressively expose the social construction of place has limited our understanding of class identities, just as it has restricted our appreciation of race, ethnicity, nationality, and gender. The contributors to this collection provide a corrective since they analyze various identities with a particular type of place in mind. Most of these places are rural because we believe the lack of attention to the rural case underlies the invisibility of place generally. Our point, however, is that rural and urban distinctions, as well as the categorical refinements of each, are important dimensions of identity and hierarchy. We have thus asked our contributors to look at their areas of expertise with the rural/urban distinction in mind, and the results speak eloquently to our point.

A PLACE FOR RESISTANCE

Underlying our interest in the manifestations of rustic identities is a belief that they are not symptoms of incomplete development or inadequate education. Rather we see a clear attempt on the part of rustic people to assert their value and place in a world dominated by urban(e) others. Such an assertion challenges the cultural preeminence of sophisticated urbanity by its very expression (Scott 1985: xvi). Furthermore, since many of the cultural markers of rusticity evoke rural poverty, they also graphically expose economic inequality. In other words, simply claiming a rustic identity has multiple resistance possibilities. With fitting irony, rustic people manipulate this potential in very sophisticated ways, as Marc Edelman shows in the case of politically savvy Central American peasants. In another powerful example, Rainer Lutz Bauer (1992) recounts how Galician peasants in the eighteenth and early nineteenth centuries asserted their "backwardness" in order to maintain cultural distinction and resist incorporation into the Spanish state. Then, from the middle of the nineteenth century, peasants used their rusticity as a basis for claims on the state, blaming it for their economic problems and demanding redress. Gavin Lewis (1978) suggests that Austrian peasants at the turn of the century may have used conservative rhetoric to advance quite progressive and economically advantageous rural programs. These examples encourage us to take a more skeptical approach to the interpretation of rusticity. While simple rural conservatism may support the political status quo, the idea that rural life and rustic lifestyles are valid and valuable, that what the world needs is a few more rednecks, is a radical attempt to upset existing cultural hierarchies, or at least to prevent further deval-uation of rusticity. Consequently, for rustic Americans, it is increas-ingly important not just to own guns, but to display them and aggres-sively defend their ownership; it is important to drive a truck as much for what it says about you as for the service and utility it provides, and it is important to listen to country music in which the cultural value of these symbols is reinforced. These symbolic representations deliber-ately politicize rusticity since they insist upon incorporating it into the public sphere.

While many analysts have discussed peasant rebellions and their equivocal outcomes (Magagna 1991, Wolf 1969), we suggest that attempts to assert identities defined by rurality and rusticity are both less and more than revolution. They may lack a utopian vision but they do claim the margins along lines that other analysts of identity politics have sketched (hooks 1990; Fuss 1991). Thus, while rustics are often identified with the right and its racist, ethnocentric or national-ist ideologies, we suggest that they are *made* conservative by others: by national ideologues seeking the primordial essence of the nation (Verdery 1991), by colonial and development experts validating their own authority and importance (Pigg 1992, Murphey 1972), by urban-ites needing a low other against which to claim their own superiority (Ching 1993, Cohen 1993), by religious leaders attempting to preserve their power over the family (Guizzardi 1976), and by reactionary mem-bers of the middle and upper classes seeking validation for their own more conservative views (Ehrenreich 1989: 101). As Osha Davidson (1990: 118) notes, "the far right understands rural peoples' alienation and exploits it, transforming their bitter desperation into political action that suits the right's own broader agenda." In other words, the marginality of rustic people renders them vulnerable to conservative maneuvering, but efforts at more self-conscious rustic resistance could challenge such manipulation. The political power of French farmers exemplifies such an effort, as does the role of rural voters in returning socialists to power in eastern Europe (Creed 1995). To the degree that rustic empowerment prevents other groups from asserting and capital-izing on their marginality, it is regressive and discriminatory. Thus, while by no means advocating tolerance of rural white supremacist groups or the rural militia movement, we argue that self-conscious rustic identities spring from conditions similar to those politicizing other marginalized groups. More importantly, we argue that without such recognition, the study of identity politics inadvertently maintains existing cultural hierarchies and contributes to the persistent lack of solidarity among those at the bottom.

The assertions of identity we discuss in this book may fulfill Charlie Daniels' call for a few more "rednecks," but the potential of these "rednecks" to redefine what is culturally valuable and respectable in their societies still seems fraught with uncertainty. Since this presentation of identity aggressively embraces many devalued stereotypes of rusticity, its performance may actually reinforce existing cultural hierarchies even when its objective is to question them. In other words, by providing ever more vivid images of rural backwardness, such resistance could actually sustain the rustic low that underwrites the relative value of the urbane high. Whether you are an East Indian in Trinidad, a Breton in France, or a "redneck" in Texas, asserting a positive rural identity courts devaluation in the larger society where rusticity remains at the bottom of the cultural heap. According to John Berger (1991), the career of Jean-François Millet exemplifies this dilemma. His paintings of the French peasantry may have gained him popularity, but they cost him critical acclaim. Berger concludes that such outcomes are inevitable "unless the hierarchy of our social and cultural values is radically altered" (85). By insisting on a place for rusticity within those areas of scholarship which purport to challenge existing canons and cultural hierarchies, our collection attempts to fulfill Berger's charge. We believe that questioning the cultural ascendancy of urbanity takes an important step towards a unified challenge to diverse systems of stratification, bringing together all those who are beyond the urbane pale, from the "redneck" to the inner city resident, from the peasant to the urban immigrant.

NOTES

1. French Situationist Guy Debord (1967: 137) placed his call for cultural and social revolution in the city because he too believed that the distinction between rural and urban areas no longer shaped experience. While he was ostensibly talking about political economy, he placed his theories of social and cultural revolution in the urban environment. More extremely, Augé argues for the increasing disappearance of meaning-saturated places altogether, claiming they have been replaced by the "non-places [which] are the real measure of our time . . . the airports and railway stations, hotel chains, leisure parks, large retail outlets, and finally the complex skein of cable and wireless networks that mobilize extraterrestrial space" (1995: 79).

2. When the popular press, especially in its more high-brow forms, reports on rural culture, it can reveal quite clearly the opprobrium still attached to any activity seen as rustic. *Harper's Magazine* trumpeted its July 1994 cover story on state fairs with this arch description: "Wherein our reporter gorges himself on corn dogs, gapes at terrifying rides, acquaints himself with the odor of pigs, exchanges unpleasantries with tattooed carnies, and admires the loveliness of cows" (Wallace 1994). Similarly, Joyce Carol Oates, reporting for *The New Yorker* from Timothy McVeigh's hometown of Pendleton, N.Y., asserts that place has no importance in identity formation: "To visit such wholly American places as Pendleton and Lockport is to be granted a revelation: how little where we have lived, with whom we have lived, and of whom we are born has any longer to do, in the public sense of who we are" (Oates 1995: 36). She strains to support this assertion despite the voices that contradict her: "Lockport, with its twenty-five thousand inhabitants, is *the* city. When Timothy McVeigh spent time there, he would have been identified as 'from the country'—that vague, just slightly pejorative designation given such boys and girls as if identity might be a matter of geography and distance" (35). Instead of openly considering the possibility that place might indeed play a role in identity formation, Oates, with her dismissive "as if," implicitly confirms our prejudices against the very people ("boys and girls") she purports to be describing.

3. Herzfeld (1987: 16) describes a similar dynamic in nineteenth-century studies of Greek folklore with "an educated mind formulating a folk culture in which it claimed participatory rights, but to which it was at the same time both exterior and superior."

4. Likewise, the vast literature on the interplay of architecture and environment constantly asserts the importance of place but consistently ignores the existence of a hierarchy of places. See, for example, E. Relph's *Place and Placelessness* (1976).

5. Perhaps for this reason it is in literature, where authors are less plagued by the social-scientific phobia of essentialism, and are more comfortable with metaphor, that the case for rural identity is most convincingly made today. Contemporary writers such as Dorothy Allison (1992), Kathleen Norris (1993), and Jane Smiley (1991), to name only a few, demonstrate in intimate ways how rural places influence a sense of self and world both in the country and away from it.

6. While this distinction may be unique to the United States inasmuch as an early president and founding father articulated it, it also has long been used to characterize the attitudes of the English toward their country; in Samuel Johnson's "London" (1738), which outlines the complaints of a poet about to leave the city to live in rural Wales, the contrast between England's corrupt urban present and her past rustic glory is stated early on (lines 99–106). Oliver Goldsmith, in "The Deserted Village" (1770), also bemoaned the urbanization of England and similarly posited a rural Golden Age:

A time there was 'ere England's griefs began,

When every rood of land maintained its man. . .

But times are altered; trade's unfeeling train

Usurp the land and dispossess the swain. (57-64)

Bell (1994: 9–10) discusses more recent explorations of this tension.

7. Jefferson's vision, of course, has never formed a national consensus, but see White and White (1962) for further examples. On the tension between the rural idyll and urban development in American culture, see Leo Marx (1964).

8. According to Richard Bernstein, the French make a similar distinction between "France Deep and France Parisian" (1990: 19-95).

9. Soja offers a West-coast version of this map (1989: 232).

10. This claim is supported empirically by Hummond's (1990) investigation of community ideology in Northern California. Only 19 percent of the suburban residents in his study self-identified as "suburbanites"—others chose standard "city" and "country" identities, or denied any place identity at all (145). He concludes that "suburban ideology lacks sufficient meaning to construct a vital suburban identity" (157). The implication is that city and country remain ideologically central even as they are increasingly qualified demographically.

11. Ron Powers, in *Far from Home* (1991), discusses a similar conflict facing the New York City exurb of Kent, Connecticut.

12. The terms themselves also carry evidence of the cultural devaluation we are discussing. The term "peasant," for example, shares a Latin root with the word "pagan," locating both outside (Christian) civilization. Until at least

the late eighteenth century, the word "rustic" was used synonymously with "clown." Interestingly, most of the rural epithets listed here continue to enjoy a degree of public approbation while epithets based upon race or ethnicity are socially censured.

13. For a discussion of the interesting case of Chinese terms and the increasing derogatory connotations of "peasant" associated with western influence see Cohen (1993).

14. The image of the suburbs also figures in this defense since while safe, they are imagined as culturally sterile, reaffirming the need for and value of urban culture.

15. V. S. Naipaul's (1989) discussion of "redneck" culture, in the travel narrative *A Turn in the South*, echoes these observations in a more serious vein.

16. While homosexual rape never occurs in *Falling Down*, according to Allison Graham (1995), the threat is evident. The makers of such films evidently assume that audiences will not experience interpretive dissonance when such suggestions are juxtaposed to stereotypes of rustic homophobia.

17. In some cases, women are sought out for *industrial* employment because of assumed feminine characteristics such as docility (Ong 1987).

18. Interestingly, this shift also helps explain the continuing value of the peasant as a unifying symbol for the Palestinian nation (Swedenburg 1990).

19. Sonya Salamon's (1992) work on seven Illinois farming communities shows important relations between rural and ethnic identities.

REFERENCES

Allison, Dorothy. 1992. *Bastard out of Carolina*. New York: Dutton.

Anderson, Benedict. 1983. *Imagined Communities: Reflections on the Origin and Spread of Nationalism*. London: Verso.

Augé, Marc. 1992. *Non-Places: Introduction to an Anthropology of Supermodernity*. London: Verso, 1995. Trans. John Howe, original 1992.

Barlett, Peggy F. 1993. *American Dreams, Rural Realities: Family Farms in Crisis*. Chapel Hill: University of North Carolina Press.

Batteau, Allen W. 1990. *The Invention of Appalachia*. Tucson: University of Arizona Press.

Bauer, Rainer Lutz. 1992. "Changing Representations of Place, Community, and Character in the Spanish Sierra del Caurel," *American Ethnologist* 19: 571–588.

Bauman, Zygmunt. 1987. *Legislators and Interpreters: On Modernity, Post-Modernity, and Intellectuals*. Ithaca, N.Y.: Cornell University Press.

Bell, Michael Mayerfield. 1994. *Childerley: Nature and Morality in a Country Village*. Chicago: University of Chicago Press.

Berger, John. 1991. *About Looking*. New York: Vintage.

Bernstein, Richard. 1990. *Fragile Glory: A Portrait of France and the French*. New York: Knopf.

Borgmann, Albert. 1992. *Crossing the Postmodern Divide*. Chicago: University of Chicago Press.

Bourdieu, Pierre. 1984. *Distinction: A Social Critique of the Judgement of Taste*. Cambridge: Harvard University Press. Trans. Richard Nice.

Brantlinger, Patrick. 1990. *Crusoe's Footprints: Cultural Studies in Britain and America*. New York: Routledge.

Bunce, Michael. 1994. *The Countryside Ideal: Anglo-American Images of Landscape*. New York: Routledge.

Caro Baroja, Julio. 1963. "The City and the Country: Reflexions on Some Ancient Commonplaces," in Julian Pitt-Rivers, ed., *Mediterranean Countrymen: Essays in the Social Anthropology of the Mediterranean*. The Hague: Mouton.

Casey, Edward S. 1993. *Getting Back into Place: Toward a Renewed Understanding of the Place-World*. Bloomington: Indiana University Press.

Cernea, Michael. 1978. "Macrosocial Change, Feminization of Agriculture and Peasant Women's Threefold Economic Role," *Sociologia Ruralis* 18: 107–124.

Chambers, Iain. 1986. *Popular Culture: The Metropolitan Experience*. London: Methuen.

Ching, Barbara. 1993. "Acting Naturally: Cultural Distinction and Critiques of Pure Country," *Arizona Quarterly* 49(3): 107–125.

Cohen, Myron L. 1993. "Cultural and Political Inventions in Modern China: The Case of the Chinese 'Peasant,'" *Daedalus* 122(2): 151–170.

Collins, Jim. 1989. *Uncommon Cultures: Popular Culture and Post-Modernism*. New York: Routledge.

Creed, Gerald W. 1993. "Rural-Urban Oppositions in the Bulgarian Political Transition," *Südosteuropa* 42: 369–382.

————. 1995. "The Politics of Agriculture: Identity and Socialist Sentiment in Bulgaria," *Slavic Review* 54: 843–868.

Davidson, Osha. 1990. *Broken Heartland*. New York: Macmillan.

Debord, Guy. 1967. *La société du spectacle*. Paris: Buchet/Chastel.

Douglas, Mary. 1966. *Purity and Danger: An Analysis of Concepts of Pollution and Taboo*. London: Routledge and Kegan Paul.

Drakulić, Slavenka. 1994. "Lav Story," *The New Republic* (April 25): 11–12.

Duncan, James and David Ley. 1993. "Introduction: Representing the Place of

Culture," in James Duncan and David Ley, eds., *Place/ Culture/ Representation*. New York: Routledge.

Ehrenreich, Barbara. 1989. *Fear of Falling: The Inner Life of the Middle Class*. New York: Pantheon.

Ferguson, James. 1992. "The Country and the City on the Copperbelt," *Cultural Anthropology* 7: 80–92.

Fitchen, Janet M. 1991. *Endangered Spaces, Enduring Places: Change, Identity, and Survival in Rural America*. Boulder: Westview.

Frykman, Jonar and Orvar Löfgren. 1979. *Culture Builders: A Historical Anthropology of Middle-Class Life*. New Brunswick: Rutgers University Press, 1987. Trans. Alan Crozier.

Fuss, Diana. 1991. "Inside/Out," in Diana Fuss, ed., *Inside/Out: Lesbian Theories, Gay Theories*. New York: Routledge.

Garreau, Joel. 1991. *Edge City: Life on the New Frontier*. New York: Doubleday.

Glenny, Misha. 1992. "Yugoslavia: The Revenger's Tragedy," *New York Review of Books*, August 13: 37–43.

Goldsmith, Oliver. 1770. "The Deserted Village." In Roger Lonsdale, ed., *The New Oxford Book of Eighteenth-Century Verse*. Oxford: Oxford University Press, 1984.

Graham, Allison. 1995. Presentation at the American Studies Colloquium, April 23, The University of Memphis, Memphis.

Grossberg, Lawrence et al. 1992. *Cultural Studies*. New York: Routledge.

Guizzardi, Gustavo. 1976. "The 'Rural Civilization' Structure of an 'Ideology for Consent'," *Social Compass* 23(2/3): 187–220.

Halperin, Rhoda H. 1990. *The Livelihood of Kin: Making Ends Meet "The Kentucky Way."* Austin: University of Texas Press.

Handler, Richard. 1994. "Romancing the Low: Anthropology vis-à-vis Cultural Studies vis-à-vis Popular Culture." *Polar: Political and Legal Anthropology Review* 17(2): 1–6.

Harvey, David. 1989. *The Condition of Postmodernity*. Cambridge: Blackwell.

———. 1993. "Class Relations, Social Justice and the Politics of Difference," in Michael Keith and Steve Pile, eds., *Place and the Politics of Identity*. New York: Routledge.

Herzfeld, Michael. 1987. *Anthropology Through the Looking-Glass: Critical Ethnography in the Margins of Europe*. New York: Cambridge University Press.

Hoffmann, David L. 1994. *Peasant Metropolis: Social Identities in Moscow, 1929–1941*. Ithaca: Cornell University Press.

hooks, bell. 1990. *Yearnings: Race, Gender, and Cultural Politics*. Boston: South End Press.

Hummon, David M. 1990. *Commonplaces: Community Ideology and Identity in American Culture*. Albany: State University of New York Press.

Huyssen, Andreas. 1986. *After the Great Divide*. Bloomington: Indiana University Press.

James, Henry. 1877. *The American*. New York: Signet, 1963.

Jameson, Fredric. 1991. *Postmodernism, or The Cultural Logic of Late Capitalism*. Durham: Duke University Press.

Johnson, Samuel. 1738. "London." in E. L. McAdam with George Milne, eds., *Poems*. Volume 6 of *The Yale Edition of the Works of Samuel Johnson*. New Haven: Yale University Press, 1964.

Keith, Michael and Steve Pile. 1993. "Introduction Part 2: The Place of Politics" in Michael Keith and Steve Pile, eds., *Place and the Politics of Identity*. New York: Routledge.

Kisbán, Eszter .1989. "From Peasant Dish to National Symbol: An Early Deliberate Example," *Ethnologia Europaea* 19: 95–105.

Kohn, Howard. 1988. *The Last Farmer*. New York: Summit.

Larson, Erik. 1995. "Unrest in the West," *Time*, October 23: 52–66.

Lass, Andrew. 1989. "What Keeps the Czech Folk 'Alive?'" *Dialectical Anthropology* 14: 7–19.

Lefebvre, Henri. 1970. *La révolution urbaine*. Paris: Gallimard.

Lewis, Gavin. 1978. "The Peasantry, Rural Change and Conservative Agrarianism: Lower Austria at the Turn of the Century," *Past and Present* 81: 119–143.

Lewis, Sinclair. 1929. *Dodsworth*. New York: Signet, 1967.

Lipton, Michael. 1982. "Why Poor People Stay Poor," in John Harriss, ed., *Rural Development: Theories of Peasant Economy and Agrarian Change*. London: Hutchinson University Library.

Magagna, Victor V. 1991. *Communities of Grain: Rural Rebellion in Comparative Perspective*. Ithaca: Cornell University Press.

Marks, Stuart A. 1991. *Southern Hunting in Black and White: Nature, History, and Ritual in a Carolina Community*. Princeton: Princeton University Press.

Marx, Leo. 1964. *The Machine in the Garden: Technology and the Pastoral Ideal in America*. Oxford: Oxford University Press.

Murphey, Rhoads. 1972. "City and Countryside as Ideological Issues: India and China," *Comparative Studies in Society and History* 14: 250–267.

Nagengast, Carole. 1991. *Reluctant Socialists, Rural Entrepreneurs: Class, Culture, and the Polish State*. Boulder: Westview.

Naipaul, V. S. 1989. *A Turn in the South*. New York: Random House.

Norris, Kathleen. 1993. *Dakota: A Spiritual Geography*. New York: Houghton Mifflin.

Oates, Joyce Carol. 1995. "American Gothic," *The New Yorker*, May 8: 35–36.

Olalquiaga, Celeste. 1992. *Megalopolis: Contemporary Cultural Sensibilities*. Minneapolis: University of Minnesota Press.

Ong, Aihwa. 1987. *Spirits of Resistance and Capitalist Discipline: Factory Women in Malaysia*. Albany: State University of New York Press.

Østergård, Uffe. 1992. "Peasants and Danes: The Danish National Identity and Political Culture," *Comparative Studies in Society and History* 34: 3–27.

Ousmane, Sembene. 1965. *The Money Order with White Genesis*. Oxford: Heinemann, 1972. Trans. Clive Wake.

Perlez, Jane. 1989. "The Proud Masai's Fate: Finally, to Be Fenced In?" *The New York Times*, October 16: A4.

Pigg, Stacy Leigh. 1992. "Inventing Social Categories Through Place: Social Representation and Development in Nepal," *Comparative Studies in Society and History* 34: 491–513.

Powers, Ron. 1991. *Far From Home: Life and Loss in Two American Towns*. New York: Random House.

Redfield, Robert. 1941. *The Folk Culture of Yucatan*. Chicago: University of Chicago Press.

Relph, E. 1976. *Place and Placelessness*. London: Pion.

Roberts, Bryan. 1978. *Cities of Peasants: The Political Economy of Urbanization in the Third World*. London: Edward Arnold, Ltd.

Said, Edward. 1979. *Orientalism*. New York: Vintage.

Salamon, Sonya. 1992. *Prairie Patrimony: Family, Farming and Community in the Midwest*. Chapel Hill: University of North Carolina Press.

Scott, James C. 1985. *Weapons of the Weak: Everday Forms of Peasant Resistance*. New Haven: Yale University Press.

Shutes, Mark T. 1993. "Rural Communities without Family Farms: Family Dairy Farming in the Post-1993 EC," in Thomas M. Wilson and M. Estellie Smith, eds., *Cultural Change and the New Europe: Perspectives on the European Community*. Boulder: Westview.

Silverman, Carol. 1983. "The Politics of Folklore in Bulgaria," *Anthropological Quarterly* 56: 55–61.

Simic, Andrei. 1973. *The Peasant Urbanites: A Study of Rural-Urban Mobility in Serbia*. New York: Seminar Press.

Smiley, Jane. 1991. *A Thousand Acres*. New York: Knopf.

Soja, Edward. 1989. *Postmodern Geographies: The Reassertion of Space in Critical Social Theory*. London: Verso.

Stallybrass, Peter and Allon White. 1986. *The Politics and Poetics of Transgression*. Ithaca: Cornell University Press.

Stegner, Wallace. 1962. *Wolf Willow: A History, A Story, and a Memory of the Last Plains Frontier*. New York: Viking.

Storey, John. 1993. *An Introductory Guide to Cultural Theory and Popular Culture*. Athens: University of Georgia Press.

Swedenburg, Ted. 1990. "The Palestinian Peasant as National Signifier," *Anthropological Quarterly* 63: 18–30.

Turner, Graeme. 1990. *Introduction to British Cultural Studies*. New York: Routledge.

Verdery, Katherine. 1991. *National Ideology Under Socialism: Identity and Cultural Politics in Ceauşescu's Romania*. Berkeley: University of California Press.

Walker, Alice. 1973. *In Love and Trouble: Stories of Black Women*. New York: Harcourt, Brace, Jovanovich.

Wallace, David Foster. 1994. "Ticket to the Fair," *Harper's* July: 35–54.

Weber, Eugen. 1976. *Peasants into Frenchmen: The Modernization of Rural France, 1870–1914*. Stanford: Stanford University Press.

Weil, Danielle and Verlyn Klinkenborg. 1995. "A Farm Farewell: The Barnyard Animals Live at a Distance from Us Now," *The New York Times Magazine*, June 18: 36–39.

Williams, Raymond. 1973. *The Country and the City*. New York: Oxford University Press.

White, Morton and Lucia White. 1962. *The Intellectual versus the City from Thomas Jefferson to Frank Lloyd Wright*. Cambridge: Harvard University Press and the M.I.T. Press.

Wolf, Eric R. 1969. *Peasant Wars of the Twentieth Century*. New York: Harper and Row.

I ~ AISHA KHAN

Rurality and "Racial" Landscapes in Trinidad

My family said don't marry an estate girl, marry a university girl. . . . Ask any family if they'd like their daughter to marry a fellow who works on a sugar estate or whose parents lived in a barracks. They'd be seen as having Madras blood in them, meaning a higher temper, quick to fight and pull arms [weapons], dark skin. For the dark part of the skin they say, 'that is the Madras in you.'

— Indo-Trinidadian friend, 1989

THIS chapter is an inquiry into social inequality and identity in Trinidad, West Indies, from a perspective still atypical in analyses of multicultural postcolonial New World societies. It argues that a significant dimension of definitions of self and other, us and them, in Trinidad is a rural/urban opposition that has not been sufficiently explored in cultural terms among Caribbean peoples. This rural/urban dyad is an essential component in a larger identity discourse which constitutes a metaphor for the tensions of empire in this postcolonial nation. In this discourse, mutually constitutive concepts of culture, race, class, and ethnicity are differentially valued, and thus comprise a cultural hierarchy that both shapes and interprets patterns of social stratification. The various stereotypes and other forms of representation that inform cultural hierarchies are constantly in dialogue, and at times in conflict with each other. In Trinidad, as elsewhere, cultural hierarchies are far from a gloss on political-economic constraints. While they interact with other dimensions of inequality to inform the way stratification is experienced by local communities and individuals (cf. Handler 1992), they do not do so in predictable or logically consistent ways. This chapter seeks to demonstrate the pivotal position of rural/urban oppositions in the cultural hierarchies of Trinidad, particularly their intimate relation to local ideas about "race" and its referents, "culture," and "ethnicity," among Indo-Trinidadians.

Occupation, too, plays a part in the discursive construction and lived experience of cultural hierarchy, and this category can also be viewed through the rural/urban opposition. Agricultural labor, whether slave or free, was a necessary factor in the establishment and maintenance of British Caribbean colonial societies; the consequent rise and importance of various forms of peasantries would become characteristic of the region. Since slave emancipation in Britain's colonies in 1838, Caribbean peoples have established many patterns of land occupancy and tenure alongside the dominant plantation system of agricultural production, a labor form which nevertheless persists in some areas today. One consequence of the intimate relationship between plantation labor and independent subsistence farming in the Caribbean is that for peoples of the region, land is both an economic and a symbolic resource (Besson 1992; Besson and Momsen 1987). Land may represent either the indignity of servitude or the dignity of autonomy and self-preservation.

Indians arrived in Trinidad in the mid-nineteenth century (1845–1917) as part of Britain's post-Emancipation indentured labor project (a policy in force throughout its sugar-producing colonies). For many decades after their arrival they remained geographically distinct from other populations because of their assignment to sugar estates (plantations). Although some Afro-Trinidadians and a few whites were also on the estates, Indians were predominant. Relegated by colonial authority to specific arenas of production, indentured Indians were literally placed in and figuratively associated with plantation agriculture. By contrast, Afro-Trinidadians became more thoroughly incorporated into town-centered occupations, and, from about the 1920s, were particularly well-represented in the petroleum refineries. Until the end of World War II, Indo-Trinidadians remained disproportionately involved in subsistence agricultural sectors; in the mid-twentieth century social and economic transformations and political independence began to reverse this concentration. The Indian immigrants initially found themselves with "black" grass-roots (poor and working-class) Trinidadians—who were socially and racially distinguished from the "colored" middle class, sharing the bottom of an ethnically segmented labor market and a cultural hierarchy fundamentally replicating British ideology. The early analogous structural positioning of "blacks" and "East Indians" and their gradual differentiation and dispersal did not, however, elide the tensions which grew between them, tensions that were a consequence of their competitive roles as workers.[1] Nor did it erase the cultural association between Indians and agriculture which developed during plantation indenture. Agricultural production and manual labor became synonymous with "Indian Culture" and, in a reverse trajectory, with Indian heritage.

The labor histories of rural proletarian Indo-Trinidadians reveal an intimate association between the physical and psychological experience of estate (plantation) labor. Among them, a sensibility about agricultural work and the natural environment as powerful and life-shaping is tacitly implied or directly projected, though the ways these associations become configured as "rural," and what "rural" signifies in social relations is not immediately obvious in this discourse. More evident are the various attributes of "rural" in identity discourse that seem to stand on their own, outside of geographic associations and, without necessary connection to actual experience in the countryside. However, the rural "countryside" constitutes a particularly resonant metaphor for Indo-Trinidadians as an ethnic group predominantly relegated through indentured labor to the rural proletarian sector of agricultural production. The countryside reveals what may be called a "racial landscape" in which the "racial" identities of ethnic groups are identified with particular types of place as a result of perceptions of cultural heritage and island social history. Through the lens of cultural hierarchy and the angle of rural/urban opposition, we can better see contradictions such as "racial" landscapes that persist in spite of demographic discrepancies. For example, in a study of contemporary agriculture in Trinidad, Harry (1993) found that almost two out of ten (18.5%) farmers in her sample were Afro-Caribbean, managing one-fourth of the cocoa and dairy farms she surveyed (1993: 208). Although there are Afro-Trinidadians involved in agricultural pursuits, and Afro-Trinidadians who have lived for generations in "rural" localities, they find their identity in imagery largely antithetical to farming—a cultural terrain preserved for Indo-Trinidadians.

Rural affiliation became an important element in Indo-Trinidadian identity for social and historical reasons linked to Indian, African, and British worldviews and to the colonial experience in Trinidad. As postcolonial conditions created a context in which racial and ethnic identities gained significance, the role of rural affiliation as a racial and ethnic marker was reinforced. Rurality was also perpetuated by its cultural connection with north/south regional divisions. However, it soon came into conflict with ideas of "modernity" and associated shifts in cultural hierarchies which disadvantaged rural affiliation and valued Western over Eastern categories. Class mobility seemed to require distance from a culturally devalued rural context, which, in turn, seemed to threaten Indo-Trinidadian ethnic authenticity. This contradiction has been overcome by the increasing cultural differentiation of negative "rusticity" from aspects of rural affiliation which are positively valued (see Creed and Ching, this volume). This distinction has been tapped by upwardly mobile Indo-Trinidadians to facilitate upward mobility within an "authentic" (read "rural") context. In turn, then, racial and ethnic distinctiveness has been bolstered by the continued validity of "rural" and "rustic" as racial markers of Indo-Trinidadians. Yet each conveys significantly different messages about group history and identity.

Despite fewer Indo-Trinidadians in agricultural production, the image of "Ram, the barefoot Indian" (Hodge 1975: 35) remains. Local stereotypes of Indo-Trinidadians as "naturally" inclined to toil and soil, to putative land greed, and to an alleged shrewdness in orchestrating upward mobility are made credible on the basis of the organization of production historically and on the concomitantly unfolding concepts of race and culture. The identity processes in postcolonial Trinidad cannot be understood without attention to how rural/urban, class, and racial/ethnic categories interact, an interaction that must be examined in terms of cultural as well as structural hierarchies. I will demonstrate the importance of rural/urban oppositions in Trinidadian cultural hierarchies by first analyzing local ideologies of "race" and "culture" and their significance for representations of rurality. Then I will examine geographic places as symbolic constructs, with particular reference to the multi-layered meanings given to the four cardinal directions, north, south, east, and west. Finally, I discuss some ethnographic examples taken from Trinidad's "south" that reveal local perceptions of race, culture, and place, which in turn inform rural/urban dyads and the cultural hierarchies they help to sustain.

COLONIAL LOGIC AND POSTCOLONIAL LEGACIES

The originally unequal participation of Afro-Trinidadians and Indo-Trinidadians in the principal sectors of the national economy resulted in a division of labor in which the urbanization of Afro and the ruralization of Indo (Sebastien 1980: 126) prevailed in many parts of the island. Concentrations of particular populations in certain sectors of the island created what would remain, in popular wisdom, a mutually exclusive geography, where an Afro-Trinidadian, urban "north" is elevated in contrast to an Indo-Trinidadian, rural "south." Therefore, even in the significant number of areas where population heterogeneity was, and is, the empirical reality, the metaphoric "racial" landscape still prevails.

As Helen Safa (1987) notes, the pivot of national identity in the Anglophone Caribbean is race. However, constructing interpretive categories of identity and distinguishing particular types of person according to these categories are complex exercises in Trinidad. Daniel Segal (1994) correctly points out that this complexity is not so much due to an "unusual degree of social heterogeneity" as it is due to an imagined pluralism, where the ancestral past is memorialized in a way that links and makes synonymous historical and contemporary diversity (1994: 223–25). As Trinidadians currently envisage their nation and the array of selves that constitute it, the cast consists of "living ancestors," categories of person created in plantation political economy, the colonial moment that both enraced and socially positioned particular constituencies who retain these ancestral identities today—"Europeans" ("masters"), "Africans" ("slaves"), "East Indians" ("indentured laborers") (1994: 223). History thereby remains a vital part of the present, rather than simply a background or a precondition.

Although these three most significant configurations—European, African, Indian—comprise a template for social identities among Trinidadians, the nature of colonial relations among the populace (notably sexual activity) was such that numerous permutations of identities based on ancestry emerged. Lacking the "one drop" rule of North American racial accounting, Caribbean societies, in general, do not operate on an exclusive binary opposition between "white" and "black." Consequently, determining and debating ethnic and racial identities is an avid activity among Trinidadians. However, as I have argued elsewhere (Khan 1993), a dual discourse is evident within which showing too much preoccupation with race comes dangerously close to appearing "racial," that is, to attributing validity to racial hierarchies, and thus evoking colonial hegemony. Hence, on the one hand, there exists the apparently self-evident structure of ranked social and cultural attributes; on the other hand there is the ideally preferable notion of democratic equality and autonomy.

Because it is a fraught construct, highly charged through the role it has played in both organizing and justifying plantation society, "race" is often glossed in terms of "color" or "culture." Color, for example, as a descriptive register, can appear merely a statement of empirical evidence and therefore not a dilemma: assessment without judgement. While such terms as "brown" or "red" signify a mix of "races" (Euro and Afro), they remain a step away from harking back to that problematic colonial moment that racial accounting generally evokes. Even as it can represent "race," therefore, color can also side-

step it; thus "color" may function as a euphemistic category of identity. The tensions of unequally evaluated cultural distinctions may, as
well, be de-fused through a putative relativism that invokes neutrali-
ty: *customs* can differ without causing (or being caused by) social conflict, if they are located outside of "racial" phenomena; that is, when
they are extra-historical with respect to New World contexts. The
rural/urban opposition plays a similar role, affirming the "fact" of
"race" and racial ranking by maintaining a discursive space that
implicitly acknowledges these while employing an alternative idiom.

"Race," as an interpretive category of identity in Trinidad, is
understood to be constituted by essential heritable traits (biological
foundations) that produce phenotypical markers (genealogical cues)
that intimately articulate with and therefore mutually constitute culture (traditions and practices of forebears), and that can thus predict
character and behavior which are perpetuated in the fundamental
locus of the family—whether "African," "European," or "East Indian."
But there is another feature emblematic of "race" in Trinidad (and
throughout the Caribbean), an additional way history remains part of
the present, informing identity and the configuration of cultural hierarchies there. In the ideology of living ancestors, the present-day "collective characters from the colonial past" (Segal 1994: 223), history
itself becomes an essential quality of personhood. That is, for those
who have experienced them in the most disempowered ways (Africans
and Indians), the social conditions of plantation political economy
become part and parcel of "self." In other words, these social conditions located in *place* become, in a sense, internalized as part of experience, not simply the site of experience.[2] While historically a domain of
industrial and other innovations connected with things urban, the
plantation is associated with the countryside in the rural/urban dyad.

The postcolonial condition in Trinidad rests on a colonial legacy
that is steeped in the plantation—an allegedly inescapable, essential
quality derived from the experience of place. The notion of plural
ancestries continues to shape Caribbean identity today, in contrast, for
example, to identity in the United States, another locality with significant heterogeneity and a heritage of immigration. There, contrary to

the Caribbean ideology of living ancestors, a sense of closure on "the time before immigration" exists, at least for those accorded a privileged status as "fully American" (Segal 1994: 222). I would add another facet to this contrast, one that bears on the relationship between "race" and "rurality" in local cultural hierarchies. Along with the prerequisite of closure for hyphenated Americans, there is the power of the "American dream." By dint of effort, success (upward social mobility) theoretically lifts one out of a previous condition, and into a new and improved one. Among Trinidadians, the ultimate former condition, the plantation, is never completely erased with upward mobility. As the consummate site of identity formation, the plantation becomes a powerful metaphor of individual and group. In the United States, history is something to be transcended, even overcome; the legacy of colonialism in the Caribbean is such that history is not separated from basic identity. For even when social mobility may project one out of the grass-roots stratum (a *class* membership linked to a heritage of slavery or indenture), place/plantation subsumes and symbolizes origins, experience, identity. What exists is a discourse of *escape* but not of *rejection*. Perhaps because Indo-Trinidadians have far more recent memories of the plantation than do Afro-Trinidadians, and because they are not included in the allegory of Middle Passage cultural loss and re-creation under slavery, for them "traditional culture" can be compromised with social mobility ("Western" lifestyle, conversion to Christianity). As my epigraph illustrates, place can become racialized through people's ambivalent assessment of their past as figured in the dark and dangerous types who are said to have populated plantations ("estates") and who carry the blood of racial inferiority into an ethnic group. But, paradoxically, in so doing, place is not denied (or closed off); rather, it is affirmed.

As the British pursued their economic ventures in the Caribbean, they established the traditional European epistemology which pitted rural against urban. For example, Barbara Bush (1981) recounts that eighteenth-century British observers of the Caribbean colonies assumed "a strong distinction between [white] country and town women." One observer argued that [country women] were exposed to the dangers of 'constant intercourse' with negro domestics; [while] ladies in and about the towns, in contact with Europeans 'and others brought up in Great Britain', were 'better mannered and more refined' (Bush 1981: 255).

Here, spatial (town/country), racial (negro/European), and gender (women/ladies) identities can transgress the social order by threatening conventional configurations—town/white/refined/high; country/ negro/coarse/low—through improper relations with (exposure to) each other. What is interesting is that this three-centuries-old perspective clearly employs the assumption that "urban" is metonymic of high culture as much as "white" is, and that "urban" has the power (through its degree of significance) to undermine high culture if it is spoiled by country ways—ways which are themselves metonymic of low culture.

Reverberations of these distinctions between rural and urban are evident in the colonial indenture project as it justified itself in the face of criticism from the Abolitionist Movement as it was monitored by the government of India since it feared potential labor unrest in the island. In doing so, part of its recourse was to "explain" the structural position of the different labor constituencies ("ethnic groups") in terms of cultural qualities and proclivities. Social hierarchy and cultural hierarchy thus came to buttress each other. In presenting Indian recruitment for Trinidad's sugar estates as culturally sensible, planters fostered the notion that indentured immigrants brought with them to the sugar colonies some kind of affinity for agricultural production through their previous experience as peasants. Often touted as naturally suited to this kind of labor, Indians were presented, in colonial depiction, among other ways, as logically filling a particular niche, one that ostensibly was similar to the way of life they had left behind. Thus, colonial assumptions about "urban" and "rural" that obtained with regard to Britain, Africa, and India also found another, quite pragmatic application in the Caribbean.[3] As Donald Wood (1968) points out, during the 1850s and 1860s, when Indians were becoming the principal sector of Trinidad's immigrants, "ideas about the Indians were freezing into a stereotype" that would set the tone for race relations up to contemporary times (1968: 154). For example, in 1901 the *Trinidad Mirror* commented that "agricultural labour in Trinidad was not attractive to those people 'who have got beyond the stage of civilisation that is satisfied with a loin cloth and a pot of rice'" (quoted in Singh 1985: 36). We can infer from this comment that an implicit contrast is being made between Afro and Indo "racial" groups as well as between grass-roots and middle-class Indo-Trinidadians. Moreover, the structural constraints within which Indo-Trinidadians and Afro-Trinidadians have established affinities and managed animosities were inflected with their respective evaluations of heritage. These evaluations formed a gradation of worth that had the potential to confirm the alleged fit of cultural predisposition to a particular form of labor, fostering their own essentialized constructions of "Indian" and "African" ("creole") culture. At the same time, each group was able to imbue its social position with dignity. Indo-Trinidadians have built upon a colonially created landscape and cultural hegemony by valorizing their own interpretations of "traditional" and "authentic" heritage and social status. These notions, such as those of rurality and rusticity, simultaneously conform to and challenge Trinidad's cultural hierarchies, thus creating permutations and contradictions within it.

THE COUNTRY AND THE CITY

Ethnographic research conducted in contemporary Caribbean societies reveals versions of rural/urban, or country versus city contrasts. For example, Lisa Douglass (1992) observes that when young Jamaican women are disapprovingly alleged to be sexually active, the assumption is that it is with socially inferior partners. It is not uncommon for this characterization to be made of "country girls" by "town people," revealing the "town view of country people," who are seen "as wild and uncivilized" (1992: 180). In Trinidad, according to John Stewart, "one of the strongest ideals . . . is to remove oneself from the

bush"; he states that urban residents rarely visit the bush and emphasize the distance separating "culturally backward bush-dwellers"
from the "civilized" city (1973: 66–67).

Social science models of social organization have also contributed
to the configuration of plantation societies in terms of a country versus city metaphor. For decades these models were often (implicitly or
otherwise) premised on the opposing world views of urban and rural
life (e.g. Redfield 1930, 1941). However, several factors characteristic
of Caribbean colonies challenge these conceptual dyads. Two have particular relevance for my present discussion. First, as Sidney Mintz
(1953) observed over forty years ago, Caribbean plantations represent
"a special kind of industrial organization. Many of the features of life
generally associated with 'urban', 'Western', or 'modern' society . . .
are introduced through plantation organization" (1953: 138). These
features represent the ingression of an "urban," Western capitalist way
of life into the countryside (see Quintero Rivera 1987; Sebastien 1980),
as most of the sugar industry has been in "rural" areas. In post-
Emancipation times, Caribbean sugar plantations, for example, have
given rise to rural proletarian communities, such as those in Puerto
Rico, where the "vast majority of people is landless, propertyless, . . .
wage-earning," with few alternatives to plantation labor (Mintz 1953:
139). As such, they conform in many respects to notions of "rustic." A
second consideration compounds this issue of plantation (industrial)
organization. Observers of the Caribbean have argued that relative to
other areas of the world, the region shows a comparatively indistinct
rural/urban divide in terms of the degree of separation (technological,
infrastructural, cultural) between the two spheres (see Momsen 1993;
Ryan 1966). Most of the islands did not have extensive urbanized
sectors and had only one "primate" city (Cross 1979). Moreover, infrastructural amenities such as transportation, entertainment, and
schools have brought an urban culture "within the rural orbit" (Rubin
1960: 119).[4] While there are core/periphery-like relations between
central and outlying areas in the Caribbean (Cross 1979), the precise
nature of these relations, and their implications for rural/urban models

are typically assumed; "rural" remains largely a prima facie aspect of Caribbean societies.

Given these factors, the questions become: why in Trinidad is a rural/urban contrast such a significant dimension of local identity and how does it inform discourses of "race," "culture," and "ethnic group"? The colonial legacy looms large, in terms of its nineteenth-century ideological predispositions toward hierarchies of all kinds and in terms of the way these assumptions were institutionalized in the form of particular social, political, and economic arrangements. However, the laborers' re-creations over time in response to these forces figure significantly as well. In other words, the rural/urban hierarchy remains, even while criteria for the categories have changed.

Contributing to the conceptual and demographic dichotomy between urban and rural have been tensions over resource competition and livelihood. As owners of sugar estates bought up the arable lands throughout the late nineteenth and early twentieth centuries, land became an increasingly scarce commodity for most people. Viewed as a kind of economic insurance by Indo and Afro alike, Afro-Trinidadians expressed their anxieties partly by decrying Indo-Trinidadian population growth and its perceived concomitant, land acquisition. Moreover, initial geographical separation was never tantamount to social anonymity. Indo-Trinidadians were often viewed with resentment by non-Indo-Trinidadian workers, particularly Afro-Trinidadians, as being not only the preferred labor of colonizers and agents of the depression of wages, but also as undue recipients of land grants, which, for a period, Indo-Trinidadians received after their terms of indenture expired or in lieu of return passage to India. For instance, the expansion of cane farming in the 1870s was an opportunity that Afro-Trinidadians seized when they were able: "the cane farmer was to some extent his own master; sugar had at last become a cash crop for the small independent Negro land-holder" (Wood 1968: 296). Yet the colonists' desire for malleable and dependent estate labor combined with the competitiveness of sugar production and market demand for wet rice (Wood 1968) to foster Indo-Trinidadian agricultural production and significantly eclipse Afro-Trinidadian farming.

Thus even as early as the 1870s, "irrigated *padi* fields became prominent in the cultural landscape" of central and southern Trinidad (Wood 1968: 276). Merely twenty-five years after the first indentured immigrants had arrived, the landscape associated with Indians had both an ecological (crop production) and cultural (symbolic) valence.

This symbolic dimension is so powerful that it holds sway in spite of contradictory knowledge. For example, according to the Protector of Immigrants, while from 1869 to 1912, 89,222 acres of Crown lands were granted to Indo-Trinidadians, if the increase in the Indo-Trinidadian population were to be factored in, the land owned by Indo-Trinidadians per head showed a clear decrease (Kondapi 1951: 310). As a friend of mine explained to me:

> First time people [original forebears] used to own a lot of land, everybody had they own land because the land was so cheap. But they give all to they children. And now people can't afford the land. And my grandmother, if she give she children she land, and them give them own children, so then they ent [is not] no more land left. First time generation not so big as now, too. And one lot [one-ninth of an acre] can only be given to one child.

It is true that declining per capita land ownership among Indo-Trinidadians does not necessarily invalidate the concerns about land concentration for Indo-Trinidadians as a group; theoretically, if the population were increasing they could take up more land even if they have less of it per person than in the past. Still, many individual Indo-Trinidadians find themselves with inadequate land. At the same time, others have expanded their holdings so that the contempoary profile of land holding among Indo-Trinidadians is quite diverse. The cultural stereotype, however, of land-hungry and land-hoarding Indo-Trinidadians remains powerful even in the face of discrepant realities.

NORTH AND SOUTH

Indo-Trinidadians have long been characterized in popular wisdom, local fiction, and scholarly literature by notions of the countryside that are generally equated with the "south," as opposed to an urban, Afro-Trinidadian "north." As recently as 1993, one scholar explained the preponderance of Indo-Caribbeans in the agricultural sector far into the twentieth century by invoking

> their social backgrounds in India, their *innate love* for and knowledge of the land and its cultivation, [which] made them over time the *classic farmers* and food producers of Trinidad and British Guiana, dominating the Black population in most key areas of rural production (Look Lai 1993: 220; my emphasis).

If the logic of this position were extended, the suggestion would be that through historical circumstances a biological predisposition (racial identity?) was exposed and harnessed. In other words, supposed rural identities are used to interpret history. Indeed, as I considered an appropriate site for my field research, I became particularly interested in the conventional wisdom that informed people's characterizations of the life and culture of various communities. Local friends and informants consistently echoed each other's advice to me that if I wanted to experience "*real* Indian culture" I must go "south," to an alleged rural heartland of authentic tradition and "long time ways." The localities repeatedly suggested were Penal, Debe, and Barrackpore (particularly Penal), all three the epitome of the rural, crucibles of "traditional ways" where progress and modernization ostensibly have not fully penetrated. There is certainly significant agricultural production in the "north," for example on the outskirts of the capital city, Port of Spain, and along the heavily populated East-West Corridor. Yet this agricultural production remains associated with modernity, beyond the bounds of heritage. In one of numerous examples from contemporary Caribbean literature, Vidia Naipaul evokes this association of countryside, "south," "race" (primal urges), and thinly disguised Indo-Trinidadians in *The Mimic Men*, where he describes the "rural workers, picturesque Asiatics . . . , ever ready to listen to the call of the blood" (1967: 206). Clearly, cultural geographies shape physical ones. As one Afro-Trinidadian woman summed it up: "Penal is behind God's back."

Ironically, Penal, where most of my research took place, historically has been a principal area of subsistence and cash crop production,
and thus a major marketing center. Situated only about thirty minutes'
drive from Trinidad's "industrial capital," San Fernando, it is in the
midst of Trinidad's oil-producing region (St. Patrick County). The contradiction of an ostensibly isolated, timeless trove of authenticity
ensconced in such a central (and thus indeed "modern") location
intrigued me. There, agriculture is an identifiable industry; "rural" is
a cultural concept. Yet the concept of "rural" depicted in literature on
the Caribbean tends to be made synonymous with "agriculture." An
empirical and a conceptual space are equated with a means of production, and it is assumed that occupations within the rubric "agricultural" do not significantly differ. The varying descriptions of Penal as a
particular kind of locality reveal people's assumptions about the
nature of Indo-Trinidadian history and the relationship between culture and class. These descriptions also reflect the ways in which history and identity are constituted in geographical spaces, which in turn
shape the identities of those persons and communities residing in
them. That "south" and "north" are metaphoric as well as literal
demarcations was brought home in an offhand remark once made to
me by a taxi driver. I had been visiting some friends near Icacos, the
southernmost area on the western side of the island, and told the driver I wanted to return to my home in Penal. He responded, "oh, you're
going *south*." I found this remarkable, considering that we were easily
three hours south of Penal. There was a cultural logic to his association, however, as beyond Penal are the fields and refineries of
Trinidad's oil industry. Although there are communities located significantly further south of this cultural "south," they are not included
conceptually within this geographic designation, largely because they
are much more ethnically heterogeneous and less involved with agriculture, whether it be cash crop or subsistence farming. Historically
employing Afro-Trinidadians, this region thus evokes a heterogeneous, cosmopolitan, and hence "modern" ethos.[5]

As metaphoric representations of space as well as literal demarcations of the cardinal directions, "south" and "north" are differently

evaluated, and in multiple ways. Both "south" and "north" comprise
respective constituencies of "grass-roots" residents, but "grass-roots"
communities "in south" have a distinctly "countryside" association,
whereas their counterparts "in the north" have an urban association.
This association tends to position northern grass-roots identity as
hierarchically superior to grass-roots characteristics in the south,
given the broader contrasts between the two regions. "South" itself
constitutes two contrasting symbols among Trinidadians. One is a relatively positively evaluated rural space that connotes cultural authenticity on the part of Indo-Trinidadians, and a relatively negatively
evaluated rural place that produces rustic persons.[6] Because these positive and negative glosses are not necessarily mutually exclusive or
fixed with respect to their referents, "south" as an index of "things
Indian" is in ambivalent flux between, in a sense, "high" and "low"
culture; that is, something to be valued or something to be eschewed.
As my friend, an elderly Afro-Trinidadian woman explained to me:

> Indians of today live a higher class life, so you won't see nothing
> Indianish in them. Real Indians live a kind of low class life. When
> you have more education and a better life [standard of living] you lose
> your life style, you live like white people, not like Indians. You have
> maids, servants, a big house.

While the "north"/"south" dichotomy is quite significantly an
implicit Afro/Indo distinction, this urban/rural symbolism also signals
distinctions among Indo-Trinidadians, distinctions that are fundamentally about class stratification and the ideologies that accompany
it. For example, a wealthy and urban young Indo-Trinidadian man
explained to me that there is a

> difference between [town dwellers] and dark Indians from Barrackpore,
> Penal, and Couva. There's a lot of class status and hierarchy in the Indian
> community. Some friends of mine say I'm not Indian because I'm living
> in town. If your father was a professor and your grandfather was a
> teacher and you have Sindi [Sind region of Pakistan] in you, well, the
> others, it's like they're only one generation from indenture.

The areas to which this speaker refers, Barrackpore, Penal, Couva, are all localities that have been profoundly associated with servitude, poverty, manual labor, and general "backwardness," if also with "authentic" tradition. That he associates "dark" and "indenture" with the rustic residents of these rural places is not coincidental.

EAST AND WEST

Also informing rural place/rustic person imagery is the distinction between "East" and "West," familiarized by a long tradition of Orientalist discourse. This distinction, too, obtains within the constructed "south," where things "Western" are associated with the modern while things "Eastern" are associated with the authentic, yet with valuations that are contingent. "East"/"West" tensions in the cultural hierarchy of "retrogressive" versus "progressive" are accompanied by "high" culture/"low" culture tensions, where "East" or "West" can represent either, depending upon how cultural authenticity is being defined and interpreted, as something to be sought or something to be transformed. In an essay meant for a wide audience, a local Indo-Trinidadian journalist relies on familiar conventional wisdom to support his point about the essential Indian:

> Urban Indians are unrepresentative of their people . . . Indians are
> largely a rural people, quiet, conservative and attached to the land.
> They live in the Western hemisphere, but they are Eastern peoples. If
> Negroes look to the Americans and Europeans and wish to be bourgeois,
> Christian, materialistic and intellectual, Indians do not. They hold to
> traditions and behaviour from India, despising all else as inferior.
> (Jagessar 1969; quoted in Ryan 1972: 9,fn. 12)

Yet this dismissal of the value of urban spheres contends with other interpretations. In my fieldnotes I recorded a casual conversation I had with an elderly acquaintance who had been a resident "of south" his entire life:

> [Gyan][7] seems sad his children didn't take up Hinduism, though he says

'if they loyal to Christ, is okay,' in a kind of resigned way. 'Just now I will pass away and everything will vanish. These days young people don't want to learn things that the Hindu people know, prayer and so on. Only English, English. It have [there are] Indian children up in the north who have a lot of Hinduism. They good in their Hindi, you know. South is semi . . . half way. South is not so progressive. The parents don't make up their mind to *learn* [teach] the children. The young people here don't know their prayers, then they join the Open Bible Church. In the North, people teach their children Hindi and bhajans [Hindu hymns].'

In one Indo-Trinidadian woman's explanation of the rural/urban opposition, Orientalist imagery was expressed largely through a religious idiom, as she characterized rural areas, on the one hand, as consisting of "the Little Tradition, rituals, folk tradition, traditional methods of income like gardening, fishing, taxis, the fringes of the economy, you are more surrounded by the culture of your own, a similar culture." Urban areas, on the other hand, are

> moving towards the Great Tradition, the Vedantic tradition, just do *hawan*[8] and focus on the *message* of the *Ramayan*,[9] no pandit [priest], greater literate people inquiring about life. You can have traditional lifestyles in urban areas but they're not *really* urban lifestyle as they still don't go to parties, everyone knows each other, family interests are more important than individual interests, parental authority exists.

Whether urban areas confer certain qualities upon Indo-Trinidadians or urbane Indo-Trinidadians aggregate in particular patterns, according to her juxtaposition rurality denotes: blind (or less informed) faith as opposed to greater literary capabilities, attention to repetitive detail in worship rather than concern with philosophical questions, the insularity of a homogeneous culture and omnipotent family authority as opposed to individual satisfactions in heterogeneous contexts, and grass-roots pursuits such as gardening, fishing, and taxi-driving. This is another point in which class constructs—grass-roots and middle class—dovetail with cultural imagery.

FROM RUSTICITY TO RURALITY

Grass-roots consciousness among Indo-Trinidadians is permeated with historical memories of real experiences of the hardships of estate barracks life, subsistence agriculture, and illiteracy. Augmenting these, however, is an oral tradition that invokes a local past in which religious and cultural forms were "closer" to original, indigenous ones. Thus, the image of the "coolie" is at once one of a localized (creolized) rural proletariat and of a culturally foreign other, ascriptions that are generally, if paradoxically, conflated. Class mobility, then, is inherently also a matter of cultural jeopardy, where cultural practices that are definitive of *being* Indian—such as ritual, aesthetic forms like dance and music, and so-called family values (essentially, moral propriety)—are made precarious, and thus are defined and negotiated accordingly.

Cultural traditions symbolizing an ancient and high (*legitimate*) culture have been employed in efforts to re-fashion the extant cultural hierarchy that relegates Indo-Trinidadians to the bottom. These traditions, however, remain subject to the hegemonic influences of colonial (and postcolonial) ideology. That is, the assertion and valorization of cultural authenticity occurs within a historically powerful discourse of denigration; constructions of identity are ambivalent and reflect broader power relations. Rather than the "south," or the countryside, subsuming and thus symbolizing both the *products* of social-cultural interaction (lifeways, ambience, quality of life) and the *people* who produce these, the notion of the "south" contains a distinction between cultural products and cultural producers.[10] This distinction between rural place and rustic persons obtains, as well, in the discourse of race and ethnicity. It is important to note, however, that neither of these concepts is necessarily expressed as a formal set of ideas. Rather, they exist as parts of the common sense and taken-for-granted categories of thought that constitute everyday relations. In this way they operate as hegemonic metaphors that inform racial constructs. Emblematic of ethnic group by virtue of labor history, the concepts of rural place and rustic person also locate cultural heritage in inherent proclivities.

Rurality is assumed by most non-Indo-Trinidadians and celebrated by most Indo-Trinidadians as a touchstone of true Indian tradition: authentic, timeless, essential culture serving as a crucible of heritage against political domination and potential cultural absorption by demographically equal and, post-independence, politically empowered urban/northern Afro-Trinidadians. "South"-as-rurality offers, in literal and figurative terms, demographic safety for those who value it. It is a niche that transcends its actual inhabitants. However, it does so insofar as its allure in offering what the urban cannot does not depend on the (presumed) nature of those who actually reside there. In other words, as the imagined cradle of cultural authenticity, the "south" as rural place exemplifies the successful (ethnic) group deflection of the onslaught of colonialism and, concomitantly, a domain of self-preservation irrespective of the pejoratively characterized (by both Indo and Afro) rustic resident. As such, the grass-roots dimension of "south"-as-rural is not subject to specific class connotations. Authenticity is, in a sense, held constant in relation to the structural inequalities of Trinidadian society.

Rusticity, however, is often denigrated as retrogressive, as inhibiting the progress and achievement availed through what are interpreted as signs of modernity: formal higher education, civil service or white collar employment, and consumption of high status consumer goods. As such, it indexes, rather than transcends, a decidedly lower class "grass-roots" position. In fact, appreciating the physical harshness of the life of rural proletarians who also must produce their own subsistence crops, Indo-Trinidadian literary figures have often portrayed "rustic" life as more or less nasty, brutish, and short. This reaches perhaps its apogee in H. Sonny Ladoo's novel, *No Pain Like This Body* (1974). The alleged disadvantages of rusticity are earmarked, for example, by certain dispositions: being *cunumunu*, a slang term for a simpleton, sometimes a cuckold,[11] often a country bumpkin; or having a *"jheel* mentality," which can be translated as a lagoon perspective, one grown backward and dull from a life spent working in the "lagoon," a local gloss for subsistence gardens of rice and vegetables usually located some distance from the house. To have a *jheel* mentality means to be traditional in one's thinking, not in the positive sense of authentic, but in the negative sense of retrograde.

As with cane fields, the lagoon is for Indo-Trinidadians a "master symbol" (Wolf 1958) of the demanding, wrenching labor of subsistence agriculture, the physical manifestation of their location in Trinidad's system of stratification. Yet it is also the means of sustaining life since access to land or provision production is what differentiates a "secure" from a "precarious" working class among all Trinidadians (Khan 1995). Rice land in the wet season and vegetable garden in the dry season, the lagoon was terrain distinct from the estates' cane fields, a significant if ambivalent domain of autonomy that most Indo-Trinidadians today have some kind of experience with, even if solely in the form of the previous generation's lore. For residents of the "south," the majority of whom are Indo-Trinidadian, the comfort of guaranteed persistence through the possibility of subsistence gardening figures significantly in their valuation of land, a possibility more realistically attainable by them than by the urban residents of the "north," who have less access to acreage. Significant at the same time, however, is the idea that "making garden" is more appealing and sensible to Indo-Trinidadians due to "natural" talents for agricultural pursuits as well as predilections for safeguarding the future, subsequently embellished (rather than stifled) under indenture. Whereas local racial ideology has Afro-Trinidadians as making the most of the present (often carelessly), Indo-Trinidadians are characterized as concerned (often to a fault) with exigencies to come. Thus, land is resonant as the safety net of ethnic group survival, as the presumed abiding passion of ancestors from the sub-continent, and, through these, as a salient attribute in the local lexicon of "race."

Ownership of land, as opposed to renting or squatting, raises prestige within Indo-Trinidadian communities. It is also a means of upward mobility. However, ownership alone does not enable Indo-Trinidadians to disrupt or opt out of the hierarchy of "high" and "low" culture. Significant modifications in class position and disassociation from rusticity come with capitalist status and education, a change in one's relation to the means of production. It is not merely that acreage is acquired; it is that one ceases to work it oneself. Transcending the linkages between livelihood and associated character traits requires more than simply improving one's status within that livelihood. But, importantly, such a transition is still possible within the category of the "rural."

This requisite for upward mobility begs the question of what happens to one's authentic culture/heritage as one becomes literally and symbolically more removed from the land. On the one hand, subtle architectural emendations (and associated lifestyle patterns) clearly attest to this attenuation. "Grass-roots" houses tend to have less distinct boundaries separating inside from outside, in contrast with middle-class houses. These often have "galleries" (balconies/porches) enclosed by glass or otherwise clearly demarcated or separated; social activities increasingly take place inside the house; rooms, and space in general, tend to be closed off; wall-to-wall carpeting often replaces *lipe* (dung and earth plaster) or covers board or cement flooring. Not only are local notions of privacy altered, but distinctions between the appropriate spaces for "natural" products as opposed to "cultural" products become sharper. However, some critical considerations remain for Indo-Trinidadians: the conceptual distinctions between "traditional" and "modern" previously discussed, and the implications these have for ethnic group viability and the security of upward class mobility against perceptions of cultural loss. As Indo-Trinidadians experience upward mobility (or the promise of it), an ideological shifting may occur, where that which is associated with rusticity becomes redefined in terms of rurality. When this process occurs it is not necessarily measurable as a consistent, predictable, historical unfolding from one to the other in a series of concrete events. Rather, it is a tendency that forms part of the experience of culture and class transformation among Indo-Trinidadians.

The equation is that a "grass-roots" position grants a higher degree of cultural authenticity, a greater proximity to indigenous heritage. In reaching a higher, say middle-class, position, what an Indo-Trinidadian lacks in "Eastern" roots s/he gains in a lifestyle more consonant with things "Western." However, this inverse correlation can be negotiated, such as when involvement with the land is glossed as indicative of rurality rather than rusticity. For example, as Indo-Trinidadians experience upward class mobility, they may find cultural solace as well as, ideally, community approbation (because she or he is trying to maintain "living good with people" through the levelling mechanism of manual labor) by continuing to garden a small plot next to the house. More a pointed gesture than an economically critical practice, continuing to garden after it becomes a superfluous enterprise conveys more than a statement about the ability to own land— itself an anchor in an otherwise stormy sea of competing resource claims. Another dimension invoked is that quintessential Indian cultural signature, working one's land, perceived as brought from the sub-continent to the Caribbean untrammeled and undisrupted, a dignified and authentic, if humble, pursuit, one that is a channel for the bonds of community.

Thus, middle-class status does not necessarily jeopardize cultural authenticity if it can be reinterpreted as rurality; that is, linked with valorized images of Indianness, and by extension, Indo-Trinidadianness, and with public contribution (whether to the neighborhood or to the nation). These efforts imply that occupations in the civil service or professions, which, along with private entrepreneurship, historically have been the means of Indo-Trinidadians' upward mobility, are seen as not offering the same dignity of autonomy that is gained by living off the land (cf. B. Williams 1991: 72). This perspective, of course, reveals contemporary Indo-Trinidadian fantasies of a somewhat idyllic independent peasantry in India, as well as the pervasive reality of rural proletarianization in the New World.

DEBE, PENAL, BODI KE DAL

The referents of a familiar folk rhyme from the "south," "Debe, Penal, Bodi ke Dal," tell us much about the conceptual linkages among landscape, identity, and history. As two communities that epitomize the "south," Debe and Penal are the consummate sites of "real" Indo-Trinidadian life and culture on the island. Bodi is a kind of string bean, commonly grown in the subsistence plots of Indo-Trinidadian households; dal is lentils. They are two common and definitively Indian foods in Trinidad, associated with the gardens and the culture that produce them. This local adage associates "south"/cultural authenticity with grass-roots class position, for "south" is evocative of kitchen gardens (and hence food) that are indexical of the Indo-Trinidadian experience commemorated by this saying. The rhyme, in turn, interprets everyday experience in the "south." Walking to "make market" one morning, my friend's young son teased her about the pair of new, bright yellow sandals she had chosen to wear on our outing. He joked, "you look like you walked through dal, like you from Barrackpore." As another community epitomizing "south," Barrackpore in this quip, though meant in jest, was not a complimentary reference; it was tantamount to saying that she must be a country bumpkin if there *had* been the telltale dal on her feet.

Indo-Trinidadians as well as non-Indo-Trinidadians who do not live in the "south" tend to perceive the area as homogeneous, and residents of Debe and Penal as uniformly rustic. Yet the perceptions that the members of these two communities have of each other reveal the multiple discourses possible even when the premise of the existing cultural hierarchy is maintained. *Intra*-regional distinctions among hierarchized diagnostic attributes tell us something about how identities are constructed and integrated, and about the relationship of these processes of construction to a particular local context. My informants in Penal, for example, distinguished themselves from their neighbors in Debe, despite important "pumpkin vine" (extended) kinship ties, informal communal labor cooperation, and generations of variously intimate social interactions. My elderly neighbor, a man who had spent his entire life in Penal doing manual labor (agriculture and road maintenance), made precise distinctions between those Indo-Trinidadians who work in the island's cocoa/citrus estates (e.g., Penal) and those who work in sugar (e.g., Debe), the latter being generally more "hardened" by life and hence, in his view, possessing a more obdurate and simple constitution.

A second, quite telling, example comes from a conversation I had with another neighbor and her teenage son. His mother and I were teasing him about the urgency of getting him married off. I mentioned facetiously that I had recently met "a nice girl from Barrackpore" (which, like Debe, has been historically characterized by sugar production and thus readily symbolizes rusticity). In response, he exclaimed, "Barrackpore? You call that *nice*?!" Surprised, I queried him about his reaction, and he elaborated,

> Barrackpore and Debe [pauses]. Fighters, for one thing. Barrackpore [is] so far down, plenty flood, so out of the way. The place ent [is not] right, not developed. Debe [pauses]. You can't play bad [there] or the people will beat you. They stick together. They would not ask any question, just want to fight.

At this moment (which I am certain was not coincidental, even if unconscious), his mother chimed in, "Debe, Penal, bodi ke dal," as if to clarify and underscore his explanation. I asked the son where, then, he would prefer to find a wife. "Well, up north, Port of Spain side, San Fernando side." While San Fernando is only about twenty-five minutes' drive from Penal, as the only other urban concentration in Trinidad of any size, this young man perceives it as synonymous with Port of Spain, the capital city, approximately three hours away. He encapsulated his wishes gleefully: "Rich people!" His mother then responded dryly, "well, I will have to look for a girl for you from Port of Spain, but when you tap [beat] she, she can't go by she family again, she too far."[12] In her comment, the mother gently rebukes her son's aspirations, which she clearly finds unlikely as well as impractical. But her retort also signals that their unlikelihood attests to the symbolic distance between the "south" and "north" among Indo-Trinidadians. As importantly, the son's fantasy clearly indicates that locality and class identity are associated and hierarchically positioned; rusticity rather than rurality is suggested, even while both are coherently constituted as "south." Moreover, as he describes the "south"—

Barrackpore, Debe—he invokes a given correlation among intemper-
ate ("fighters"), impoverished ("not developed"), and clannish ("stick
together")—i.e., those who cannot "live good with people." If asked,
this young man would likely not extend his cognitive model to a claim
that people in the south, the "south" *he* delineates (absenting his own
locality of Penal), are of a distinct "race." However, he is nonetheless
relying on the inherently linked, and thus predictive attributes of geographic place and group identity. In the cultural hierarchy of rural and
urban, "racial" identity is in part constructed in connection with
locality, a "south" of subsistence agriculture and "traditional" ways.

CONCLUSION

As I stated at the outset of this chapter, cultural hierarchies
and their related discourses are multivocal. Notions of rusticity and
rurality mediate each other, and thus tensions between authenticity/
rurality and backwardness/rusticity diffract (uniform constructions) of
Indo-Trinidadians as an "ethnic group" with particular "racial" characteristics. These notions also challenge models of Caribbean "race
relations" that approach the structural as if it were given, independent
of local interpretation and contradictory ideologies.

While the Caribbean provides a compelling reason not to confuse
urbanization with industrialization, it also provides an example of the
contingent (if not arbitrary) connection between "agricultural" and
"rural." The former is a historically and empirically identifiable industry in the region; the latter is in most cases an ideologically charged
category. The implicit assumption contained in conceptually linking
agricultural and rural is that a point in literal and symbolic space
("rural") is equated with a type of production ("agriculture"), and that
occupations within the rubric "agricultural" supposedly do not *significantly* differ. However, while *occupation* is distinct conceptually from
production, in Trinidad's ethnically segmented labor market agricultural occupations form a metaphor for cultural quality that informs cultural hierarchies and the contours of racial identity. In this metaphor,
the cultural landscape of padi fields and seas of sugar cane are juxta-

posed with the cultural landscape of urbanized modernity. In various communities these landscapes become translated into "ethnic" terms by virtue of the historical tensions among groups specifically positioned in competitive labor arrangements. They are translated into "racial" terms in being essentialized into reduced and congealed representations that are seen as natural and imbued with predictive power, rather than as social and contingent.

However, the meanings people in changing circumstances assign to the constituent attributes that obtain in categories of identity are always creatively re-tooled. They are also, like ideology in general, self-justifying in masking their own internal contradictions and appearing conventional and given. For example, "rural" and "rustic" are not consistently mutually exclusive places/qualities, but are complexly imagined, overlapping, and simultaneously mutually affirming and negating symbols. Thus, the role of cultural hierarchies in social stratification is not one of the simple promotion or contestation of certain images of identity and their significance. Cultural hierarchies variously arrange identities and their imagery as these are absorbed and embellished by local groups. In other words, everyday life is organized around and understood through them. In Trinidad, and, I would argue, the wider Caribbean, the contrast between "rural" and "urban" places is a salient feature of the cultural hierarchies that inform the configuration and experience of social stratification on the ground. "Race," a key underpinning of Caribbean identities, takes a fundamental cue from rural/urban oppositions in its colonial and postcolonial associations with a culturally as well as economically charged domain, the land. These associations negotiate social inequality in the name of "rural" places and the "rustic" persons who live in them.

NOTES

I am grateful to Gerald Creed, Barbara Ching, and Daniel Segal for conscientious attention to this chapter, which benefitted greatly from their astute critiques. And, once again, Stephen Stuempfle helped me to clarify some of my thoughts. Always most helpful with useful comments in addition to incisive editing is Allyson Purpura, to whom I owe a great deal for invariably reading with such a keen eye. The fieldwork on which this chapter is based was part of a larger research project funded by Fulbright, Wenner-Gren Foundation, and Sigma Xi Society grants.

1. Also significant in the formation of allegedly mutually exclusive ethnic groups out of this diverse population was the advent of post-independence (1962) party politics. By the 1950s, the appeal to race was a key aspect of mass political mobilization (Hintzen 1989).

2. This is not to say that Euro-Caribbeans have not also had their sense of group and self shaped by the plantation in complex ways. However, far less often subordinate than were Afro-Caribbean and Indo-Caribbean peoples, Euro-Caribbeans's relationship to the plantation was not a matter of survival and oppression in a way comparable to enslaved and indentured populations. Thus the memory and meaning of the plantation have a distinct role in Euro-Caribbean identities.

3. Compare Mbilinyi's (1985) discussion of the significance of "city" and "country" in colonial Tanganyika, where "a contrast between city and country permeates colonial commentary on the society its agents found, and the one they struggled to create and rule. . . . The city was associated with non-Africans. . . . According to colonial ideology, the country was 'home' for Africans . . . and the African in town was considered an 'alien' in 'foreign' territory. . . . Colonial . . . presume that the past was rural and agricultural" (1985: 88).

4. An exception to this in Trinidad (and elsewhere in the Caribbean) is the recent arrival of electricity and pipe-borne water to many relatively remote areas (such as the one where I conducted my fieldwork). However, this attests to the marginalized status of these outlying areas relative to more central ones, rather than to their insularity from urbanization.

5. Former Prime Minister Eric Williams alluded to this demographic and symbolic distinction in his much quoted dichotomy between Africans/oil and Indians/sugar (e.g., Williams 1969).

6. It is my impression that this idea of cultural authenticity and the "true" core of identity being traceable to rurality does not apply to Afro-Trinidadians. As a Trinidadian might phrase it, the "rootsy" foundations (i.e., roots) of Afro-Caribbean racial and cultural identity do not lie in the land the way they do for Indo-Caribbeans—although the peasant and rural proletarian heritage of Afro-Caribbean peoples is, of course, recognized.

7. This is a pseudonym.

8. A sacred fire, in which *ghee* (clarified butter) is offered in devotional worship, and does not require the intervention of a *pandit* (priest).

9. The *Ramayana*, the Hindu epic involving the adventures of Ram, Sita, Latchman, and Rawan.

10. See Ferguson's (1992) discussion of Zambian conceptions of the "country as ideal" and the "country as locale" for a similar observation.

11. It is widely, if implicitly, recognized that men are deceived in this manner by women, as well as the obverse; thus, *cunumunu* includes both genders.

12. The subtext of this mother's statement is the knowledge among women that many men do eventually "tap" their wives (if only on occasion), that women need and continue to make use of nearby kin to help protect or support them during marital stress, and that therefore a bride's putting distance (geographic, emotional) between herself and her family can be detrimental.

REFERENCES

Besson, Jean. 1992. "Freedom and Community: The British West Indies." In Frank McGlynn and Seymour Drescher, eds., *The Meaning of Freedom: Economics, Politics, and Culture after Slavery.* Pittsburgh: University of Pittsburgh Press.

Besson, Jean and Janet Momsen, eds. 1987. *Land and Land Development in the Caribbean.* London: Macmillan.

Bush, Barbara. 1981. "White 'Ladies,' Colored 'Favorites,' and Black 'Wenches': Some Considerations on Sex, Race, and Class Factors in Social Relations in White Creole Society in the British Caribbean." *Slavery and Abolition* 2(3): 245–62.

Cross, Malcolm. 1979. *Urbanization and Urban Growth in the Caribbean.* London: Cambridge University Press.

Douglass, Lisa. 1992. *The Power of Sentiment: Love, Hierarchy, and the Jamaican Family Elite.* Boulder: Westview.

Fardon, Richard. 1990. *Localizing Strategies: Regional Traditions of Ethnographic Writing.* Washington, DC: Smithsonian Institution Press.

Ferguson, James. 1992. "The Country and the City on the Copperbelt." *Cultural Anthropology* 7: 80–92.

Handler, Richard. 1992. "High Culture, Hegemony, and Historical Causality." *American Ethnologist* 19: 818–24.

Harry, Indra. 1993. "Women in Agriculture in Trinidad: An Overview." In Janet Momsen, ed., *Women and Change in the Caribbean.* London: James Currey.

Hintzen, Percy. 1989. *The Costs of Regime Survival.* Cambridge: Cambridge University Press.

Hodge, Merle. 1975. "The Peoples of Trinidad and Tobago." In Michael Anthony and Andrew Carr, eds., *David Frost Introduces Trinidad and Tobago*. London: Andre Deutsch.

Jagessar, Ramdath. 1969. "Indian Iceberg." *Tapia*, November 16.

Khan, Aisha. 1993. "What is 'a Spanish'?: Ambiguity and 'Mixed' Ethnicity in Trinidad." In Kevin Yelvington, ed., *Trinidad Ethnicity*. London: Macmillan.

————. 1995. "Purity, Piety, and Power: Culture and Identity Among Hindus and Muslims in Trinidad. Ph.D. dissertation. City University of New York Graduate School.

Kondapi, C. 1951. *Indians Overseas, 1838—1949*. London: Oxford.

Ladoo, Harold Sonny. 1974. *No Pain Like This Body*. London: Heinemann.

Look Lai, Walton. 1993. *Indentured Labor, Caribbean Sugar*. Baltimore: Johns Hopkins University Press.

Lowenthal, David. 1961. "Caribbean Views of Caribbean Land." *Canadian Geographer* 5(2): 1–9.

Mbilinyi, Marjorie. 1985. "'City' and 'Countryside' in Colonial Tanganyika." *Economic and Political Weekly* 20(43): 88–96.

Mintz, Sidney. 1953. "The Folk-Urban Continuum and the Rural Proletarian Community." *American Journal of Sociology* 59: 136–43.

————. 1985. "From Plantations to Peasantries in the Caribbean." In Sidney Mintz and Sally Price, eds., *Caribbean Contours*. Baltimore: Johns Hopkins University Press.

Momsen, Janet. 1993. "Development and Gender Divisions of Labour in the Rural Eastern Caribbean." In Janet Momsen, ed., *Women and Change in the Caribbean*. London: James Currey.

Naipaul, V. S. 1967 *The Mimic Men*. N.Y.: Vintage.

Quintero Rivera, Angel. 1987. "The Rural-Urban Dichotomy in the Formation of Puerto Rico's Cultural Identity." *New West Indian Guide* 61(3–4): 127–44.

Redfield, Robert. 1930. *Tepoztlan*. Chicago: University of Chicago Press.

————. 1941. *The Folk Culture of Yucatan*. Chicago: University of Chicago Press.

Rubin, Vera. 1960. "Cultural Prospectives in Caribbean Research." In Vera Rubin, ed., *Caribbean Studies: A Symposium*. Seattle: University of Washington Press.

Ryan, Selwyn. 1966. "The Transition to Nationhood in Trinidad and Tobago, 1797–1962." Ph.D. dissertation. Cornell University.

————. 1972. *Race and Nationalism in Trinidad and Tobago*. Toronto: University of Toronto Press.

Safa, Helen. 1987. "Popular Culture, National Identity, and Race in the Caribbean." *New West Indian Guide* 61(3–4): 115–126.

Sebastien, Raphael. 1980. "A Typology of the Caribbean Peasantry—The Development of the Peasantry in Trinidad, 1845–1917." *Social and Economic Studies* 29(2–3): 107–133.

Segal, Daniel. 1994. "Living Ancestors: Nationalism and the Past in Postcolonial Trinidad and Tobago." In Jonathan Boyarin, ed., *Remapping Memory: The Politics of TimeSpace*. Minneapolis: University of Minnesota Press.

Singh, Kelvin. 1985. "Indians and the Larger Society." In John La Guerre, ed., *From Calcutta to Caroni*. St. Augustine: University of the West Indies Press: 33–60.

Stewart, John. 1973. "Coolie and Creole: Differential Adaptation in a Neo-Colonial Plantation Village, Trinidad, West Indies." Ph.D. dissertation. University of California Los Angeles.

Trouillot, Michel-Rolph. 1984. "Caribbean Peasantries and World Capitalism." *New West Indian Guide* 58(1–2): 37–59.

Williams, Brackette. 1991. *Stains On My Name, War In My Veins*. Durham: Duke University Press.

Williams, Eric. 1969. *Inward Hunger: The Education of a Prime Minister*. London: Andre Deutsch.

Wolf, Eric. 1958. "The Virgin of Guadalupe: A Mexican National Symbol." *Journal of American Folklore* 71: 34–9.

Wood, Donald. 1968. *Trinidad in Transition*. London: Cambridge University Press.

"Is It True What They Say About Dixie?"

Richard Wright, Zora Neale Hurston, and Rural/Urban Exchange in Modern African-American Literature

Is it true what they say about Dixie?
Does the sun really shine all the time?
Do sweet magnolias blossom at everybody's door,
Do folks keep eating 'possum, till they can't eat no more?
Is it true what they say about Swanee?
Is a dream by that stream so sublime?
Do they laugh, do they love, like they say in ev'ry song? . . .
If it's true that's where I belong.

—"Is it True What They Say About Dixie?" (1936), popular song written
by Irving Caesar, Sammy Lerner, and Gerald Marks, quoted by Richard
Wright in an epigraph to *Uncle Tom's Children* (1938)

I

Although the urban-bound gaze of much contemporary rap music
and rap-saturated black film sometimes makes it hard to see, the postmodern moment of African-American expressive culture is one in
which the rural South rivals the urban North as the imaginary homeland of black America. Since the Civil Rights movement's qualified
victory over white supremacy in the region, the South has been on the
receiving end of a major remigration of black artistic attention, its
rural terrain revisited in literature, film, and music as the fountain,
touchstone, and graveyard of Afro-American identity. In *"Who Set
You Flowin'?"* (1995), a recent study of twentieth-century African-
American migration narratives, Farah Jasmine Griffin extensively cat-

alogues this new episode in black reconstruction. Starting in the 1970s, Griffin notes, many prominent black artists favorably reappraised the South's countryside, from musicians such as Gladys Knight and the Pips, to filmmakers such as Julie Dash, to writers such as Maya Angelou, Ernest Gaines, James McPherson, Toni Morrison, Albert Murray, and Alice Walker (1995: 142–83). After decades in which representations of the agrarian South as an invitation to flight were common, such artists produced work framing it as a site of racial history and possibility, a refuge as valuable and even more livable than the northern cities that had been envisioned as black "promised lands" during much of the century. As the atypically rural-minded rap group Arrested Development phrase it in their hit song "Tennessee" (1992), the desire for knowledge of self and community now seems to demand that African-Americans "Walk the roads [our] forefathers walked/ Climb the trees [our] forefathers hung from" (qtd. in Griffin 1995: 178).

Yet not every black intellectual is overjoyed by what can be called the "rural turn" in black expressive culture, with its desire to transform lynching trees into learning trees and country roads into paths of wisdom. For much of the last decade, literary critic Hazel Carby has contended that the rural turn is a classic case of art as false consciousness. In a series of essays touching on the redeemed reputation of modernist novelist-anthropologist Zora Neale Hurston, Carby has argued that it is no accident that an intense interest in Hurston and other proponents of rural black folks and landscapes arose during a time of unprecedented crisis in the life-world of black cities. "Large parts of black urban America [are] under siege," Carby reminds us, "the number of black males in jail in the 1980s doubled; the news media have recently confirmed what has been so obvious to many of us for some time—that one in four young black males are in prison, on probation, on parole, or awaiting trial; and young black children face the prospect of little, inadequate or no health care" (1990: 89). The focus on the rural South thus is not just "a convenient method for ignoring the specific contradictions of an urban existence in which most of us live" (1994: 331); it is also a "discursive displacement of contemporary conflict," a suicidally imaginary diversion from the urban emergency of Afro-America offering "assurance that, really, the black folk are happy and healthy" (1990: 90).

Carby's stance is a crucial corrective to more frequent, less searching accounts of the rural turn, many of which shade the Romantic-nationalist idealization of rustic bearers of a people's genius into appreciation of the authentic blackness of African-American country folk. Nonetheless, she neglects the possibility that the lack of exclusive attention to the crisis of black urban life stems from an acknowledgement, not a denial, of the current state of Afro-America. Carby's use of the pronoun "us" in her comments on "the specific contradictions of an urban existence" rightly assumes that many black Americans are city dwellers. Yet recent data indicate that the "Great Migration" of millions of blacks from the South to the urban North launched during World War I was not just stemmed, but reversed, in the 1970s. The years between 1975 and 1989 saw a net migration of some 637,000 African-Americans into a less violently segregated post-Civil Rights South that called itself "New" (Griffin 1995: 145). For a significant number of these migrants, the move meant a literal return to the rural roads of the ancestors rappers Arrested Development declare their intention to walk. According to an analysis of the 1980 census by John Cromartie and Carol B. Stack, a full 69 percent of all black arrivals between 1975 and 1980 were "return movers," defined as new residents of households including southern natives, frequently relatives who never undertook the trek North (1989: 306–307). For forty-five percent of these return movers who rejoined sites of family history, their destination was a nonmetropolitan area, despite the superior economic opportunities offered by the booming cities of the region (1989: 308). Not all of these returnees were middle-class professionals seeking what Carby might call a physical displacement of the crisis of the black poor. One-third of black return movers "were living well below the poverty level in 1980" (1989: 305). Contemporary black art identifying the rural South as the locus of Afro-American destiny thus plays accompaniment to the travels of a cross-class group of African-Americans who have begun to stand one of the largest mass migrations in modern history on its head.

Pointing out these ties between the "facts" and "fictions" of recent black remigration to the rural South is not intended to blunt Carby's criticism and launch an argument for the inevitability and accuracy of contemporary reappraisals of the region, or the excellence of their effects. Like her, I have particular reservations about the way in which advocates of the rural turn have recentered the canon of African-American literature around [Hurston and her flattering portraits of rustic black spaces.] Yet criticism of this turn and its consequences cannot begin and end with the proposition that the recent glance outside the city is a form of blindness comforting to those who would write off, even cordon off, black urban communities. What I offer here, then, is a skeptical look at the primary effect of the rural turn on African-American literary history which nevertheless recognizes that "the specific contradictions of an urban existence" are not the sole defensible concern for contemporary black intellectuals seeking to face reality. Through a challenge to recent accounts of the debate between the mid-twentieth-century African-American authors Zora Neale Hurston (1901?–60) and Richard Wright (1908–60), I take issue with the way in which the map of modern black literature is now being redrawn in accord with the postmodern reconstruction of the rural South as black *terra firma.* While the ongoing effort to give Hurston her due as a precursor of both black women's writing and black return migration is laudable and highly valuable, her reemergence has been predicated on a dismissive caricature of Wright that replicates the either/or evaluative logic of the earlier critics who proclaimed him a literary kingpin at Hurston's expense. I argue that the construction of a hard and permanent opposition between Hurston and Wright obscures more than it reveals about the writers' own experiences, conceptualizations, and representations of rural/urban relations. The buried affinities between the two authors indeed ultimately suggest that the rural turn in black expressive culture should be met with a revision of modern black literature that recognizes the dynamic reciprocity of black rural and urban spaces and the mutual construction of black rural and urban identities.

2

In a brief 1938 piece at the back of the *Saturday Review*, Zora Neale Hurston administered a stern talking down to a younger and relatively obscure African-American radical who had given the same to her novel *Their Eyes Were Watching God* (1937) a few months earlier in the *New Masses*, the American Communist Party's cultural journal of record. While admitting that some of newcomer Richard Wright's "sentences had the shocking-power of a forty-four" (1938: 32), Hurston complained that his short story collection *Uncle Tom's Children* (1938) betrayed a disturbing fondness for gun play. Wright had devoted his considerable talent to spectacular scenes of interracial violence rather than to the "fundamental phases of Negro life," and as a result had fabricated "a book about hatreds" (1938: 32). "There is lavish killing here," she dryly noted of one story, and the tally of virtuous black counterattacks was "perhaps enough to satisfy all male black readers" (1938: 32). Despite the equal-opportunity blood and guts, Wright could not claim a brave self-direction while in Hurston's company. Her review argued that Wright was content to derive his tales of black-white conflict from "the picture of the South that the Communists have been passing around of late," a portrait of a "dismal, hopeless section ruled by brutish hatred and nothing else" (1938: 32). Hurston here implied that Wright's acceptance of the Communist Party's red-colored glasses generated work guilty of the same minstrel technique he had charged her with in his review of *Their Eyes*. Under the spell of a secondhand vision of the South as a "Dismal Swamp of race hatred" (1938: 32), Wright took up the minstrel's burden of indulging a white racial fantasy—in this case, a proletarian version of Southern Gothic authored by white Communists.

For a protest against literary violence, Hurston's review was incongruously combative. Behind its toughness was not just the distemper of Wright's earlier review, but a quarrel over literary turf fed by serious differences of perspective and principle. Hurston's emphasis on Wright's supposed distortion of southern reality suggests that she considered *Uncle Tom's Children* a threat to her position as perhaps the leading African-American literary voice of the southern "Black Belt." One undeniable bone of contention between the two writers in 1937–38 was the question of how best to represent the black South in the wake of the Great Migration, the mass resettlement that saw over one million southern blacks arrive in the urban Northeast and Midwest between 1910 and 1930 alone (Douglas 1995: 73). In distinction to the compound of lyrical modernism, confessional ethnography, and traditional pastoral topoi through which *Their Eyes* affirmed the continued viability of rural black communities "down home," *Uncle Tom's Children* imported a sociological naturalism into the black South, a brand of social realism steeped in the urban sociology that saw the Great Migration as part of the epochal modernizing trend of urbanization. Wright's text also may have revived Hurston's old frustrations with the unthinking masculinism of much black protest literature and the notion of black cultural deprivation she saw as its corollary. Like W. E. B. Du Bois's "Of the Coming of John" (1903) and Jean Toomer's "Blood-Burning Moon" (1923) before it, Wright's story "Long Black Song" at first glance figures American race relations as a blood feud between white and black men fought over the terrain of the black woman's body. The remainder of Wright's collection, displaying a range of uncringing black responses to white violence, might be read as the product of the assumption that black life was finally a brutal response to white stimulus. *Uncle Tom's Children* was thus likely to have run afoul of Hurston's core conviction, her absolute faith in the health, richness, and autonomy of the African-American culture which she had absorbed as a child in the all-black village of Eatonville, Florida, and had learned to defend as an anthropologist trained at New York's Columbia University.

Whatever the precise motivations behind Hurston's review, its stringency has not been lost on contemporary literary criticism. With the rediscovery of Hurston during the last two decades by those seeking a usable past for the rural remigration of black expressive culture and the remarkable outpouring of contemporary black women's writing, her run-in with Wright has become the most famous exchange within African-American literature. Few of the many recent studies of

Hurston's work fail to include an account of the debate attributing the clash to Wright's weaknesses. In her introduction to Alice Walker's pioneering Hurston anthology *I Love Myself When I am Laughing* . . . (1979), Mary Helen Washington explains the dispute as the product of Wright's blinkered view of African-American life: "Being black was such grimly serious business to Wright that he was incapable of judging Hurston's characters, who laugh and tease as well as suffer and who do not hate themselves or their blackness" (1979: 18). Barbara Johnson's article "Metaphor, Metonymy, and Voice in *Their Eyes Were Watching God*" (1984), an influential attempt to make peace between the sometime hostile camps of deconstructive and African-American criticism, attributes the gap between the two writers to something different, but no less Wright's problem: his inability to acknowledge the black woman's complex subject position (1984: 167). In *The Signifying Monkey* (1988), Henry Louis Gates, Jr.'s prize-winning articulation of a theory of black literature drawn from the text milieu of this literature itself, Hurston's literary executor ups the ante by asserting that "[n]o two authors in the tradition are more dissimilar than Hurston and Wright" (1988: 183). Their quarrel, and their contradictory theories of black narrative and black subjectivity, Gates concludes, are markers of the "great divide in black literature" (182). Since Wright is seen to reject the same black vernacular expression that Gates boosts from a subject to a principle of black criticism, this great divide seems to compel a leap onto Hurston's side.

As the divergent emphases of these critics indicate, the idea that Hurston versus Wright names the crucial division in African-American literature now does a wide variety of cultural work. The vision of near-epic conflict between the two writers not only authorizes a tradition of audacious black women's writing, but may be called on to dramatize several enabling oppositions of contemporary African-American criticism: oppositions such as race versus class, modernism versus realism, black nationalism versus Marxism, Harlem Renaissance versus Chicago Renaissance. It is the rare critic, however, who fails to use the Hurston-Wright difference as shorthand and ballast for what is perceived as the dichotomy between black rural and urban selves and cultures, and the affiliated binaries of South and North, folk and mass. The plentiful retellings of the Hurston-Wright debate that readjudicate the dispute in favor of Hurston and the terms associated with her have indeed become a major staging area for what Carby calls the "ideology of the 'folk'" (1989: 126). In this construction of black cultural identity invigorated by the recent rural turn, African-Americans are envisioned as—at bottom—a rural, southern folk; black culture is equated with rural, southern folk culture, and this culture's purest utterances are identified as songs, stories, and other vernacular practices, which successful black writers like Hurston are thought to translate into formal literary discourse without pretense to elevation.

Despite all the investments in an irresolvable Hurston-Wright difference, I believe that the participants in and explicators of the debate have overlooked more-than-trivial points of contact between the two writers. In particular, all have failed to grant that Wright as well as Hurston was attracted to a self-conscious version of black folk ideology following personal removal from its rural, southern ground, and under the influence of a northern, metropolitan education. During the 1930s, both Hurston and Wright harnessed folk ideology to provide an urban-based symbolic counterforce to a mass migration that threatened to empty the rural population and cultural power of the southern Black Belt. Exploring this point of convergence is a means practically to deconstruct the overloaded heap of antitheses that the Hurston-Wright dispute has become. It is also a means to question narratives of twentieth-century black literary history that imagine the rural and the urban as sites in strict opposition, automatically switching polarity with changes in the direction of black migration. For all their differences, the Hurston and Wright of the 1930s made themselves public proof of the shaping presence of the rural in the urban, and vice versa.

3

Perhaps the most important relationship to the Great Migration that Wright and Hurston shared was their direct participation in it.

Unlike most prominent African-American writers of the 1920s and 1930s, the pair arrived in the urban North after childhoods spent in the rural deep South. Hurston's path took her from the black-governed agricultural town of Eatonville, Florida, through education with a touring musical theater and at Howard University in Washington, D.C., to Manhattan in 1925, where, like the typical African-American migrant of historical accounts, she immediately sought assistance at the offices of the National Urban League. Wright conducted himself from Natchez, Mississippi, a place the WPA guidebook to the state would describe as "pastoral terrain" (qtd. in Davis 1986: 469), to a risky self-education in Memphis, to Chicago in 1927, where he was met by relatives who introduced him to the "Bronzeville" of the South Side.

Despite this common record of travel, Hurston's and Wright's autobiographies, both written in the early 1940s, imagine the meaning of their participation in the Great Migration in markedly different ways. Hurston's *Dust Tracks on a Road* (1942) addresses her move to New York in just three compressed paragraphs, the most substantial of which skips from a description of immediate reasons for coming to a portrait of a new arrival bereft of external resources, but otherwise untouched by the transition: "Being out of school for lack of funds, and wanting to be in New York, I decided to go there and try to get back in school in that city. So the first week of January, 1925, found me in New York with $1.50, no job, no friends and a lot of hope" (1942: 122). Despite the familiar list of the city migrant's grounds for reinvention—"$1.50, no job, no friends and a lot of hope"—earlier jaunts with a light opera company and later folklore-collecting expeditions into Florida and the Caribbean are seen as more significant transformations. Her journey to the northern city is figured not as part of a mass migration, but as the product of a compulsive individual wanderlust whose contours are visible as early as a poetic childhood dream of "sitting astride of a fine horse . . . [and] riding off to look at the belly-band of the world" (1942: 28). Somewhat paradoxically, Hurston's cutting of her bonds to the group experience of the Great Migration preserves a conception of black community tied to the continued accessibility of rural southern folk. By casting her flight to New York as the out-growth of an inborn desire to ramble rather than as part of a large-scale labor migration thinning out the black South, she retains the ability to view the Eatonvilles of the region as ripe for reconnections during which folklore and more intimate memories could be secured.

Wright's autobiography similarly poses his departure from the South as an episode of heroism, but unlike Hurston, he delineates a resistant northern landscape that frustrates hopes for easy self-making. The images of Chicago that open *American Hunger* (1977), the lesser-known continuation of Wright's *Black Boy* (1945), may have migrated directly from the impenetrable yet insubstantial urban spaces of T. S. Eliot's best-known poems. Like the mysterious, dismal cities of "Preludes" and "The Love Song of J. Alfred Prufrock" (1917), the "flat black stretches" of Wright's Chicago are "wreathed in palls of gray smoke" that signify shifting limits to perception and a kind of spiritual miasma as much as the presence of belching slaughterhouses (1977: 1). Like the London of *The Waste Land* (1922), Wright's Chicago is "an unreal city" whose effects on the mind nevertheless cannot be evaded. "The din of the city entered my consciousness," he asserts, "entered to remain for years to come" (1977: 1). This depiction of Wright's encounter with the Eliotic urban landscape is followed by a discussion of its effect on his Aunt Maggie, a physical and psychological modification measurable in the "frantic light in her eyes" (1977: 2). The entrance of the city's din into the consciousness of migrant Wright is thus not due to any extraordinary receptive capacity on his part. With its imagery of Chicago as alienating-modernist-wasteland, and its insistence on the city's renovation of representatives of two generations of a black family, *American Hunger* sketches Wright's arrival in the urban North as emblematic of a large-scale rupture with the knowable territory of the rural black South and the selves developed there. Unlike Hurston's *Dust Tracks on a Road*, which personalizes northward migration and so maintains the aura of an unchanging rural southern folk community, Wright's autobiography casts the trek North as a literally transforming transindividual experience. The Great Migration has made it hard to go down home again, a place from which whole black families and their subjectivities have decamped.

One might assume that the differences between Hurston's and Wright's representations of arrival in the northern city can be explained with reference to the different intellectual and/or disciplinary practices the writers drew upon once settled there—for Hurston, rural-minded Boasian anthropology; for Wright, urban-minded Chicago School sociology crossed with Communist Party theory on the "Negro Question." In Hurston's case, her work as an anthropologist and an anthropologically minded fiction writer appears to have mandated that she spurn the notion that the Great Migration meant rupture with the rural South. The anthropology to which Hurston was introduced while at New York's Columbia University initially involved her in anthropometric studies designed to show the fallacies of the nineteenth century's pet science of race. Even as an undergraduate, she aided German-Jewish émigré Franz Boas's campaign to strangle racist phrenology with its own statistics, on one occasion carrying a pair of callipers to Harlem and buttonholing passers-by for skull measurements. According to her biographer Robert Hemenway, this was "an act that many contemporaries felt only Zora Hurston, with her relaxed insouciance, could have gotten away with" (1977: 63). Hurston thought the act worth the expenditure of charm because she considered Boas "the king of kings" (1942: 123). In his favor was not only his influential explanation of human differences in terms of culture rather than "racial genius," but also his ability to stimulate academically valuable self-knowledge in Hurston. Through an extended metaphor of self-disrobing, Hurston once explained that her Eatonville birth-culture could not truly be apprehended until her contact with Boas's discipline: "[It] was fitting me like a tight chemise. . . . It was only when I was off in college, away from my native surroundings, that I could see myself like somebody else and stand off and look at my garment. Then I had to have the spy-glass of Anthropology to look through at that" (1935: 9). In 1927, after Boas encouraged her to focus this spy-glass by going South in search of black folklore, Hurston seized a chance to return to her birthplace in rural Florida, only the first of many trips during which she shuttled between the positions of field-worker and native informant, and collected the material that would be worked up in nearly all her ethnographic and/or literary texts. Hurston's very career as an anthroplogist and imaginative writer thus came to depend on the same possibility of easy transit between rural South and urban North preserved in her autobiography's account of Manhattan arrival.

In Wright's case, however, the connection between intellectual training and autobiographical account of an introduction to the city is less apparent. The representation of the black migrant's disconnection from the rural South that opens Wright's *American Hunger* is succeeded by evidence that the purportedly anti-rural intellectual practices of Chicago School sociology and (especially) Communist theory may have encouraged him to revisit and revalue his rural Mississippi past. Unlike Saul Bellow and James T. Farrell, novelists familiarized with the Chicago School while undergraduates at the University of Chicago, Wright was introduced to the first of these practices as an object of a social worker's ministration. Mary Wirth, the wife of the Chicago School's Louis Wirth, was the Wright family's case worker for a few months in the early 1930s when Richard, often the family's sole source of income, could not find a job. Along with E. Franklin Frazier, Robert Redfield, and Chicago School founder Robert Park, the Wirths became Wright's own Boases, intellectual elders and admirers similar to Hurston's "Papa Franz" who taught how the dangerous absurdities of race thinking could be dismantled with scientific tools. The adjustment pains of black migrants to the northern city were not indices of special racial dysfunction, advised the Chicago School, but conventional symptoms of a community undergoing the near-compulsory modernizing experience of urbanization.

Wright's autobiography explicitly testifies that the Chicago School provided part of the intellectual foundation for his effort to understand black urbanization, especially what "the urban environment exacted from the black peasant" (1977: 26). His use of the term "peasant," however, suggests that the mountains of empirical material the School compiled on the urban environment did not completely bury its nostalgic vision of African-American life before the homogenizing modern city. Robert Park, for one, had been convinced during his early years traveling the South as Booker T. Washington's emissary that rural African-Americans were "the New World equivalent of the European peasant" (Bone 1986: 455). The mature Park's Darwinian scheme of modernization, which Robert Bone describes as a narrative of "inexorable progression from simple to complex, homogeneous to heterogeneous, naive to sophisticated, rural to urban, agrarian to industrial, static to dynamic" (1986: 455), did not preclude an attachment to African-American and other supposed peasant groups whose societies were thought to be marked by a preponderance of communal ties. Significantly, Park's muted fondness for the ways of peasant folk colors Wright's favorite Chicago School statement, Louis Wirth's essay "Urbanism as a Way of Life" (1938). Wirth's text has been labeled the low point in the Chicago School's progressive oversimplification of German sociologist Ferdinand Tönnies's famous typology of *Gemeinschaft* (community) and *Gesellschaft* (society). In "Urbanism as a Way of Life," two concepts that in Tönnies's hands had been coexisting "forms of human interaction" are reduced to descriptions of two places, the country and the city (Bender 1978: 33). The latter of these places, the city, in which fragile, voluntary, "social" ties have supplanted the "communal" kinship relations of the country, is now thought less the country's cousin than its gravedigger; for Wirth, the city has become the single evolutionary destination of modern society. But even Wirth cannot fully repress the suspicion that the human costs of urbanization are exorbitant. "Urbanism as a Way of Life" ruefully admits that "[t]he bonds of kinship, of neighborliness, and the sentiments arising out of living together for generations under a common folk tradition are likely to be absent, or, at best, relatively weak, in [a city] aggregate the members of which have such diverse origins and backgrounds" (1938: 70). As Carla Cappetti acutely observes, "[h]aving split country and city in order to foretell the urbanization of the world, the part that was suppressed, the rural world of community, intimacy, and being-at-home . . . [returns] under the guise of nostalgia" (1993: 69). Wright's best-loved Chicago School essay could not place the rural on the endangered list without intimating that a campaign for its preservation was in order. The urban sociology which Wright discovered in Chicago in the early 1930s—usually described as a major source of tension with anthropologist Hurston (Lenz 1981; Bone 1986; Sollors 1990; Cappetti 1993)—was thus not immune to sympathies of the kind to which Hurston was exposed in her more formal northern, metropolitan academic training in the late 1920s. Recommendations for the protection and retrieval of the rural-communal as a way of life hovered around the margins of even those Chicago School texts which saw the city as the end of modern history.

In the theory of the American Communist Party, the second of the intellectual practices he came upon in Chicago, Wright confronted a body of knowledge that was struggling to politicize the recovery of rural black folk culture which the Chicago School whispered about and that Hurston actively pursued in the field. In her 1938 dressing-down of *Uncle Tom's Children*, Hurston numbered among Communism's errors the misconception that the South was "a dismal, hopeless section ruled by brutish hatred and nothing else" (1938: 32). To her mind, it followed that Wright's portrait of the region was more phantasm than documentary, the necessary delusion of a figure whose prospects for political domination and pretensions to social realism were hindered by the South's true identity as a bulwark against socialism. Hurston's take on the Party's position on the South was incomplete, however. She neglected the controversial centerpiece of Communist policy on Afro-America in the 1930s, the doctrine of "Self-Determination in the Southern Black Belt," or the "Black Belt Nation Thesis" that was reaffirmed just as Wright entered the Party's orbit in 1932. From 1928 to 1939, the Communist International conspicuously broke with the socialist slighting of racism. In distinction to Eugene Debs' 1903 declaration that socialists "have nothing special to offer the Negro" (qtd. in Draper 1960: 316), a 1928 resolution of the Comintern formally redefined the so-called "Negro Question" as the question of an oppressed nation. Blacks living in the heavily African-American, largely rural Black Belt stretching from Virginia to Mississippi were thought to have met all the requirements of a nation as defined by Stalin, comprising "a historically constituted, stable community of people, formed on the basis of a common language, territory, economic life, and psychological make-up manifested in a common culture" (1913: 16). The Depression-era American Communist Party was thus obliged not only to accept the idea that African-Americans possessed a specific and worthy culture whose locus was the rural South, but to bless the possibility that this culture might grow into nationhood on the model of Soviet socialist republics.

In his autobiography, Wright in fact suggests that it was the Black Belt Nation Thesis which won him completely to the Party. *American Hunger* provides present-day readers with a heady experience of historical estrangement as it praises Joseph Stalin's *The National and Colonial Question*, a long essay defending the doctrine of self-determination for oppressed nations which Wright swears he "read with awe" (1977: 82). By creatively delineating a Soviet Union in which various "forgotten folk had been encouraged to keep their old cultures, to see in their ancient customs meaning and satisfactions as deep as those contained in supposedly superior ways of living," the essay inspired what Wright calls "the first total emotional commitment of my life" (1977: 82). "[H]ow different this was from the way in which Negroes were sneered at in America," he remembers exclaiming to himself (1977: 82). Taken as a whole, Stalin's essay impressed Wright as a revelation of "a new way of looking upon lost and beaten peoples" (1977: 82). As he expressed it even in the thick of his later campaign to dismiss the significance of his association with the Party, he became a Communist not in spite of his blackness, but "because [he] was a Negro" (qtd. in Fabre 1973: 230).

Wright's declaration that Stalin helped him to recognize the value of African-American folk culture is likely to strike most present-day readers as something between distasteful and obscene, too bizarre and distant to represent more than a dusty tableau in a gallery of Depression excesses. Wright was not the only black intellectual of the 1930s, however, to interpret Stalin's state as a model of cultural pluralism with lessons for racist America. Alain Locke, Harlem Renaissance midwife and editor of the famous *New Negro* (1925) anthology, was by 1937 endorsing "the cultural minorities art programs being consistently and brilliantly developed in the Soviet Federation for the various racial and cultural folk traditions of that vast land" (1937). As late as the 1960s, an unapologetic Paul Robeson remembered how he had discovered in the young Soviet Union that "there was no such thing on earth as a backward people" (qtd. in Duberman 1988: 188). Nearly sixty years before a succession of national independence movements helped to overthrow the Soviet Union, Wright and the African-American left could see its non-Russian republics in much the same way that Hurston saw Eatonville: (as guarantors of minority cultural health in the midst of rapid modernization.)

Despite the patent differences between Communism and anthropology, the former consequently gave Wright what the latter had given Zora Neale Hurston: [a defamiliarizing second sight] through which the culture of the African-American folk could be seen as an intricate, functioning whole. Just as what Hurston figured as the "spy glass of Anthropology" allowed her to examine her own folk culture, Communism offered Wright what he called his "first full-bodied vision of Negro life in America" (qtd. in Naison 1984: 211), a wide-angle view that throughout the 1930s would complement the perspective offered by Chicago School sociology. Both anthropology and Communism seemed to allow a constructive sort of African-American double consciousness: an untorturous two-ness allowing one to see one's own birth culture as both subject and object and thus insuring that black difference could not be interpreted as black deficiency. Both anthropology and Communism seemed to confirm black folk culture's status as something as worthy as supposedly more sophisticated ways of life. In its refusal of the discourse of the primitive with its nightmares and idylls, the Communists' Black Nation Thesis showed a debt to the anthropological concept of cultural relativism among whose most effective popularizers was Hurston's mentor Boas. Finally, both anthropology and Communism seemed to confer upon African-American folk culture a compelling significance which nimbly and seductively leaped from the local to the global. The anthropological promise that cultural difference ultimately proved a shared human creativity was matched by the Communist claim that southern African-American and other minority cultures ultimately advanced the cause of world revolution.

The overwhelming preference of contemporary literary critics for Hurston's involvement with anthropology over Wright's with Communism cannot rest on the premise that the latter inevitably demanded a compromise of supposedly authentic folk blackness which the former managed to avoid. For both Wright and Hurston, contact with a modern Western intellectual practice with claims to scientific authority and universality stoked a positively charged sense of African-American cultural difference. James Clifford and other postmodern critics of ethnographic authority have persuasively argued that "the rural folk" and other supposed bearers of cultural purity, rootedness, and authenticity are constructs born of modernity, in which mobility and cultural "inauthenticity"—the experience of being "caught between cultures, implicated in others"—are increasingly common fates (1988: 11). In the case of the engagements with anthropology or sociology and Communism that the Great Migration enabled in the lives of Hurston and Wright, we find versions of African-American cultural identity centered upon the rural folk arising in instances of interracial-intercultural intellectual contact in the modern city, instances which promoted a certain self-consciousness about the reciprocal nature of southern and northern, folk and mass, rural and urban identities. Whatever the dissimilarities between the scenes of arrival in the city in their autobiographies, both writers experienced migration to the urban North as a process that provoked desires and provided directions for reconstructing black southern folk culture, first by denying this culture, then by offering privileged intellectual access to it. For both Hurston and Wright, going up North introduced an alluring way of going down home through a career as an imaginative writer who recreated the rural South with metropolitan knowledge—a career promising urban success by means of a clarifying double vision of the rural culture left behind, and an unusual recognition of this culture's commerce with the urban.

4

The involved vision of the rural black South that Hurston and Wright developed in New York and Chicago is displayed in two closely similar stories written in the 1930s: Hurston's "The Gilded Six-Bits," a 1933 text that led to the contract for her first novel; and Wright's "Long Black Song," a text included in the 1938 collection *Uncle Tom's Children*. In a spirit of harmony absent from the writers' dueling book reviews, both these stories represent the black South as a soberly utopian counter to the anti-utopian aspects of the Great Migration that were becoming visible by the time of the Great Depression. This is not to say that either story imagines the South as a pristine, conflict-free retreat from northern ghettos and urban unemployment. Instead, both present narratives of social antagonism in which the urge to migrate is represented as a fatal temptation to be resisted. Both situate their narratives in the early years of the Great Migration, yet cheat historicism by reinventing the moment as one in which the costs of the removal North can somehow be seen as plainly as the potential benefits. The final goal of Hurston's and Wright's humble fantasy machinery is to propose imaginary alternatives to the Great Migration, to resupply its losses without assuming that the rural South and the urban North are related only through opposition.

Hurston's "The Gilded Six-Bits" is a story of invasion, seduction, and the final victory of love, set in Florida around the 1920s, and filled with the rural southern black dialect she was among the first African-American writers to employ in both dialogue and narration. The text begins with a sensual tableau of a black woman, a cabin, and natural surroundings that seems idyllic even in the shadow (and smelling range) of "the G. and G. Fertilizer Works" mentioned in the first sentence (1933: 86). Missie May, young, strong, and pretty, is pictured bathing herself in the metal washtub in a small, cheerful cabin, surrounded by honey flowers and chinaberry trees, within a black settlement supported by G. and G.'s payroll. She eagerly awaits her husband Joe, and the ritual with which they mark Saturday: Joe is to throw silver dollars he has earned at the plant through the door of the cabin, and hurry to a hiding place where he will wait until she discovers him and the candy kisses he has planted in his clothing. The game takes place as always, but Joe has news to report. A Mister Otis D. Slemmons from Chicago and other points North has come to town, a flashy entrepreneur who flaunts what Joe describes as "'a five-dollar gold piece for a stick-pin . . . a ten-dollar gold piece on his watch chain and [a] mouf . . . jes' crammed full of gold teethes'" (1933: 90). Joe idolizes Slemmons as a black Rockefeller and an icon of city sophistication, and insists that the couple visit the newcomer's ice-cream parlor. After the trip, Missie May claims to be unimpressed. Slemmons' gold, she tells Joe, would "'look a whole heap better on you'" (1933: 91). A few weeks later, however, Joe's high opinion of his wife and Slemmons is shaken when he finds them together in bed. He rousts Slemmons out, in the process snatching the coin from his watch-chain. Despite Missie May's regretful cry that "'Ah love you so hard and Ah know you don't love *me* no more'" (1933: 94), time ticks by with Joe refusing to return to the marriage bed, clutching onto the gold in his trousers as a sign of the household's depressed sexual economy and a moribund but threatening substitute for the phallus. "[T]he yellow coin in his trousers," thinks Missie May, "was like a monster hiding in the cave of his pockets to destroy her" (1933: 95). Joe eventually relents, however, and leaves Slemmons' glitter behind in the sheets. After the lovemaking, Missie May fears that what was once a game with coins has become prostitution: "He had come home to buy from her," she worries, "as if she were any woman in the long house" (1933: 96). Yet she also discovers that Slemmons' coin is in truth just a gilded half-dollar, and, soon enough, that she is pregnant. When Joe is assured that the baby is his, he travels to Orlando and trades Slemmons' trick money for an oversized bag of candy kisses. The story ends as Joe approaches Missie May back in Eatonville and inaugurates the ritual that signals the return of time as it was before Slemmons' arrival. "'Joe Banks,'" Missie May greets her husband in the final lines, "'Ah hear you chunkin' money in mah do'way'" (1933: 98), happy to know that silver coins have taken the place of gilded ones, and love the place of sex-for-cash.

The opening pages of Wright's "Long Black Song," a text set during the First World War and perhaps directly indebted to Hurston's, whet the appetite for southern pastoral that Wright saw as the lasting contribution of white regional apologists like Joel Chandler Harris. He begins with a young black mother named Sarah singing a lullaby and nursing a baby in a farmhouse overlooking fields that "whispered a green prayer" (1938b: 106). This bucolic scene is soon spoiled by the appearance of a young and lecherous white salesman from Chicago peddling a combination clock-gramophone with a gilded edge, an item reminiscent of Hurston's gilded coins and one well-chosen to symbolize both urban-industrial time and urban-industrial leisure. Although Sarah, shown to answer to natural rural rhythms in a number of interior monologues, is initially resistant to this commodity and the existential shift it represents—she explains that "'[w]e just don need no time, Mistah'" (1938b: 108)—she eventually surrenders to its temptations. Almost at once, the clock-gramophone's white salesman makes a sexual advance, and opens a scene that remains controversial. Sarah first resists, then responds to his hands, and is seduced and/or raped. When Sarah's farmer husband Silas returns from selling crops in town and discovers signs of the salesman in their bed, he becomes violent with jealousy, smashing the clock-gramophone, whipping Sarah until she runs off, and vowing to meet the white intruder with gun in hand. On the following morning, the salesman is killed when he returns to collect a payment on his product, reduced in price from fifty dollars to forty dollars after his night with Sarah. Within hours, Silas himself is cut down firing at a white posse as Sarah and the baby look on from a safe distance as if watching a film. Both Hurston and Wright's texts, Werner Sollors notes,

> contrast natural time with clocked time and focus on the intrusion of the
> capitalist ethos as a sexual seduction. Both imagine the seducer as a man
> from outside (in both cases with a Chicago dimension), portray the
> *female* character as the more traditional one who yet yields to the snake
> of the salesman of leisure (whether he be in the gramophone or ice-
> cream line), and show that the glitter of modern capitalism is not made

of gold but merely gilded (1990: 30–31).

Yet Sollors' perceptive reading of the parallels between the stories stops before it analogizes the seducers from the North with the seductions of the Great Migration. Both northerners arrive on the southern scene around the period of World War I, the moment when the boll weevil invasion, the increasing dependency of the southern economy, a worsening of Jim Crow violence, and a labor shortage in the North combined to spark major out-migration (Marks 1989: 3). With their urban slickness, talents for promotion, and connections to Chicago— home of the *Defender*, the black newspaper that was among the most powerful propagandists for migration—the two invaders are allied with the agents sent South by northern industry to recruit black labor. Admittedly, they are labor agents with a difference. Rather than courting male field hands, they direct their efforts toward women working in the home who are represented as at once more firmly rooted in the rural southern soil and more attracted to the new regime of consumption than their men. Rather than guaranteeing train fare and lucrative wage work in the city, these agents promise the pleasures of eroticized mass leisure that such work could buy. Rather than collecting the reward a large head count of migrants could bring, they are left without a following when the price of their pleasures is magically revealed before they can drag blacks North. As Joe exults near the end of "The Gilded Six-Bits," the Chicago intruder's lies are revealed before he "'[s]tole off folkses wives from home'" (1933: 98).

Contrary to Sollors' reading, the agents are not so much salesman of "the capitalist ethos," already up and running in the rural South, as flacks for a mass migration that threatened the few remaining folk practices actively battling this ethos from within. The resistance to the temptations of migration that concludes both stories—tragic and violent in the case of Wright's—accordingly does not restore an arcadian scene in which "natural relationships" rout "money relationships." As mentioned above, the conclusion of Hurston's "Gilded Six-Bits" sees Joe once again throwing the silver dollars he has earned at the G. and

G. Fertilizer plant "in the door for [Missie May] to pick up and pile beside her plate at dinner" (1933: 87). Even in its happy romance ending, Hurston's story highlights the inescapable presence of exactly what Susan Willis observes is absent from most recent black women's fiction constructing the rural South as an alternative to the urban North: the wage (1987: 11). Yet the ritual of Hurston's couple does not conclude with the chucking and arrangement of coins. Missie May will go on to search Joe's pockets for candy kisses, the freely chosen coin of love they win the luxury to employ after satirizing their dependence on the general equivalent—money. The resilience of Hurston's couple is indicated through their ability to restore an ironic game which reveals and defuses the unavoidable mediation of their marriage by an industrial capitalist economy which has entered the South before the arrival of Slemmons. The imaginary alternative to the Great Migration offered in "The Gilded Six-Bits" is thus a restrained fantasy of a rural black folk whose freedom lies in an ability to resist the utter victory of the cash nexus that migration promises. Ironically, the very tokens of this freedom—candy kisses—are secured through work at the G. and G. Fertilizer plant, which processes the natural agricultural product of manure into a manageable, portable, cash-producing commodity.

The gory defeat of the salesman which concludes Wright's "Long Black Song" similarly does not spell the defeat of a completely alien capitalist ethos. Through Sarah's reflections, Wright reveals Silas to be a rigid, would-be entrepreneur who understands intimately the relationship between the Protestant ethic and the spirit of capitalism, methodically saves his money to invest in land, and generally covets the status of a Slemmons. Instead of the capitalist ethos *per se*, Wright's salesman peddles what the Chicago School defined as modernization—the epic transition of peoples from magical to scientific thinking, rural to urban social organization, and agricultural to industrial production. As Sollors notes, Wright's introduction to St. Clair Drake and Horace K. Cayton's *Black Metropolis* (1945), a study of black Chicago written in the grain of Park and Wirth, strongly suggests that the socio-historical collisions articulated through the meeting of Sarah and the salesman are derived from the Chicago School. "Holy days became holidays," notes Wright in a summary of the School's account of modernization, "clocks replaced the sun as a symbolic measurement of time" (1945: xxii). Mindful of the Chicago School's teleology, the alternative to the Great Migration offered in Wright's story of clocks replacing the sun is, if anything, more modest than that offered in Hurston's "The Gilded Six-Bits." Wright's representative of the temptations of migration—in this case a young white man—is, like Hurston's, successfully repelled, but at the cost of interracial murder and the destruction of a black family. If there is literary "signifyin(g)" on Hurston's text in Wright's—a use of the vernacular-derived forms of repetition with a difference that Henry Louis Gates, Jr. identifies in *The Signifying Monkey*—then it consists in his rewriting of the earlier work's comic conclusion as a bloody interracial clash. Still, Wright's borrowing from the Chicago School's scheme of urbanizing modernization does not neglect its nostalgia for the rural. "Long Black Song" at once denies the School's conflation of the rural with the pre-capitalist, and inflates its fond visions of doomed black peasants into scenes of a black farmer who takes up armed resistance to agents of urbanization. Like Hurston, Wright imposes a taxing defeat on the booster for migration in a rural southern setting which is familiar with capitalist relations, yet shows the damages of the Great Migration in relief.

5

Imaginary refusal of the Great Migration, rife in Hurston's work of the 1930s, is not confined to "Long Black Song" in Wright's. "Fire and Cloud," the story that follows "Long Black Song" in *Uncle Tom's Children* and concludes the first, 1938 edition of the collection, rewrites Silas's isolated battle according to a less macho design. Rather than beginning with a seductive scene of at least temporary pastoral fulfillment, the text opens with Depression suffering. Wright represents the Reverend Dan Taylor hurrying home as he agonizes over how best to lead his black congregation in the rural South through a time of hunger. He must choose between two frightening alternatives:

instructing his church to trust in God and the good intentions of the town's white bosses, or advising it to join in a demonstration organized by a pair of Communists, one black and one white, who have arrived from the North. As Taylor sees it, he is a forsaken Moses expected to lead "his people out of the wilderness into the Promised Land" without help from the signs of fire and cloud that God provided the Israelites (1938a: 131). In the absence of higher guidance, he is inclined to counsel acceptance, but is troubled by what he sees around him as he makes his way home. Instead of barren fields, he passes acres of land on which "[t]he grass was dark and green" (1938a: 131). Not natural disaster, but economic device has caused Taylor's community to go hungry. The market in its mystery has declared that crops cannot be sold, and the laws erected to protect it declare that blacks may not grow their own food on land on which they have worked all their lives. In a passage steeped in the territorial imperative of the Communist Party's Black Nation Thesis, Taylor informs God that the South has become an open-air prison for blacks dispossessed from the land: "'The white folks say we cant raise nothing on Yo earth! They done put the lans of the worl in their pockets! They don fenced em off n nailed em down! Theys a-trying t take Yo place, Lawd! '" (1938a: 138).

What Taylor decides is not to decide at all. After receiving a long-awaited sign during a night spent being humiliated by white thugs, he realizes that the choice between the road of the black church and the road of the Communists is unnecessary. As he informs his son Jimmy, he has learned that the sins of Jim Crow can be erased only when the indigenous faith of the black church is integrated with the imported faith of mass protest:

"Membuh whut Ah tol yuh prayer wuz, son?"

There was silence, then Jimmy answered slowly:

"Yuh mean lettin Gawd be so real in yo life tha everything yuh do is cause of Im?"

"Yeah, but its different now, son. Its the *people*! Theys whut mus be real t us! Gawds with the people! N the peoples gotta be real as Gawd to us! We cant hep ourselves or the people when wes erlone." (1938a:

171–72)

Like many proletarian texts of the 1930s, "Fire and Cloud" ends with a strike scene. Taylor finds his calling as a new kind of Moses by joining the throng that marches to the heart of town demanding bread. Even when asked to speak with the town's white mayor "up front" (1938a: 179), he refuses to leave its ranks, instead spontaneously reproducing Lenin's maxim that *"Freedom belongs t the strong!"* ([sic] 1938a: 180). What is most interesting about the ending of "Fire and Cloud," however, is the absence of some of the common components of proletarian literature. Wright's setting is not a shop floor or city street, but the center of a small southern town. His hero is not a newly radicalized industrial worker or a previously vacillating middle-class intellectual, but a black sharecropper-preacher who learns that "'Gawds with the people!'" The liberated social space prefigured by the moment of victory is not an egalitarian factory, but a yeoman's paradise in the tradition of both Jeffersonian pastoralism and black folk ideology that should have made Hurston proud. As Taylor envisions it, Communism in action would look something like a farm and a folk culture of one's own:

> Lawd, we could make them ol fiels bloom ergin. We could make em feed us. Thas whut Gawd put em there fer. Plows could break and hoes could chop and hands could pick and arms could carry. . . . On and on that could happen and people could eat and feel as he had felt with the plow handles trembling in his hands, following old Bess, hearing the earth cracking and breaking because he wanted it to crack and break; because he willed it, because the earth was his. And they could sing as he had sung when he and May were first married; sing about picking cotton, fishing, hunting, about sun and rain. (1938a: 132)

Despite Wright's current standing as the archenemy of the rural black South, "Fire and Cloud" reimagines the Black Belt as the breeding ground of collective resistance to the racial-economic forces that menace it. Like "The Gilded Six-Bits" and "Long Black Song," Wright's text flaunts leaks in the rural/urban, South/North opposition: here, an interracial pair of northern, urban Communists spark rural blacks to draw on their own cultural resources and protect their place in the South. Again, as in these two stories, Wright's text proposes an alternative to the Great Migration: here, the iconography of Moses and the black Christian trope of northward exodus as a "Flight out of Egypt" is rewritten to propose a political journey to overturn the conditions that inspire black flight. For a trek North, "Fire and Cloud" substitutes a southern movement to synthesize northern Communism and black folk culture and overturn the inequities of sharecropping. In this, Wright's story suggests that self-destructive or purely imaginary violence against the temptations of migration shown in "Long Black Song" should give way to massive political opposition to the forces depopulating the Black Belt. "Fire and Cloud"'s place at the conclusion of *Uncle Tom's Children* positions the text as the end of the cycle of interracial killing traced in the collection's first three stories; it also situates it as the most complete "solution" to the dilemma of migration addressed throughout. Moving from the opening "Big Boy Leaves Home"—an implicit account of the Great Migration as an escape from the threat of death at the heart of the sharecropping system—through "Long Black Song," to "Fire and Cloud," we travel from sympathetic explanation of a migrant's need to abandon the South, to wish-fulfilling masculine defiance of the migration's corrupt promoters, to a blueprint for staying put down South with revolutionary intent. Only by isolating this progression's starting point—the well-known, sometimes separately anthologized story "Big Boy Leaves Home"—can Wright's *Uncle Tom's Children* be seen to clinch his recent reputation as a Soviet-supplied General Sherman laying waste to Hurston's Dixie.

"Fire and Cloud" suggests that it was the hint of hermeticism that Wright found most troubling about Hurston's black rural South. When he remarks in his review of *Their Eyes Were Watching God* that Hurston is content to confine her folk within "a safe and narrow orbit which America likes" (1937: 25), he is referring to the supposedly minstrel-like emotional range of her novel's characters. The metaphor of unthreatening enclosure also provides a clue, however, to understanding his critique of the intraracial focus of her rural southern fiction. Moved by the Communist Party's project of combining disparate southern black communities into a greater collectivity, Wright imagined that widening the orbit of the folk to encompass the extent of the Black Belt was a key task in the struggle for black liberation. Hurston's welcome challenge to pathologizing accounts of rural black communities thus had to be accompanied by a challenge to the facts of white ownership that at best prevented the full flowering of rural black folk culture into black political self-determination, and at worst threatened the folk's existence by causing starvation and necessitating removal North. When Reverend Taylor in "Fire and Cloud" chooses to integrate black prophetic traditions and Communist tactics and act on his dreams of black land, he signals Wright's desire to redeem the ideology of the rural black folk, to revise what he regards as a finally compensatory Eatonville of the mind into a spur to collective action that would make this ideology's symbolic resolutions to social contradictions real. To the writer who offered Taylor as a standard of black rhetorical skill, both Party politics and common sense demanded that African-American literature aid the effort to expand Eatonville's borders and transform a threatened enclave into a Black Nation. It was this difference as to the proper political pitch of the ideology of the folk, rather than Wright's supposedly less organic connection to this ideology's living representatives, which created one of the few unbridgeable gaps between Hurston and Wright during the 1930s.

It is telling, however, that the method of "Fire and Cloud"'s revision of Hurston's folk may have been suggested by Hurston herself. In 1934, she published a very short story entitled "The Fire and the Cloud" in Dorothy West's *Challenge* magazine. Wright knew West and her publication well; both were mainstays on the compact black literary scene in Chicago during the 1930s. When the magazine was revived as *New Challenge* in 1937, he thought enough of its past to assume the position of associate editor under West and Marian Minus. It is more than likely, then, that Wright read Hurston's tale of a dead but lucid Moses who evaluates his career bringing monotheism to the Jews while waiting to ascend from Mount Nebo. The main business of "The Fire and the Cloud" is demystifying the Old Testament prophet as a half-man, half-god with an affinity for the culture of rural southern blacks, a concern which shows it as the germ of the novel *Moses: Man of the Mountain*, the long rewriting of Exodus Hurston published in 1939. Like the novel, the story recontextualizes Moses from the scripture to the folklore of the African diaspora in which he was accepted "as the fountain of mystic power" (Hurston 1939: xxii). In this folklore, the Old Testament deliverer in whom European exegetes had seen a shadow of Jesus was given typological primacy. For some of the "children of Africa," reports Hurston, "the stories of the miracles of Jesus [were] but Mosaic legends told again" (1939: xxii). For others, Moses was both of this world, and not of it, associated with significant historical events in the present as well as in the past. The folk Moses of "The Fire and the Cloud" is appropriately not without human frailty. The Old Testament's shining instrument of God becomes a blessed but weary old man whose divine mandate does not keep him from complaining that he gets no respect. "Look now upon the plain of Moab," he exclaims, "A great people! They shall rule over nations and dwell in cities they have not builded. Yet they have rebelled against me ever" (1934: 11). Neither is this Moses above the occasional joke in colloquial language that functions, as Robert Hemenway notes of *Moses: Man of the Mountain*, to puncture "the high seriousness of biblical rhetoric" (1977: 266). On one occasion, he parodies his biblical tags of "nation-maker" and "law-giver" with the declaration that he is "Moses, The-drawn-out" (1934: 10). Though "The Fire and the Cloud" is not lengthy enough to develop the transition from standard English to black dialect through which the novel's Moses manifests his increasing identification with the Afro-Israelites, the story's emancipator places himself within the black folk tradition by conversing familiarly with a lizard, a creature reminiscent of the talking buzzards borrowed from the animal stories of black folklore who make a surreal appearance in *Their Eyes Were Watching God*. Muttering to the lizard about the "stiff-necked race of people" he was commanded to lead (1934: 11),

Hurston's Moses adopts the proud if irritated tone she associated with black leaders privately musing on their community.

Oddly, the lines between Hurston's Moses story and Wright's have barely been traced. "Lines of Descent/Dissenting Lines," Deborah E. McDowell's introduction to a 1991 reprinting of Hurston's *Moses*, is the single critical text I have encountered in which "The Fire and the Cloud" and "Fire and Cloud" are paired. McDowell maintains that Hurston's story "might be read as a short answer to Wright's version" in which she "liberates her pen from . . . the 'literary religion of socialist realism'" (1991: 232). It might well be read this way, but only with reference to some ideal order of texts: the publication of Hurston's "answer" predates the appearance of Wright's story by four years. It seems more fruitful, then, to refrain from projecting upon the past Wright's current status as Hurston's looming, true-believing predecessor, and to read his take on the Moses story as a response to hers. Wright's title is of course almost identical to Hurston's, as is his use of colloquial language to deflate the distancing solemnity of the rhetoric of Exodus. From Hurston's text, Wright seems to have learned that black Christianity's revision of the Moses story invited further revisions that preached dissenting sermons on the meaning of black emancipation. As Robert Hemenway has suggested, Hurston's portrait of the disaffection of Moses and the ungratefulness of the Afro-Israelites crystallizes the irony of turning to another to provide freedom for the self (1977: 268–69). Through his depiction of Taylor's final decision to stand among the folk and embrace the "many-limbed, many-legged, many-handed crowd that was he" (1938a: 179), Wright makes the complementary point that black leaders should reconceive their mandate as an obligation to aid the self-organization of those they represent. Even with its "correction" of Hurston's under-Communized construction of the black folk, Wright's "Fire and Cloud" thus appears to revise "The Fire and the Cloud" in an indebted and respectful style close to that associated with the black woman writers who have explicitly claimed her as a foremother. Here, if not in his scathing review of *Their Eyes Were Watching God*, Wright renders a Hurston similar to the precursor created in the novels of later black women—"a literary forbear," notes Michael Awkward, "whose texts are celebrated even as they are revised, praised for their insights even when these insights are deemed inadequate" (1989: 8). Despite Wright's fighting words about Hurston's "minstrelsy" and his consistent inability to see her feminism as a legitimate intellectual or political concern, "Fire and Cloud" testifies that it was possible for him to appreciate (and appropriate) the literary results of her conclusion that the Great Migration demanded reinvestment down home.

6

By the 1940s, the covert entente between Hurston's and Wright's fictional texts had disappeared along with any overt airing of their disagreements. Hurston's construction of a resilient black folk survived the change of decade largely intact. As Wright distanced himself from the Communist Party in the 1940s, however, he seems to have abandoned hopes for a syncretic African-American folk socialism strong enough to battle the Great Migration. The black migrants to northern cities who dominate Wright's fictional texts of the 1940s and after neither pine for the South, nor resettle in it. As Farah Jasmine Griffin observes, "[t]he closing pages of *Native Son* [1940] portray the final moments of Bigger's life [in Chicago] prior to his execution. Cross Damon of *The Outsider* [1953] goes to Europe to lead an existential existence" (1995: 160–61). Wright's historical text for *12 Million Black Voices* (1941), meanwhile, a WPA-style essay in documentary photography, is quiet on the prospects of the Black Belt Nation Thesis, even as it concludes with a Party-friendly depiction of black city dwellers who "look forward to the dawn of a new day where they along with their poor white comrades forge a different world" (Griffin 1995: 161).

Recent reconsiderations of the Hurston-Wright relationship affected by the rural turn in black expressive culture fail to recognize the possibility that there were any affinities between the two to fade in the 1940s. Casting the Hurston-Wright debate as the pivot point of a freighted set of critical oppositions, these reconsiderations have relied on a historically undifferentiated account of the writers' dealings that reads whole careers (and whole tendencies in modern black literature) in the light of their trading of nasty reviews in 1937–38. Yet there is nothing to stop us from testing the pages of Hurston's and Wright's texts against these reviews, save our desire to accept them as writ. Close comparison of Hurston's and Wright's southern fiction of the 1930s reveals not just signs of what Gates declares "the great divide in black literature," but a shared endeavor to protect the rural black folk from the worst of the Great Migration. Ironically, Hurston and Wright each marked the decade of the public eruption of their rivalry by issuing texts imaginatively repelling black flight North. From the angle of these restrained pastorals, uncommonly forthright about the codependence of city and country in twentieth-century black life, the effort of contemporary criticism to enlist the Hurston-Wright debate for a rural-only revision of the field of modern black literature looks exactly inappropriate. If the two writers' parallel fictions can be heard to issue a warning to critics enamored by the rural turn, they do so in the name of a vision of more fluid, less hierarchical black rural/urban relations. In their analysis of black remigration, John Cromartie and Carol B. Stack note that

> there is evidence that for most black families throughout [even the period of large-scale movement from North to South], migration was a drawn-out affair. Complex cyclical migration patterns developed, shaped as much by familial circumstance and kinship as by economic need. Many considered the move temporary and planned to return. There is evidence of back-and-forth movement reflecting the needs of families, of seasonal shifts between factories and farms, and of a persistent, general pattern of cyclical migrations even after blacks left the farm. (1989: 299–300)

In the family of black literary migrants composed of Hurston and Wright, only the former, with her many lengthy folklore-collecting trips, joined the families described above and literally engaged in "a persistent, general pattern of cyclical migrations" from rural South to urban North. With each of the two writers, however, rural fiction "is evidence of [a] back-and-forth movement" in which metropolitan literary and intellectual practices feed and feed upon reconstructions of rural folk culture. Hurston's and Wright's work thus suggests that placing the rural in the driver's seat of a still-rigid rural/urban opposition need not be the rural turn's final legacy to literary history. Forty years before the waning of the Great Migration drew the attention of black artists and critics Southward, the most famous rivals in modern African-American literature seemed to agree that black rural and urban life were linked through cycles of exchanges, exchanges not just of white capital, but of restless black populations, and the intercultural, yet ethnicizing knowledges necessary to see them clearly. It is these cycles, illuminated and intensified by recent black return migration to the rural South, that offer a model for literary-historical revision worthy of the rural turn, a development that itself is indebted to the persistent travels of black identity cityward, countryward, and back again.

REFERENCES

Awkward, Michael. 1989. *Inspiriting Influences: Tradition, Revision, and Afro-American Women's Novels.* New York: Columbia University Press.

Bender, Thomas. 1978. *Community and Social Change in America.* New Brunswick, N.J.: Rutgers University Press.

Bone, Robert. 1986. "Richard Wright and the Chicago Renaissance." *Callaloo* 9: 446–468.

Cappetti, Carla. 1993. *Writing Chicago: Modernism, Ethnography, and the Novel.* New York: Columbia University Press.

Carby, Hazel V. 1989. "Ideologies of Black Folk: The Historical Novel of Slavery." In Deborah E. McDowell and Arnold Rampersad, eds., *Slavery and the Literary Imagination.* Baltimore: The Johns Hopkins University Press: 125–143.

———. 1990. "The Politics of Fiction, Anthropology, and the Folk: Zora Neale Hurston." In Michael Awkward, ed., *New Essays on Their Eyes Were Watching God.* New York: Cambridge University Press: 71–93.

———. 1994. "'It Just Be's Dat Way Sometime': The Sexual Politics of Women's Blues." In Vicki L. Ruiz and Ellen Carol DuBois, eds., *Unequal Sisters: A Multi-Cultural Reader in U.S. Women's History.* New York: Routledge. 330–341.

Clifford, James. 1988. *The Predicament of Culture: Twentieth-Century Ethnog-*

raphy, Literature, and Art. Cambridge: Harvard University Press.

Cromartie, John, and Carol B. Stack. 1989. "Reinterpretation of Black Return and Nonreturn Migration to the South, 1975–1980." *The Geographical Review* 79.3 (July): 297–310.

Davis, Thadious. 1986. "Wright, Faulkner and the South: Reconstitution and Transfiguration." *Callaloo* 9: 469–80.

Douglas, Ann. 1995. *Terrible Honesty: Mongrel Manhattan in the 1920s.* New York: Farrar, Strauss and Giroux.

Draper, Theodore. 1960. *American Communism and Soviet Russia: The Formative Period.* New York: Vintage, 1986.

Duberman, Martin Bauml. 1988. *Paul Robeson.* New York: Alfred A. Knopf.

Fabre, Michel. 1973. *The Unfinished Quest of Richard Wright.* Trans. Isabel Barzun. New York: William Morrow.

Gates, Henry Louis Jr. 1988. *The Signifying Monkey: A Theory of Afro-American Literary Criticism.* New York: Oxford University Press.

Griffin, Farah Jasmine. 1995. *"Who Set You Flowin'?": The African-American Migration Narrative.* New York: Oxford University Press.

Hemenway, Robert E. 1977. *Zora Neale Hurston: A Literary Biography.* Chicago: University of Illinois Press.

Hurston, Zora Neale. 1933. "The Gilded Six-Bits." *The Complete Stories.* New York: Harper Collins, 1995. 86–98.

———. 1934. "The Fire and the Cloud." *Challenge* 1.2: 10–12.

———. 1935. *Mules and Men. Folklore, Memoirs, and Other Writings.* New York: The Library of America, 1995. 1–267.

———. 1938. "Stories of Conflict." *The Saturday Review of Literature* 2 April: 32.

———. 1939. *Moses: Man of the Mountain.* Chicago: University of Illinois Press, 1984.

———. 1942. *Dust Tracks on a Road: An Autobiography.* New York: Harper Perennial, 1991.

Johnson, Barbara. 1984. "Metaphor, Metonymy, and Voice in *Their Eyes Were Watching God.*" *A World of Difference.* Baltimore: The Johns Hopkins University Press. 155–171.

Lenz, Gunter H. 1981. "Southern Exposures: The Urban Experience and the Re-Construction of Black Folk Culture and Community in the Works of Richard Wright and Zora Neale Hurston." *New York Folklore* 6.8 (Summer): 3–39.

Locke, Alain. 1937. "Resume of Talk and Discussion: Alain Locke: Sunday Afternoon Session: National Negro Congress." *Official Proceedings: Second National Negro Congress.* Philadelphia: Metropolitan Opera House.

Marks, Carole. 1989. *Farewell—We're Good and Gone: The Great Black Migration.* Bloomington: Indiana University Press.

McDowell, Deborah E. 1991. "Lines of Descent/Dissenting Lines." Introduction to Zora Neale Hurston, *Moses: Man of the Mountain.* In Henry Louis Gates, Jr. and K. A. Appiah, eds., *Zora Neale Hurston: Critical Perspectives Past and Present.* New York: Amistad, 1993: 230–40.

Naison, Mark. 1984. *Communists in Harlem During the Depression.* New York: Grove.

Sollors, Werner. 1990. "Anthropological and Sociological Tendencies in American Literature of the 1930s and 1940s: Richard Wright, Zora Neale Hurston, and American Culture." In Steve Ickringill, ed., *Looking Inward, Looking Outward: From the 1920s through the 1940s.* Amsterdam: VU University Press: 22–75.

Stalin, J. V. 1913. *Marxism and the National [and Colonial] Question.* Tirana, Albania: 8 Nentori, 1979.

Washington, Mary Helen. 1979. "Introduction. Zora Neale Hurston: A Woman Half in Shadow." Zora Neale Hurston. *I Love Myself When I am Laughing . . .* (Alice Walker, ed.) New York: The Feminist Press: 7–25.

Willis, Susan. 1987. *Specifying: Black Women Writing the American Experience.* Madison: University of Wisconsin Press.

Wirth, Louis. 1938. "Urbanism as a Way of Life." *Louis Wirth: On Cities and Social Life.* Ed. Albert J. Reiss, Jr. Chicago: University of Chicago Press, 1964: 60–83.

Wright, Richard. 1937. "Between Laughter and Tears." *New Masses* 5 Oct.: 22, 25.

———. 1938a. "Fire and Cloud." *Uncle Tom's Children.* New York: Perennial Library, 1965. 129–180.

———. 1938b. "Long Black Song." *Uncle Tom's Children.* New York: Perennial Library, 1965. 103–128.

———. 1945. "Introduction." St. Clair Drake and Horace R. Cayton. *Black Metropolis: A Study of Negro Life in a Northern City.* 2 vols. New York: Harcourt Brace & World, 1970. xvii–xxxiv.

———. 1977. *American Hunger.* New York: Harper & Row.

3 ~ AARON A. FOX

"Ain't It Funny How Time Slips Away?"

Talk, Trash, and Technology in a Texas "Redneck" Bar

It's been so long now, yet it seems like it was only yesterday
Ain't it funny how time slips away?

—Willie Nelson

SAMMY, Donna, Ann, and I were sitting around Ann's bar talkin' shit, as usual. On this rainy weeknight, our voices and soft old country music on the jukebox were the only sounds in the low-ceilinged, windowless beer joint which sat in the middle of a rolling plain dotted with pastures, farmhouses, trailers, junk-car lots, and cotton fields on a state highway some thirty miles outside of the city of Austin.[1] As it so often did, the conversation turned to the old days, the way things used to be. And somehow, and again as usual, that led us on to talk about music, and into a conversation saturated, as so many always were in this place, with bits of singing and lovingly caressed memories of singers and songs. As we talked, nostalgic memories and fascination with technology blended into the effort to salvage and repair a suddenly obsolete musical medium: the 33-RPM LP record.

My middle-aged interlocutors, it seemed, valued this phono/graphical medium, with its archaically iconic transduction of sound into a shaped, grooved materiality, precisely *because* of its obsolescence. As such, it provided a mnemonic evocation of symbolically loaded working-class social practices centered on talk and mutuality and a disappearing social order.

We talked of early live radio and phonograph machines, of the vivid novelty those now antiquated technologies had once had within my friends' own lifetimes, growing up in rural, working-class homes where families would gather around radios and phonographs as they now gather around televisions and VCRs. As we considered the recent and decisive rise of the compact disc, and the sudden awareness of once again witnessing a discontinuous shift in the aural and material and social experience of music, my friends allegorically remembered an earlier transition, from 78-RPM to 33-RPM records. Miss Ann, who owned the beer joint and worked behind the bar, opened the topic:

> ANN: See we were raised[2]
>
> BAPtist . . .
>
> and . . .
>
> so of course
>
> DANcin' was out of the QUEStion
>
> MOther,
>
> all her life,
>
> she liked to dance . . .   [Donna laughs]
>
> And we used to have
>
> HOUSE dances.
>
> We were one of the FIRST people to
>
> ever HAVE
>
> e-LECtric . . .
>
> ol' . . .
>
> 78-type
>
> (thing that you play) records (on)   DONNA: uhuh?
>
> and she . . .

we'd have HOUSE dances for us girls . . .
and we could have dancin'
(we two)
us girls
providing we would do all this
WORK! . . .
[laughing]
we could have 'em   [Donna laughs]
MAN we would WORK

SAMMY: GOD you're OLD, Ann!
[laughs]

ANN: (I am)
We worked our BUTTS off
to get to have that . . .
PARty
that DANCE

SAMMY: I had a friend . . .
that I worked with,
when I was workin for Dover,
and he collected Victrolas
and stuff (like that)   ANN: mmmmmm?
He just hunted for them
ALL the time . . .
he'd spend all his MOney on it . . .
an' he had a ROOM
FULL of em . . .   ANN: yeah!
but he'd also
he also had his
his uh . . .
disc,
disc players?
Something like that

I mean you talk about somebody into music!

He listened to music   ANN: I 'MAgine! I
                                                    'MAgine![3]

ALL the time!

ANN: Y'know

I'VE got some of those ol albums over there
are WARped and everythin else
at forty years OLD!

SAMMY: mmhmm . . .

Seventy-eights,
an' stuff like that?

ANN: Oh I HAD

hundreds of them things
but I think they gotten burn(ed) up . . .
But I 've got some of those ol'
ALbums
of those ol'
Well, when seven,
whatever,
thirty-THREES just came out   SAMMY: mmhmm?

ANN: I remember the first thirty-three *I* ever bought
was uh . . .
Webb Pierce,
"Wandering Woman"   DONNA: oh YEAH!

SAMMY: Was it WARped?

ANN: I think it's warped . . .

SAMMY: They can be fixed   DONNA: I LIKE him too
                                          I like Webb Pierce

AARON: How do you fix em?

SAMMY: They can be fixed!

ANN: Can they?   SAMMY: No,   AARON: Just
  I've got several of 'em   YOU can fix 'em   put some
  I don know what   weight on'em?
  oh
  in the OVEN?

SAMMY: ALL you gotta do
  is just stick 'em in th'OVen

ANN: I HEARD that . . .

SAMMY: Put em in the gas OVen
  with just
  JUST the uh . . .
  the PIlot . . . .
  and PRESS it   ANN: oh yeah
  just leave it in there
  jus let it set   DONNA: (you need like a)
  get it warm enough   big old ROUND
  get it warm enough . . .   Iron SKILLET or somethin!?
  just let it SIT

SAMMY: No you don't use skil . . .
  ol' IRon skillet
  you use somethin FLAT
  and you
  put WEIGHT on it
  then when
  you leave it there for a while
  when it gets,
  you know it's been there for a good while,
  then you jus take it out
  an' let it COOL,
  leave the WEIGHT on it,
  all the warp'll come out of it

DONNA: Seems like bein layed on that wire rack'd . . .

SAMMY: [Interrupting] You don't LAY it on a wire rack . . .

DONNA: What do you LAY it on?

SAMMY: You got to lay it on somethin FLAT　　ANN: You would have
　　an you put somethin' FLAT on top of it!　　　to, yeah

DONNA: yeah . . .

ANN: But wouldn't the GROOVES melt
　　on the gas?

SAMMY: Uh uh . . .　　　　　　　　　　　　AARON: don't run it too hot . . .
　　You don' get
　　you don'
　　See you jus' talkin' about heat like,
　　you're jus' talkin about
　　the uh PIlot
　　an y'know it keeps that oven . . .　　　　DONNA: Well I wonder how
　　Well,　　　　　　　　　　　　　　　　long you, how long you
　　the oven　　　　　　　　　　　　　　leave it IN there?
　　a pilot
　　just a PIlot on that oven'll make it
　　keeps it pretty warm
　　and you
　　just like the sun y'know
　　—'swhat cause it to warp
　　the heat—
　　so you put it on there
　　and just leave it in there for a while
　　—a good while—
　　you may(be) leave it in there for a . . .
　　DAY
　　and you take it out
　　keep it together
　　jus set it up and let it COOL
　　and it'll be fine . . .

DONNA: hmm!

SAMMY: There's a lot of little tricks you can do! . . .
    take care o' stuff . . .
    it'll amaze you!
    [laughs]

TALKIN' REDNECK BLUES

What do we make of such talk, with its dense, hilarious and skill-ful tropes? Its apparent interactional artistry and its nostalgic tonality combine to signify an unmistakably rural aura, a working-class *ethos,* the discourse of marginal participants in the headlong rush of novelty and replacement that constitutes (capitalist culture's orientation) to musical commodities and the ever-shifting mediating technologies from which these commodities are inseparable.

For working-class Americans whose trailers and beer joints and churches occupy the peri-urban and semi-rural boundaries of the postmodern city with its information-driven economy, stereotypically derided and celebrated in popular culture and sometimes, polemically, in their own discourse as "rednecks," everyday life foregrounds a struggle between two powerful logics: the commodity's alienation and talk's sociability. Figured as a "country" way of life in opposition to the encroaching presence of the urban economy, and symbolized by the adoption of self-conscious emblems of a remembered (if sometimes re-imagined) rural past such as "country" music, "redneck" working-class sociability works a dialogic alchemy on the leaden commodity form. This sociability reinvests the commodity with a resonant sense of social meaning, talking its mystifying inscrutability back into a known, inhabited space and time, until space and time become a lived-in *place* and a memorable *moment.* Sociability embeds the ephemeral, trans-local commodity in the fertile muck of the local, the everyday, the "ordinary." It modulates the lure of the new, constructed in a dis-course of desire, with nostalgia for the old, for what these people often polemically call "REAL life," constructed in a discourse of loss (Fox

1992). The commodified object dissolves in dialogue and re-appears as an image in a local poetics of sentimental over-attachment, revealing a startling and critical irony: ain't it funny how capitalist time slips away faster than the human lives it disciplines and organizes?

But ain't it funny how the commodity sometimes will *not* slip away? And this is especially true of the highly symbolic musical commodity, with its associated practices of sociable participation and consumption. The musical commodity may live on past its planned obsolescence, especially among people insulated (if only marginally and by an ambiguous choice) from the market's accelerating oscillations between nostalgia and novelty, miniature and gigantic, decrepit and futuristic. Among "rednecks" I have known, and specifically among low-wage working-class people living on the mixed-use agricultural and industrial margins of postmodernizing cities (see Fox 1995b), musical commodities may be re-mediated over the circuits of talk that define a well-known place, a place these people inhabit, a *topos* these people figure with the trope of "outness" when they refer to it, as they often do, as "out the country."[4] In a fusion of culture, identity, and location, this marginally rural place comes to stand for the selective retention and re-invention of "country" life, rusticity deployed as a marker of class and a strategy of resistance.

Sociable *talk,* defined by a deeply engaged, tropically saturated, and aesthetically cultivated quality is the catalyst in this alchemy. Social life and emotionally vivid experience are promoted "out the country" in a verbal flow of conversation, gossip, persuasion, reflection, and narration. Talk in this sense is, here as everywhere, the modality of the local, the personal, the interested, and the experienced. Talk looks at and into *everything* around it—relationships, objects, the natural world, and the world of feeling. Talk appropriates all of this to the social, the present, the flowing moment of experience, the "real," a "real" which is materially grounded and experientially located in a rustic place.

But talk is never guaranteed to bear this phenomenological weight. Talk is an art form in and of itself in the "redneck" social world. Talk is ironically figured as trash: "Aaaaaaaaah, we jus'

ASSholes talkin' shit," old Rusty once told me, dismissing my attempt to analyze the intricacies of his verbal creativity, the tightly woven prosodic and tropological density of his three-hour dialogues with his best friend Jerry, another old man, with whom he had been talking every day for years as they sat drinking beer at Ann's Other Place. To objectify talk, Rusty implied, is to run the risk of mimetic displacement beyond a lived-in place and moment, beyond the "ordinary." Thus, talk's alchemical authenticity is perhaps most evident on the margins of the geographic *and* metaphysical edifice of postmodernity, an evasive, invisible presence around which instrumental debasements and technological simulacra of talk swirl. Fully co-present talk, the primordial foundation of shared human meaning and community, has in an increasingly displaced social world ironically become a privilege of the powerful, a guilty pleasure for workers, and a simulated spectacle on "talk radio," on the Internet, at conferences and board meetings, and in popular "infotainments" where it is conjoined to the spectacle of social otherness predicated on race, class, and rusticity. The rural and peri-urban working poor in particular appear, in their talkative excessiveness, as "rednecks" and "trailer trash." They appear as a dangerous, over-sexed rabble on the ubiquitous television talk shows (e.g. "The Ricki Lake Show") and "reality" police shows (e.g. "C.O.P. S."), and as unselfconscious, debased clowns devoid of style and sophistication in the plethora of interchangeable television situation comedies which foreground the American obsession with social distinction (e.g. "Delta" and "The Jeff Foxworthy Show").[5]

These representations of "redneck" rusticity as simultaneously dangerous and foolish saturate the political unconscious of the American middle-class, itself anxiously positioned "in between" the country and the city in the expanding utopian universe of the suburb, the shopping mall, the "edge city," and even more anxiously positioned between the agricultural and industrial political economy of modernity and the blossoming informational and cultural political economy of American postmodernity. Like inner-city African-Americans, tenuously rural "rednecks" are marked by a suite of commodified cultural orientations (music, religion, violence, recreation, clothing, vehicles, politics) which comprise a codified "style," a style which can be detached from the gritty reality of working-class social experience (an experience diverging ever more sharply from a normative middle-class existence) and marketed as commodity and fashion. And these cultural orientations are powerfully evoked by language, by rhetorical and prosodic tropes, by the lexical and grammatical and phonological "deviations" from middle-class speech which comprise regional and ethnic and class "accents" ("dialects," "registers," "styles," "codes"), and by the poetic foregrounding of an oddly non-instrumental orality and interactional prowess, a tendency to talk for talk's sake. Class positions are, at least in part, mapped onto the geography of residuality by *talk*.

Such marked talk is much more than a stereotyped index, paradoxically inhabited and seen from afar by its subjects as a medium for the experience of self as other. At "redneck" bars like Ann's Other Place, talk is an expressive and experiential resource which resists alienation from the living local world it instantiates. In order to hold closed the door against postmodernity's avalanche of desire and replacement, against the newest and latest and next best thing, talk must throw itself between the commodity and the flow of time, between "obsolescence" and "progress," between loss and desire. Talk must brace itself against the material world *as it is* in order to articulate a vision of the moral world *as it could be,* which in the local, working-class idiom means a world in the image of life *as it was,* before Wal-Marts, before CDs, before the deluge.

SONG AND THE RURAL, WORKING-CLASS LIFEWORLD

In places like Ann's Other Place, *song* is the archetypal object of talk's resistant scrutiny, at once the aesthetic condensation of talk's artistry and the essence of the commodity form. As I have argued elsewhere (Fox 1992, 1993, 1995a, 1995b; Feld and Fox 1994), the boundaries between talk and song are fluid and constantly traversed in Texas rural working-class culture; speech is saturated with the potential for song at every turn, and song richly and pervasively informs the texture and tonality and content of "ordinary" talk. Song's textuality seduces talk, and reinvigorates the "ordinary." Song disgraces, restores, and glorifies the here-and-now, the conversation over a beer or two or three, an exchange about the weather, and gossip about the town drunk.

Though precious, song is also, always, and already a commodity and it is known as such, recognized and even interrogated as such. Through the mediated appropriation of rural working-class style as "redneck" stereotype (see Keil 1985), the orality and musicality of the rural, working-class lifeworld is continually alienated from its participatory roots and the essential dialogism of everyday working-class social practice, even as it signifies these roots as a claim to authenticity. It is thereby continually stripped of local meaning, stripped of its organic "participatory discrepancies" (see Keil 1987) which link it to the intimate unfolding of real moments in real lives in real places. These markers of working-class participation and cultural authenticity are transformed into technologically sophisticated simulacra; they are cleaned up, rationalized, re-packaged to be sold to an ever larger and more politically and spatially and historically diluted market, though this audience includes the very working-class people for whom this appropriation is such an ambivalent loss.

With each movement through these cycles of commodification and re-appropriation, the logic of capital and the logic of working-class sociolinguistic and sociomusical practice become more interpenetrated, and a fundamental irony is elevated to a covert criterion of an evasive authenticity that confounds critics and locals alike (Fox 1992). Is Hank Williams, Jr., *kidding* when he spins an over-the-top backwoods survivalist fantasy in "A Country Boy Can Survive"? Does the urban, college-radio fascination with classic "honky-tonk" country depend upon the continued existence of a place where such music is listened to *without* irony or a sense of pastiche? Do the wildly popular pop-rock FM-radio-oriented sounds of "Hot New Country" signify the end of "real country," or simply the latest in a long line of encounters between an "authentic" tradition and the musical market's most ephemeral possibilities?

The vertiginous irony of "real country music" engenders—at its extremes—both the explosive genre-blurring aesthetics of postmodern urban popular culture and the middle-class cultivation of an impossibly pure and necrophilic "folkloristic" standard which disguises the mass-mediated commodity as a handicraft from another place and time, serving the ideological function the "rural" has traditionally served in relation to bourgeois social experience.[6] At the center of this opposition between the ironic and the nostalgic, "Hot New Country" radio thrives and country artists in cowboy hats have pages on the World Wide Web and digital pitch-correctors for their voices. This tension supplies the energy behind the capitalist edifice of the country music industry and its vast and growing market.

Yet I remember, at a party above a humble shade-tree garage on a dirt road in Texas, hearing an old beer-joint country singer spin a fantasy about taking up arms and seizing, terrorist fashion, the 100 thousand watt "Hot New Country" station in Austin. "We'll make them fuckers listen to OUR music for a change," this man concluded to delighted laughter and applause from the rest of those present. By "OUR music," he referred to a negotiable yet well-defined canon of "hard" country music, reaching back to Jimmie Rodgers, centered on the massive presence of Merle Haggard, and selectively drawing on contemporary hits which reveal a carefully evaluated mastery of classic tropes. That canon, to be sure, is filled with songs which were created as ephemeral commodities in their day. But the criterion is more than stylistic. Working-class "rednecks" continue to clutch at "country" song even in its most apparently debased and diluted form, to insist on its inalienability from local worlds and the authenticity of their sociable feeling. For these "rednecks," song is something worth fighting for as a form of participatory experience and practice. Its appropriation, its entrapment in the sweeping, searching beam of the market, is something to be resisted.

There are many specific practices through which this critical reappropriation of the musical commodity is pursued (see Fox 1995b). Song is embedded in the local lifeworld of rural working-class talk by the seamless integration of singing into everyday ways of speaking. Rural working-class people use song to mark highly potent meanings, to intensify a moment, to mend a rupture of sense. Songs are detected running below the surface of everyday speech, in the sudden emergence of a euphemism or a cliché as an object of poetic contemplation and delight. Songs are apprehended in deeply felt ways by heartbroken, "tore-up fools," whose personal immersion in an imaginary world of emotional mirrors spun by the sad song on the jukebox defies the abstraction of feeling so crucial to the circulation and exchange of the commodity form (see Fox 1993).

Song is more explicitly reappropriated for the local in practices of re-writing the words to the latest radio hits so that they refer to local people, local places, and local problems. I remember the time some teenagers in a small town in Illinois transformed Travis Tritt's hit song "Country Club" into an anthem about the local beer joint, the "Pub and Grub."[7] They played the song on tape, and dropped the volume at the end of each line of the refrain, where they would shout out locally salient revisions to the delighted cheers of the bar's other patrons. At one point, they took a vote among the patrons, asking whether they should change the song's reference to a Ford truck ("I drive an old Ford pickup truck") to a Chevy, since this was a GM factory town, or to "a beater with a heater," (the local term for a rusted, worthless old junker) which won, hands down. The GM plant had been laying people off that winter.

Song is many more things in this local world. Song is an instrument for situated, performative social critique, in the form of poetic inversions of class and gender hierarchies (Fox 1995a). Song is a resource for parody and narration, for the exchange of feelings, for the participatory cultivation of an altered state of awareness through the song-linked pleasures of drink, dance, and deep emotion. Country song and "ordinary" talk are intertwined in everyday expression and musical experience is something good to talk *about*. Song provides fodder for endless conversations over beer and jukebox music. During the conversation that began this paper, for example, Ann told us about the time she was working as a waitress at the Western Steakhouse when the great singer Jim Reeves came in. She told us how Reeves was "just a gentle, caring, loving man," a man who ate alone in working-class restaurants and, without saying a word in that magnificent baritone, spoke volumes to a tired waitress:

SAMMY: To me,
    Roger Miller is a storyteller . . .

ANN: He IS!

SAMMY: And that's . . .
    And there's a lot more to it than just . . .

ANN: But you could dance to his music . . .

SAMMY: Ya,
    but he was still a storyteller . . . [pounds on bar to make point] . . .
    every . . . song . . . he . . . ever . . . sang . . . told . . . a story.

ANN: Well SO did Jim Reeves.

DONNA: Oh, I LOVE Jim Reeves,
    God I still love him . . .

SAMMY: But he's a storyteller.
    He woulda been a . . .
    If he couldn't 'a sang,
    he'd a been a storyteller.   ANN: Yeah

SAMMY: He'd'a sat down and told you the SAME story
    in VERSE rather than in song, y'know

ANN: Right before Jim Reeves died,
    I was workin' at the Western Steakhouse?

DONNA: uhhuh?

ANN: And he'd come in,
    come in there and . . .
    I didn't know Jim Reeves from a big-eyed bug!

But he walked up to the counter,
and he handed me a card,
and on the card it said
"I'm Jim Reeves,"
"Hello,"
or somethin' like that,
"I'm Jim Reeves,
"and I would like to . . .
have dinner and would like
not like to be disturbed."   SAMMY: mmm, yeah

ANN: Real *nice* man,
   real *pleasant,*
   and just wanted to eat and be on his way . . .

DONNA: Quietly!

ANN: Uh huh!
   And so,
   I put him over in a corner,
   and turned his back to everybody,
   and he had his dinner,
   and he was a *very very* sweet . . .
   gentle, loving, caring man . . .

SAMMY: [reverently] That was my MOther's
   favorite ARtist of all time . . .

ANN: And he was a perfect gentleman . . .

DONNA: He was real good

SAMMY: Oh yeah

ANN: . . . and he just had his dinner,
   and he went his merry way,
   but I guess . . .
   [trailing off]
   it wasn't too long before he was dead . . .

Country stars like Reeves populate the imaginatively extended world of the everyday in such oft-told stories, as intimate friends, as "ordinary" people, as someone "you can relate to." Sometimes this is explicitly about reclaiming music from the logic of capital. Singers like Johnny Cash can become symbols of resistance to the increasingly corporate and commodified character of country music. Many of the working-class bars in the small towns of South Texas pay no licensing fees to the performing rights organizations (ASCAP and BMI), although as live-music venues they are legally obliged to do so, since semi-professional and amateur musicians play ASCAP- and BMI-licensed songs in these bars, and presumably contribute thereby to the generation of revenue by these tiny beer joints. ASCAP in particular had undertaken a vigorous enforcement campaign during the years of my fieldwork, and bar-owners routinely received threatening letters, calls, and visits from ASCAP lawyers and field representatives working for a percentage of whatever they could collect.

Like many bars, Ann's received regular letters, visits, and phone calls, offering various terms and threatening lawsuits for non-compliance. This infuriated Ann and her patrons. The concept of "intellectual property" rights did not extend, for these fans, into the *live* performance of "cover" songs by well-known country artists, although they acknowledged the rights of an artist to receive royalties from the sale of recordings and for live appearances. They reasoned, correctly, that "cover" performances of popular songs contribute to the general and enduring popularity of particular artists as well as country music more generally, and hence have an incalculable positive effect on the revenue artists *do* earn from public appearances and recordings. More than this, these fans and musicians understood the nature of musical "property" and its "ownership" very differently from music-business institutions like ASCAP. They were shocked to hear that I (or my university press publisher, unwilling to test the limits of the "fair use" provision of the copyright law) had to pay money in royalties to publish quotations from classic country songs in an academic article (Fox 1992). They were even more furious when an ASCAP representative told them which songs they were technically not allowed to play without payment of license fees. Although I didn't witness it, a defining moment came when Ann asked a visiting ASCAP agent *who* would get the hundreds of dollars she was being asked to pay as a yearly fee. The agent, I was told, showed Ann and some other patrons at the bar a brochure with pictures of ASCAP artists, including one of Johnny Cash. The agent left the brochure at the bar, where it was circulated with disbelieving remarks for days after the visit.

The sentiment which this inspired was crystallized in phrases I heard several times as this story was retold in subsequent weeks. People said things like "Johnny Cash wouldn't stand for this," or "If Johnny knew who was playin' his songs, he'd let us have them for free." Ann talked of writing to Johnny Cash to explain the whole situation. The incident seemed to energize anti-ASCAP sentiment. Ann discovered that record stores were exempt from live-performance licensing fees, since music played in such stores could be legitimately described as advertising and promotion for particular artists' recordings. Within days, a large bin of old country records appeared at the back of the bar, under a hand-painted yellow plastic insert stuck onto an electric beer-sign: "ANN'S LITTLE RECORD SHOP."

It wasn't long, too, before a huge white banner was draped across the graffiti-covered wall behind the band stage, which said: "NO ASCAP MUSIC PLAYED HERE." This sign didn't mean what it entailed; I offered to do some research and make a list of artists and songs licensed by ASCAP so that we could, indeed, avoid these songs when we were playing music in the bar, but the suggestion was laughed off. The sign meant, of course, that music played "here" was by definition not "ASCAP music," but the intellectual property of the people who patronized this bar. It was simply unimaginable to the patrons and musicians of this humble working-class establishment "out the country" that Johnny Cash, whose voice stood for so much to these people, would expect money from them before he would allow them to play "Folsom Prison Blues" as they sat around unsteady tables on old plastic chairs drinking cheap beer and talkin' shit. Everybody knew, deep in their hearts, that Johnny would probably join us around the table if he were coming through town, and that even if he never came through this particular town, he would be pleased to hear that his voice still mattered here.

LITTLE TRICKS

Let me now return to my opening example to show how song is explicitly linked to a sociable re-appropriation of the alienated commodity in a set of intertwined practices and discourses that might be called "redneck low-tech." These practices and discourses are, of course, embedded in a complicated social history of the relationship between class, sophistication, and technology. The rehearsal of this history is beyond the scope of this paper, but the images of the discourse are familiar parts of the national iconographic imaginary (the wheezing Okie jalopy full of children and animals and the huge satellite dish next to the mobile home being only two stereotypical extremes).

Country music has often foregrounded working-class ambivalence about technology, using idioms of nostalgia for the old ways and the foolish misuse of new machines. More complex versions of this idea emerge in the ubiquity of the speaking mechanical object (especially the jukebox) in country's textual poetics (Fox 1992). This finds its local discursive counterpart in talk which incorporates the voice of the jukebox into the flow of speech, as the song swells up to fill a poignant painful silence, and the song's lyrics are suddenly foregrounded as a voice in the conversation. More explicitly, angry polemics against the class valences of technological change have long been part of country's generic narrative trope of class inversion. Randy Travis, for example, sings of going back to a "better class of losers," a song which had enormous appeal in beer joints, even if Randy was relaxing on his horse farm in between digital recording sessions. "I need friends," the song (co-written with Alan Jackson) insists, "who don't pay their bills on home computers," and who buy coffee with the "beans already ground."[8]

These technological polemics, too, rise on occasion to the surface of everyday working-class talk. Here, the focus is often on outwitting personalized, insidious machines, and rejecting the regime of de-personalized social life they foreshadow and enable. One night, for example, I bragged to Texas beer-joint singer Larry "Hoppy" Hopkins about the new computerized digital effects unit I'd bought to play the music that I played for a living, music Hopkins always called "that top 40 crap." My boast was an invitation for critique, of course, although Hopkins delivered it gently with a story. And the story in turn suggested a song, which served as the kind of lyrical *denouement* which makes narrative successful in this social world, where songs and stories and jokes overlap and interpenetrate in quick succession, amplifying one another with intertextual references across the speech/song boundary:

AARON: It's ah,
    like a comPUter that I put
    between my guitar and my amp
    and it's got about THIRteen different effects on it
    and you can put
    ninety-nine different combinations of them together
    boy it's WILD
    First few days
    I sat there in my room
    Pressin' buttons
    Makin' sounds

LH: [Laughs] I don know,
    those things SCARE me sometimes!
    That's like . . .
    We was playin one night at a
    th'American Legion and ol . . .
    Everett
    Johnny Mac's BROther,
    was playin bass
    —they like to pull . . .
    PRANKS—

Now Everett was the type of guy,

he played bass,

but he had EVERY-thing you could imagine,

all kinds a little buttons and hookups,

and I was not suspicious at all

of this stuff he was hookin' up,

see?

And . . .

what he DID,

he hooked an ECho chamber up

Now, boy I went out there and . . .

[sings]

"Smoke smoke smoke that cigarette"

[Strums a chord]

Anyway,

pretty soon I hear this

[slightly sung, repeating and fading away]

"Smoke smoke smoke smoke smoke smoke . . ."[9]

[Reporting his own reaction, scratching his head]

"What in the hell?"

[laughter]

At this climactic moment, Hopkins punctuated his point by breaking into a full performance of the song he was invoking: "Smoke, Smoke, Smoke that Cigarette."[10] Among rural, working-class Texans, this lyrical crystallization is a standard rhetorical function of song in relation to artful narration.

This anti-technological polemic has another side, of course: the rube's Goldbergian delight in complicated technology. A recent example of this is the title figure in George Jones's hit, "High-Tech

Redneck." Kicking back in his trailer surrounded by satellite dishes and delighting in a computerized entertainment center, he watches professional wrestling on his "satellite send . . . big screen TV with stereo," controlled by a two-hundred-function remote with which he can produce a "picture-in-a-picture" so that "it's all in view." "Mayberry meets *Star Trek*" as this "high-tech redneck" surveys his subwoofers, power amplifiers, CD, CB, cassette, digital tape machine, radar and short-wave radio. He may be a "bumpkin," but he's "plugged in," and he may not listen to hip-hop or rap music, but he'll "rattle them speakers to [a decidedly unhip] Ronnie Milsap."[11]

This image invokes the time-honored trope of the fantastic "redneck" mechanical *bricolage*, the trashed-out machine fitted with an impossible array of devices and decorative additions. But the hardscrabble economic reality of rural, working-class life as I have known it marks this as clearly a fantasy, and it is not quite clear whose version of the fantasy this is, and to whom it is being projected. Compared to George Jones's stereotype, the "entertainment center" at Ann's bar was pretty low-tech: a cart piled high with half-working VCRs and a crumbly old TV, the sound running through an old Fender Princeton tube guitar amp, its speaker grill torn off. And when we could get it to work, we watched amateur videos of local singers and stolen tapes of field sobriety tests given to suspected drunken drivers.

Like any good stereotype, however, there is something true about this song, and its "high-tech redneck's" delight in technology. The rural working-class fascination with re-appropriating the machine for local sociability through an intense, deconstructive scrutiny of the machine's possibilities emerges clearly in a culturally stylized "workin' on things," including, for example, the way men work on cars and trucks, and the way women work on elaborate decorations of clothing and decorative crafts. Among musicians, it emerges in huge assemblages of broken-down equipment, wired together, piled high, and invested with a certain combinatorial magic in proportion to the complexity and idiosyncrasy of the system. And it emerges in the way musicians *talk* about equipment too, verbally "taking it apart" and putting it back together, assaying the value of a particular guitar or amplifier in terms of some quirky, excessive addition that has been fitted to it, individualizing its mechanical identity.

But it's not just musicians who talk this way, and this brings me back, in conclusion, to a consideration of the conversation with which I began this paper. Talk itself is a mode of "workin' on things," and of appropriating technologies to the mechanics of local discourse. This fragment of talk shows, I think, how "low tech" is an embedded trope of rural, working-class musical discourse, and how musical discourse is itself embedded in a more generalized flow of comfortable, dialogic sociability, a feeling of locality and of life lived, slowly and carefully, in the backwaters of fashion and taste, a life lived "out the country." The conversation between Sammy, Donna, Ann, and me, revolves around a tacit acknowledgment that the LP record is itself now an obsolete medium, and this acknowledgment informs the foregrounding of an earlier transition from 78 RPM to 33 RPM records. But the salvageability of old technology—the restoration of value to trash—is also explicitly invoked as a tactic for sidestepping the lure of the new, and for curating the forms of sociability which have been so painstakingly and lovingly assembled out of an earlier generation of musical commodities. And most basically, the commodity is re-appropriated as something good to talk about and "work on," through talk and through practices of restoration and repair, rather than something to buy and replace, in an endless cycle of alienating desire to move out of the restraining nexus of sociability.

Talk is vividly poeticized here, in ways that are both pervasive and casually ubiquitous. Talk becomes verbal art, a graspable, palpable, beautiful object in its own right through strategies such as alliteration (note, for example, the piled-up "W"s of "warped," "Webb Pierce," and "Wandering Woman"). This talk is poeticized through repetition, and through stylized and gendered forms of friendly dispute. Striking too is the mutual co-refinement of a vivid visual image which haunts this conversation: the image of a melting record, foreshadowed in Ann's remembering the burning of her record collection early in the example. This objectified poetic talk replaces even the de-commodified object constructed through talk. Talk's sociability and the nostalgic affect this talk <u>instantiates</u>, then, become the true objects of our desire, while the musical commodity becomes merely talk's predicate, something good to talk *about*. A past in which commodities like radios and records were still rare treasures, possessed of a magic that had the power to transform the experience of a life of labor, is brought back to life in the time and space of this talk. Our conversation is braced against the door of time, and it's cold outside. Sammy makes this feeling explicit for all of us when he observes, with a self-conscious laugh, "God you're OLD, Ann."

In this ubiquitous "redneck" way of talking about musical commodities, we can see how the eccentric object, the commodity, is talked back into a known working-class life-world. Once it is in that world, through what Sammy calls "little tricks" it can be melted back into shape, repaired and re-invested with meanings which anchor it firmly in a local, social space.

CONCLUSION

But ain't it funny how papers slip away? Some questions follow from these ethnographic observations. What do these musical and discursive practices say about the transformation of "rural" experience in the present moment, with its blurry expansions of the (sub)urban sphere, its accelerating social reconfigurations of the relationship between class and place, and its emergent modes of cultural standardization and hyper-consumption? Why is *music* so emblematic of the struggle for local meaning among these people, and are there parallel cultivations of resistant rusticity among other people on the tenuously rural margins of the postmodern economy?

In the trailer-parks and small towns and beer joints surrounding American cities like Austin, Texas, a working-class social world is constituted in the nostalgic image of "rural" culture. This world is in an uneasy standoff, separated only by a few miles of pasture and farmland and landfill from the homogenizing middle-class culture of the city's expanding suburban sprawl. The elaboration of this "redneck" culture draws on mediated representations of ordinariness and rusticity that circulate under the master trope of "country," a trope that finds its apotheosis in the intertwined musical and verbal discourses of this community. Working-class life "out the country" materializes as a distinctive discursive ecology in which a highly cultivated mode of everyday talk and the interpretive practices that define "country" music are densely interpenetrated aspects of "redneck" identity, and in which the evanescent, elusive musical commodity is enfolded by a defensive local sociability, and only reluctantly released to time's slipping away.

NOTES

I am especially grateful, as always, to my working-class interlocutors and consultants in Texas and Illinois. In addition, this paper has benefited from discussions with Barbara Ching, Steven Feld, Sandra Hayslette, Charles Keil, Susan Lepselter, Louise Meintjes, Tom Porcello, David Samuels, Tom Solomon, Katie Stewart, and Chris Waterman.

1. Materials in this paper are based on four years of ethnographic fieldwork in small towns and working-class bars outside of Austin, Texas, and in central Illinois. This fieldwork is reported more fully in Fox (1995). Quoted dialogue is transcribed from tape-recordings made with full knowledge and permission of the participants. Some names are pseudonyms.

2. I use the following transcription conventions (see Fox 1995):

Notation	Interpretation
Line breaks	—prosodic junctures (usually pause-marked)
CAPS	—syllables marked by strong prosodic stress
Italics	—voice quality marked by heightened intonation
. . .	—lengthy pauses
[Brackets]	—contextual glosses, and paralinguistic descriptions
(Parentheses)	—Inaudible or questionable on tape.

3. "I 'MAgine" is a widely used local affirmative expression. It is a contraction of "I imagine."

4. Short for "out *in* the country."

5. Ironically, these representations of rural "redneck" existence are paralleled (often on the same television shows) with representations of inner-city "minority" culture, complicating the meaning of the rural/urban distinction

with the politics of race and class.

6. College radio rock shows, intending to reach a young, urban audience, often mix the astonishingly archaic yodelling of a bespectacled, 60-year-old Don Walser with the raging hardcore strains of the Butthole Surfers. The same stations may devote other time segments to "A Prairie Home Companion" and earnest "folk music" shows.

7. "Country Club" by Catesby Jones and Dennis Lord. Copyright 1988 by Triumvirate Music, Inc., C/O New Clarion Music Group (BMI).

8. "A Better Class of Losers" by Randy Travis and Alan Jackson. Copyright 1991 by Sometimes You Win Music (adm. by All Nations Music)/Seventh Son Music, Inc./Mattie Ruth Musick (ASCAP).

9. This acoustic icon of the sound of a word fading away on an "Echoplex" (a tape-loop echo machine popular in the 1960s) is itself a version of the trope of narrative conclusion, a timeless summational device designed to bring a narrative to poetic closure. "Fading away" is an essential predicate of this trope. Hopkins's choice of the "Echoplex" sound for this function is inspired.

10. "Smoke, Smoke, Smoke (That Cigarette)" by Merle Travis and Tex Williams. Copyright 1947 by American Music, Inc. Copyright renewed, assigned to Unichappell Music, Inc. (Rightsong Music, publisher) and Elvis Presley Music, Inc. International copyright secured. All rights reserved.

11. "High-Tech Redneck" copyright 1993 by Byron Hill and Zack Turner.

REFERENCES

Feld, Steven, and Aaron Fox. 1994. "Music and Language." *Annual Review of Anthropology* 23: 25–53.

Fox, Aaron. 1992. "The Jukebox of History: Narratives of Loss and Desire in the Discourse of Country Music." *Popular Music* 11(1): 53–72.

———. 1993. "Split Subjectivity in Country Music and Honky-tonk Discourse." In G. Lewis, ed., *All That Glitters: Country Music in America*. Bowling Green: Bowling Green State University Press: 131–139.

———. 1995a. "The 'Redneck' Reverse: Language and Gender in American Working-Class Women's Verbal Art." *SALSA II Conference Proceedings*. 189–199.

———. 1995b. "Out the Country: Language, Music, Feeling and Sociability in American Rural Working-Class Culture." Ph.D. Dissertation, Department of Anthropology, University of Texas at Austin.

Keil, Charles. 1985. "People's Music Comparatively: Style and Stereotype, Class and Hegemony." *Dialectical Anthropology* 10: 119–130.

———. 1987. "Participatory Discrepancies and the Power of Music." *Cultural Anthropology* 2(3): 275–283.

"Campesinos" and "Técnicos"

New Peasant Intellectuals in Central American Politics

Al principio pensábamos que
teníamos lo mejor para los
campesinos
entonces les informábamos . . .
y yo me sentía muy bondadoso.
Cuando teníamos algunas dudas
les consultábamos . . . y yo me
sentía democrático.
Para mejorarlo pedíamos
sugerencias a los
campesinos . . . y yo me sentía
más democrático.
Pensábamos que era mejor para
nuestros objetivos contar con
algunos delegados
campesinos . . . y yo me sentía
muy participativo.
Ahora todo lo decidimos
juntos campesinos y
técnicos . . . y me doy cuenta
que fue recién empezamos a
comunicarnos.
Me pregunto: ¿Qué hacíamos
realmente al principio?

At first we thought that we
knew best for the
campesinos, so we informed
them . . . and I felt very
generous.
When we had some doubts, we
consulted them . . . and I
felt democratic.
To improve things, we asked
the peasants for
suggestions . . . and I felt
more democratic.
We thought it was best for
our objectives to have some
peasant delegates . . . and I
felt very participatory.
Now we decide everything
together, campesinos and
técnicos . . . and I realize
it's only recently that we
began to communicate.
I ask myself: What were we
really doing at the
beginning?

—Anonymous poem on the office wall at the Consejo Campesino Justicia y
Desarrollo (Justice and Development Peasant Council), Costa Rica, 1993

THE epigraph of this essay describes with unusual candor—or
"*transparencia,*" as the unknown author might say—a process of
growing convergence between "*campesinos*" (peasants) and "*técnicos*"
(technicians or specialists) in Central America. The poem also hints at
another related—and somewhat politically sensitive—reality: the
efforts in the 1970s and 1980s of thousands of Central American young
people, many of urban origin but usually children or grandchildren of

campesinos, to bring change to the countryside—as cadres of revolutionary organizations, liberation theology catechists, rural educators and literacy workers, health providers, cooperative movement organizers, or even government functionaries. These "outside agitators," like those who tried to instigate agrarian upheavals in other times and places, often failed to achieve their objectives (see Thorner 1986: xi). Sometimes, however, they succeeded in spurring the formation of, or at least shaping durable movements with genuine and profound roots among the rural poor.[1] By the early 1990s, the lines between *campesinos* and "outsiders," whether *técnicos* or activists, had become blurred, and rural organizing had become transnational, with the emergence of a seven-country, Central America-wide peasant association led by a new generation of peasant intellectuals.

I use the term "peasant intellectuals" to highlight commonalities of knowledge and practice that link not only campesinos and *técnicos* in Central America, but also the academic readers of this paper in North America or Europe—anthropologists and others—many of whom would likely be surprised to meet peasants who know more about macroeconomics and international trade agreements than they do. My use of the phrase differs, however, from Steven Feierman's in *Peasant Intellectuals* (1990); this superb study of how Tanzanian rainmakers' discourses about "healing the land" change over time concerns a type of "peasant intellectual" whose very exoticism seems almost to unintentionally confirm old social-scientific (and popular) stereotypes about rural people. Today's Central American "peasant intellectuals"—certainly more than earlier Tanzanian rainmakers—are very much like what Antonio Gramsci yearned for when he spoke of "organic intellectuals" (Gramsci 1967). Though they reject, in most cases, any "organic" connection to a revolutionary party, they nonetheless constitute a sector of highly politicized, articulate, and committed activists who have surged forth from among the rural poor. In the 1990s, they have also become the bearers of alternative political projects that would have been impossible to imagine during the wars and crises of the previous decade.

This paper examines how the civil wars, repression and economic crises since the late 1970s have affected Central American peasants and led to new kinds of campesino politics. It looks in particular at the emergence of increasingly sophisticated peasant leaders and of "peasantized" *técnicos*. Finally, it describes the rise of transnational campesino organizing in the 1990s and outlines the advantages and risks accompanying peasant participation in the "high" politics of lobbying and international negotiations.

RUBBER BOOTS AND BANANA REPUBLICS

In Central America, as elsewhere, the rural poor find themselves at the bottom of the cultural hierarchy. The lexicon is replete with pejorative expressions for campesino "hicks": *"polo"* in Costa Rica, *"bayunco"* in El Salvador, *"botas de hule"* ("rubber boots") in Nicaragua. Even where few peasants are indigenous, as in most of the region outside Guatemala and Panama, derisive terms for Indians serve as put-downs for those whose speech, bearing, dress, or dark skin betray rural origins. Frequently, "Indian-ness" or even "Indian blood" is associated with violence in the elite imagination. But images of rustics—which served, since the conquest, to degrade and control the peasant population—were contradictory, also surfacing at times as romanticized national icons. The unaffected, picturesque campesino as the embodiment of an older, purer, and more honest national essence is a theme found to some degree in all the Central American countries and, of course, elsewhere as well.

In the late 1970s and throughout the 1980s, Central America was in the spotlight. This region of small states—which poet Pablo Neruda described in the 1940s as sorrowful "comic opera . . . banana republics" set along "the sweet waist of the Americas" (1980: 443)—underwent social upheavals of gigantic proportions and became a major arena of superpower geopolitical competition. The 1979 Sandinista revolution and subsequent *contra* war in Nicaragua, the civil war in El Salvador, the extraordinarily bloody repression in Guatemala, and the 1989 U.S. invasion of Panama all made headlines outside the region. Honduras, which avoided large-scale civil conflict and thus rarely appeared on the front pages, was, as some said at the time, occupied by three armies: the U.S. military with its new operational and training bases, the Nicaraguan *contras* ensconced along the border, and the Honduran armed forces which, despite a nominal return to civilian rule in 1981, engaged in a campaign of brutal repression, "disappearing" 179 activists in popular movements during the 1980s (Comisionado Nacional 1994). Even army-less, democratic Costa Rica had its worst economic crisis since the 1930s depression; when the international financial institutions came to the rescue they imposed stabilization and structural adjustment programs that began to undermine the Costa Rican state's traditional—and for the region, highly atypical—commitment to the well-being of its citizens.

In Central America's wars, peasants were those who suffered most—as fighters on both sides, as non-combatants in the main zones of conflict, as victims of state and landlord repression, and as refugees who often spent years hiding in the mountains or in exile. In countries such as Costa Rica and Honduras, where social tensions did not erupt into war, the peasantry was typically the sector most immediately and drastically affected by new free-market policies that slashed production credit and price supports, privatized state-run extension and marketing agencies, stalled or reversed hard-won agrarian reforms, and encouraged grain imports that undermined domestic producers (Edelman 1991; Román Vega 1994; Thorpe et al. 1995). In Panama—with its Canal- and banking-based economy—the peasantry was small and its organizations weak; nonetheless, following the U.S. invasion it was one of the sectors most subject to repression (interview, Julio Bermúdez, *Asociación de Pequeños y Medianos Productores de Panamá-*APEMEP, Panama, 27/VI/1994; Leis 1994: 104–105)

Less noticed during the 1980s than the wars, violence, and foreign interventions was the emergence throughout Central America of a new kind of peasant politics. Derived in some cases from earlier peasant movements and rooted everywhere in age-old agrarian struggles, the campesino organizations of the 1980s and 1990s nonetheless mark a qualitative break with previous forms of rural activism. First, with few exceptions, they adamantly reject ties to parties of the left, right, and center, which they view as having cynically manipulated peasants in order to achieve narrow party objectives, election victories, or other political advantages.[2] Second, even though many peasant activists have military experience, they eschew guerrilla violence, a strategy now seen as having had tragically high human and social costs. Third, everywhere in the region they have attempted to move beyond the short-term, narrowly economic and agrarian demands of traditional peasant organizations to a concern with lobbying, influencing macroeconomic policies that affect the agricultural sector, and offering concrete development proposals. Finally, peasant organizations from different Central American countries have increasingly formed links with each other, as well as with non-peasant networks of labor unions, NGOs, and human rights, environmentalist, women's, and indigenous peoples' organizations (Biekart and Jelsma 1994; Edelman 1995; Hernández Cascante 1994).

A NEW KIND OF PEASANT

The unprecedented economic growth of the 1950s–1970s and the political upheavals of the late 1970s and 1980s complicated traditional images of peasants in Central America, making it increasingly difficult to conceive of them as either dull yet potentially violent rustics or as laborious and virtuous cultivators of the soil. Rural and urban culture converged to an unprecedented degree—and not only because radio and television reached into remote zones or because of migration from the countryside to the cities, though these were—of course—major transformative forces; in much of the region, a significant proportion of the economically active population involved in agriculture now resides in urban areas, and a growing portion of the economically active rural population engages in non-agricultural activities (Ortega 1992).

Those who remained in agriculture had to adapt to major technological shifts and become more knowledgeable about a wide variety of issues. The introduction of improved seed varieties and chemical fertilizers, herbicides, fungicides, and pesticides, even when integrated into traditional cultivation systems, involved ever larger numbers of rural people more deeply in the cash economy. Frequently this required them to deal with public- or private-sector financial, extension, and marketing agencies. The rapid expansion of agricultural, purchasing, services, and savings and loan cooperatives after the 1950s also created new forms of organization and consciousness in the countryside (Rojas Víquez 1994). Interacting with these institutions, peasants perforce had to learn more about modern agronomy, agricultural machinery, business administration, interest rates, agroindustry, and fluctuating prices. In the 1980s, as country after country adopted free-market macroeconomic policies, small-scale agriculturalists frequently began to cultivate delicate, high-risk "non-traditional exports," such as cut flowers, ornamental plants, winter fruits and vegetables, tubers for the U.S. Latino market, and cashew and macadamia nuts. Most of these crops, even more than the earlier "green revolution" in basic grains, demanded meticulous attention to administrative and agronomic detail. They literally compelled producers to become "more sophisticated."

At the same time, the revolutions in agriculture created a new social group in the countryside: service providers or *"técnicos"*—a term which in this context refers to a wide variety of specialized personnel, including agronomists, agricultural economists, rural sociologists, administrators, and certain kinds of professional consultants. Often urban-based but generally intimately familiar with conditions in the countryside, *técnicos* found full- or part-time employment with cooperatives, public-sector agencies, universities and private research institutions, agronomic consulting firms, large-scale agribusinesses, and, at times, peasant organizations. Some entered agricultural technical fields simply because these seemed promising careers, but a significant number did so as a result of their own experiences as producers and more deeply felt commitments to, and identification with the rural poor. One Honduran *técnico*—with a degree in business administration—described the mix of motives that led him to work for the Central America-wide association of peasant groups:

I have always identified with social struggles and hoped to contribute to resolving the problems of the campesinos. Even though I'm not from the countryside, I do have experience there as part of a family of medium-size agricultural producers. And it's not as if I'm working here without receiving any salary . . . (interview, Managua, 28/VI/1994).

Another *técnico*, a Costa Rican rural sociologist from a family that farmed tomatoes and chile peppers, had worked for government housing and community development programs and met peasant activists in his trips around the countryside.

Little by little we entered into contact, into dialogue, into working together, and I came to see what they were promoting in the communities, at the national and Central American levels. I'm from a rural zone myself and I knew the justice of what they were promoting . . . (interview, San José, 14/VI/1994).

"CAMPESINOS" AND "TÉCNICOS"

This kind of convergence and collaboration between *"campesinos"* and *"técnicos"* is an important part of Central America's new peasant politics and an outcome of the changes that shook the region in the 1970s and 1980s. Campesinos in general, and the campesino political leadership in particular, became vastly more cosmopolitan in this period. In part this resulted from the kinds of changes in agricultural production mentioned above, which reshaped peasants' understandings and practice of their main economic activity. In some countries—especially in Costa Rica during the 1970s heyday of social democracy, in Sandinista Nicaragua (1979–90) and in Panama under the populist regime of General Omar Torrijos (1968–81)—young people from poor or lower middle-class rural backgrounds were sometimes able to enter public universities. This not only prepared them in specialized fields, but also immersed them in the most politicized sector of Central American society, providing them with analytical tools, contacts and organizing skills that they then brought back to their communities and to the peasant organizations. But certainly more important in the overall process of change than university education, which was ultimately limited to relatively small numbers of campesinos, were the numerous new opportunities for specialized training from the cooperative movement, church and government institutions, political parties, guerrilla movements, NGOs, and the peasant organizations themselves.

This profusion of seminars and courses, which often involved travel abroad, was far from being simple indoctrination. Indeed, Salvadorans with covert ties to the guerrillas attended government training schools and travelled to Israel to study irrigation and cooperative administration; Nicaraguan peasants sometimes learned to read in the Sandinista-sponsored mass literacy campaign and then became contras; Honduran land reform beneficiaries studied in classes sponsored by one peasant union and then switched allegiances to another. More commonly, the courses led not to political gyrations such as these, but to vastly greater levels of knowledge, self-confidence, and technical expertise. In Costa Rica, Nicaragua, Honduras, and more recently El Salvador, peasant representatives sat down to negotiate with government ministers over such thorny issues as the availability of bank credit, the privatization of public-sector agroindustries and marketing boards, and plans for Central American economic integration.

The increasing availability of computers also contributed to innovative practices within the peasant organizations. Costa Rican cooperativists, for example, acquired modems and dialed in to the Public Property Registry data base to check on loan applicants' collateral. Salvadoran coffee producers cooperatives connected via satellite to the New York coffee market to follow the latest international price fluctuations. A Central America-wide association of campesino organizations headquartered in Nicaragua (see below) used electronic mail to arrange lobbying and fund-raising trips to North America and Europe. Everywhere in the isthmus, some campesino leaders acquired at least minimal computer literacy; word processing, typesetting, spread sheets, and e-mail became part of their administrative and organizing tool kit.

The themes of the courses that peasant activists took in the 1980s are remarkably varied. Not surprisingly, these included basic literacy, agronomic topics of all kinds, agroforestry, agricultural marketing, cooperative administration, and agrarian law. But campesino leaders interviewed in 1994 and 1995, some of whom had no more than a fourth-grade education, also reported attending workshops on sociology, philosophy, economic planning, statistics, microeconomics, macroeconomics, political theory, and a range of software packages.[3] A number have become modest bibliophiles, collecting volumes on technical and political subjects, as well as poetry and fiction. And several who never finished high school proudly—and not inaccurately—suggest that their lengthy curriculum vitae constitute the equivalent of a university education (interviews in San Salvador with Amanda Villatoro, *Unión Comunal Salvadoreña*, 21/VII/1994 and René Hernández, *Sociedad de Cooperativas Cafetaleras de la Reforma Agraria*, 14/VII/94). Increasingly, these highly accomplished campesinos were on an equal footing with the *técnicos* (and at times the government officials) with whom they came in contact. Their social origins were usually different, but they could understand, discuss and debate *técnicos'* and government officials' expertise in ways of which earlier generations of peasants had rarely been capable. This growing competence accompanied a widening of peasant leaders' political vision. At the same time, Central American regional arenas assumed growing significance in the design and implementation of agricultural sector and other policies.

TRANSNATIONAL PEASANT POLITICS

As Central America's civil wars ebbed or ended in the late 1980s and early 1990s, regional governments took swift steps toward political and economic integration. Powerful business lobbies in the different countries also united in a regional federation (*Federación de Entidades Privadas de Centroamérica y Panamá*-FEDIPRICAP) to defend their interests (Echeverría 1993). In contrast to the Central American Common Market (CACM) of the 1960s, which relied on high extra-regional tariffs to stimulate manufacturing for regional markets, these recent integration efforts are anti-protectionist and emphasize non-traditional agricultural exports and garment assembly industries (*maquiladoras*) as the engines of growth. Earlier integration efforts, such as the CACM, created relatively few Central America-wide institutions. But the steps toward regional unity taken after the 1987 Esquipulas Peace Accords led to the formation of powerful new supranational entities, most importantly the Central American Integration System (*Sistema de la Integración Centroamericana*-SICA) which replaced earlier, largely symbolic regional bodies and incorporated the periodic meetings of presidents and ministers and the new Central American Parliament (*Parlamento Centroamericano*-PARLACEN). SICA represented a new locus of decision-making above the national states that was a major political challenge to grass-roots sectors, especially small agricultural producers, who were only used to struggling around national-level policies.

During the 1980s, peasant organizations from throughout the isthmus had come into increasing contact with one another.[4] Sandinista Nicaragua, and particularly the National Union of Agriculturalists and Livestock Producers (*Unión Nacional de Agricultores y Ganaderos*-UNAG), founded in 1981, served as a key pole of attraction, especially for organizations sympathetic to the revolutionary Left. The regional cooperative movement too, however, through the Cooperative Confederation of the Caribbean and Central America (*Confederación de Cooperativas del Caribe y Centroamérica*—CCC-CA), established in 1980, sponsored seminars and meetings that involved campesino leaders from different countries. The Central American Workers Coordination (*Coordinadora Centroamericana de Trabajadores*-COCENTRA), a labor group formed after the 1987 Esquipulas Accords, held regional gatherings that included representatives of agricultural workers' unions. Numerous NGOs also sponsored Central America-wide seminars and visits to development projects. In many cases, peasant refugees or exiles simply sought out or met their counterparts while they were abroad. These encounters, in combination with the processes of growing sophistication described above, generated a new understanding among campesino leaders that many of their problems were shared by their counterparts in other countries.

The implementation of economic structural adjustment programs (SAPs), in particular, first in Costa Rica and then in the other countries, slashed social services (including farm extension) and agricultural credit, reduced crop price supports and subsidies for loans and inputs, stalled or reversed hard-won agrarian reforms, lowered tariffs on imported grain, and facilitated the penetration of transnational capital in the agricultural sector (Fallas 1993; FONDAD 1993; Stahler-Sholk 1990; Thorpe et al. 1995). Some of these measures were, the peasant activists realized, decided upon to a large extent in extra-regional or supra-national institutions—the World Bank or the Central American presidents' summits—where they had not previously made their voices heard.

By the late 1980s, campesino activists, especially in Nicaragua and Costa Rica, had begun to think about the formation of a Central America-wide association of campesino organizations that would defend their interests at the national, regional, and international levels. In 1990, the European Economic Community (EEC) provided funds for a regional food security education program and the sponsoring organization invited the participation of peasant groups from Honduras, El Salvador, Nicaragua, Costa Rica, and Panama.[5] Several of the invitees indicated that they would attend only if extra time were allotted so that peasant representatives from different countries could meet on their own and discuss common issues. In early 1991, at the food security education program's second meeting in Panama, the assembled peasant delegates agreed to begin forming the Association of Central American Peasant Organizations for Cooperation and Development (*Asociación Centroamericana de Organizaciones Campesinas para la Cooperación y el Desarrollo*—ASOCODE).[6]

From the beginning, the EEC and individual European governments and donor NGOs nurtured the process with substantial infusions of "cooperation" funds. This support grew out of a notion of democratization which, in contrast to the United States' near exclusive stress on free elections and institutional reform, emphasized the participation of civil society in decision-making and politics. It also reflected European (and Canadian) concern about some of the destructive effects of the macroeconomic policies encouraged by the United States Agency for International Development and multilateral financial institutions such as the World Bank.

The pace of unity between the campesino organizations was conditioned as well by the rapidity of the integration process at the Central American level. In the first half of 1991, several ministerial-level meetings began to chart a new Central American system of free trade in basic grains; the presidents were due to have a summit in July 1991 that would finalize the details of the new system (Segovia 1993). Peasants viewed the presidents' plans with skepticism, in part because structural adjustment plans had already severely affected small-scale grain producers. They argued that small producers should receive resources for technological reconversion before market openings forced them to compete with developed-country farmers who, they pointed out, generally enjoyed substantial subsidies from their governments.

Even before ASOCODE was formally founded, it sent peasant lobbyists to the July 1991 presidents' summit in San Salvador. Most of the presidents' decisions involved major steps to liberalize agricultural trade, such as the elimination of state involvement in marketing agricultural products and the implementation of the expected measures for free trade in basic grains. But the presidents' final summit declaration also resolved, to the surprise of many, "to receive with special interest the proposals of the Association of Central American Peasant Organizations for Cooperation and Development and to instruct the appropriate [government] institutions to consider and analyze them in order to find adequate responses to the issues they raise" (quoted in ASOCODE 1991: 23). This gesture was, of course, largely rhetorical, but it nonetheless represented a degree of recognition as a legitimate political force that few of the campesino activists had expected.

Since 1991, this transnational peasant association has been a frequent presence not only at the Central American presidents' summits, but at regional meetings of the ministers of economy and of agriculture, at international conferences on environment and development, and even at the World Bank and Inter-American Development Bank in Washington. ASOCODE has sponsored a continual series of workshops and seminars for peasant leaders on credit, marketing opportunities, agricultural and agroforestry technology, administrative and lobbying skills, and other needs. The Association has also produced a constant flow of proposals, position papers and newsletters. Together with other networks of cooperative, community, labor, NGO, and small enterprise organizations, it has become a highly visible force in the ongoing contention over the shape of the Central American integration process (Edelman 1995; Hernández Cascante 1994).

CONCLUSION

In Central America in the 1980s and 1990s a variety of factors permitted the emergence of a new kind of campesino movement that requires revising much of the received social scientific wisdom about peasants' capabilities and vision. Today's Central American peasant politics is transnational rather than localistic, farsighted rather than based on short-term immediate demands, centered around alternative development proposals instead of debilitating protests or violence, and assertive rather than deferential. It has arisen in part out of the extraordinary _concientización_ or coming to awareness of broad sectors of the rural poor that started with, but was by no means limited to, the revolutionary movements, liberation theology, and other grass-roots organizing and education that took place over the past two decades. It has also emerged from years of local and national struggles for land and water, credit and debt forgiveness, and technical assistance and environmental conservation, as well as from demands that governments consider the welfare of the rural poor in their agreements with international financial institutions.

In several respects, ASOCODE has achieved remarkable successes. The Central American presidents recognize this transnational association as a legitimate voice of the rural poor and accord at least lip service to its demands, thereby broadening the range of debate about agricultural and development policies. In several countries, ASOCODE's organizational and material aid has strengthened national coalitions of peasant organizations; in Guatemala, in particular, its international connections have provided an umbrella of protection for peasant groups threatened by political repression. At the same time, Central America's new peasant movements have managed to convince some sectors of the dominant groups that they are not inveterately confrontational, and that they are willing to negotiate, lobby, and play by the rules of liberal democracy.

The campesinos' presence at regional agriculture ministers' meetings, at presidents' summits, at the EEC in Brussels, at the World Bank in Washington, and at the United Nations in New York involves a substantial mobilization of resources and complicated, contradictory claims about representation. On this terrain of "high" politics, the peasant leadership now moves with striking self-confidence and with ample recognition from their new friends in international cooperation agencies and from their traditional, powerful adversaries in the state and landowning class. It is an increasingly complex affair, however, to play to these diverse audiences and to traditional constituencies among the rural poor. As campesino leaders become more and more specialized politically, they have to continue to demonstrate their authenticity—their "peasantness"—to both the people they left at home and to the dominant groups.[7]

The daily practice of this kind of politics has contributed to a blurring of campesino and *técnico* identities and to the rise of a new kind of peasant intellectual. It has also generated significant flows of foreign funds for the peasant organizations and brought some small concessions from the dominant groups. Often, however, the peasant intellectuals' international connections and their grudging acceptance among the dominant groups have a political cost at home on the farm. The specialization, professionalization, and seemingly high salaries of the leadership, as well as the continuing difficulty of translating abstract development plans into concrete results, have fueled grumbling and suspicion at the grass roots (Candanedo and Madrigal 1994). At best, the peasant intellectuals and ASOCODE, their new transnational political association, are engaged in a holding action against neoliberalism run amuck, in which the living standards of the majority of the region's campesinos will almost inevitably decline. At worst—and this is the fear of many people in the countryside—the leaders are occupied with and seduced by new opportunities for individual upward social mobility. Surmounting or managing these tensions and contradictions may turn out to be almost as much of a challenge for Central America's peasant organizations as the free-market onslaught itself.

NOTES

This paper grew out of a larger study on peasant organizations supported by the National Science Foundation (grant #SBR-9319905), the National Endowment for the Humanities (#FA-32493), and the Wenner-Gren Foundation for Anthropological Research (#5627). I gratefully acknowledge the contribution of León Arredondo, Mauricio Claudio, Alcira Forero-Peña, Néstor Hincapié, and Víctor Ortiz, who transcribed taped interviews. The friendship, trust, and logistical support of numerous peasant activists and *técnicos* from throughout Central America made this project possible. To all, many thanks.

1. The extent to which outsiders were responsible for the turmoil in Central America is highly controversial. Some analysts highlight the role of external actors (e.g. Castañeda 1993; Stoll 1993), while others acknowledge their presence but downplay their significance as catalysts (Cabezas 1982; Falla 1993; López Vigil 1993). This discussion over causality is less important for the purposes of this paper than the uncontroversial observation that rural activists in the 1980s had social origins and life experiences that were much more varied than those of earlier peasant leaders.

2. The Salvadorans are a significant exception to this generalization. Most are guerrilla veterans and remain members of the five parties (or their successor organizations) that made up the Farabundo Martí National Liberation Front (*Frente Farabundo Martí para la Liberación Nacional*, FMLN). They claim nevertheless to separate their party loyalties and obligations from their peasant movement activities.

3. In 1994 and 1995, I carried out lengthy interviews with nearly fifty campesino activists and *técnicos* in Central American peasant organizations.

4. This complex process is discussed in more detail in Edelman (1995).

5. The program's sponsor was the Support Committee for the Economic and Social Development of Central America (*Comité de Apoyo al Desarrollo Económico y Social de Centroamérica*-CADESCA), an intergovernmental body headquartered in Panama that was subject to the Latin American Economic

System (*Sistema Económico Latinoamericano*-SELA), the consultative body of Latin American Economics Ministers. CADESCA was set up as part of the Contadora peace process in 1983–84 with funds from European governments that hoped to provide an alternative to Washington's emphasis on military solutions to Central American crises.

6. ASOCODE was intended to be a "meeting table" (*mesa de encuentro*) for national coalitions of peasant organizations in each Central American country, rather than a formal confederation or a large supra-national bureaucracy. By the end of 1992, coalitions from all seven countries of the isthmus participated (see Edelman 1995).

7. This game of representation is at times quite subtle and is possibly most successful when the degree of intentionality involved is ambiguous enough so as to obscure or call into question the existence of the game itself. In 1995, for example, I accompanied one campesino leader on visits to the United Nations and to several foundations in New York. During one meeting in a fancy upper-floor suite, I was especially moved by my companion's eloquent presentation about the current situation in the region. I glanced over and thought to myself how far he had come since I first met him seven years earlier, when we sat around a knotted pine table in a grubby peasant council office. Dressed in freshly ironed slacks and a short-sleeved shirt, but facing bureaucrats in suits and power ties, he seemed totally self-confident. Then, to my horror, I noticed that he didn't have on any socks, just the same pair of slip-on shoes he was wearing when I last saw him on his own turf. Surely he knew that he ought to wear socks to New York appointments. Or did he? Or had he forgotten out of ingrained, tropical habit? Or by "forgetting" socks, was he intentionally emphasizing his "peasantness" to an audience (perhaps, he may have thought, including me) which might be inclined to doubt it? Wasn't my initial shock at his unseemly bare ankles misplaced, a result of momentarily identifying too much with my guest from Central America? Naturally, I would wear socks to a foundation or U.N. office, as a university professor would be expected to do. Whether my companion's lack of socks was deliberate or unintentional, however, he would not be judged by the same standard.

REFERENCES

ASOCODE [Asociación de Organizaciones Campesinas Centroamericanas para la Cooperación y el Desarrollo]. 1991. "Memoria [Primer Congreso ASOCODE]. 4, 5 y 6 de diciembre de 1991. Managua." Photocopy.

Biekart, Kees, and Martin Jelsma, eds. 1994. *Peasants Beyond Protest in Central America: Challenges for ASOCODE, Strategies towards Europe.* Amsterdam: Transnational Institute.

Cabezas, Omar. 1982. *La montaña es algo más que una inmensa estepa verde.* Managua: Editorial Nueva Nicaragua.

Candanedo, Diana, and Víctor Julio Madrigal. 1994. "Informe final. Evaluación externa de ASOCODE. Período julio 91–diciembre 93. Agosto 1994." Photocopy.

Castañeda, Jorge G. 1993. *Utopia Unarmed: The Latin Ameican Left After the Cold War.* New York: Alfred A. Knopf.

Comisionado Nacional de Protección de los Derechos Humanos. 1994. *Los hechos hablan por sí mismos: informe preliminar sobre los desaparecidos en Honduras 1980–1993.* Tegucigalpa: Editorial Guaymuras.

Echeverría, Carlos Manuel. 1993. "La integración centroamericana y las relaciones extrarregionales fundamentales: la visión de FEDEPRICAP." *Presencia* [El Salvador] 5, no. 19: 100–105.

Edelman, Marc. 1991. "Shifting Legitimacies and Economic Change: The State and Contemporary Costa Rican Peasant Movements." *Peasant Studies* 18 (4): 221–49.

———. 1995. "Organizing Across Borders: The Rise of a Transnational Peasant Movement in Central America." Paper presented to the Latin American Studies Association, Washington, D.C., 28–30 September.

Falla, Ricardo. 1994. *Massacres in the Jungle: Ixcán, Guatemala, 1975–1982.* Boulder: Westview.

Fallas, Helio. 1993. *Centroamérica: pobreza y desarrollo rural ante la liberalización económica.* San José: IICA.

Feierman, Steven. 1990. *Peasant Intellectuals: Anthropology and History in Tanzania.* Madison: University of Wisconsin Press.

FONDAD (Foro sobre la Deuda y el Desarrollo). 1993. *Campesinos y ajustes estructurales. Informe Encuentro Campesino: Pequeños y Medianos Productores de Panamá.* Panama: FONDAD.

Gramsci, Antonio. 1967. *La formación de los intelectuales.* Mexico: Editorial Grijalbo.

Hernández Cascante, Jorge Luis. 1994. "ASOCODE: los retos y perspectivas del movimiento campesino centroamericano." In Klaus-Dieter Tangermann and Ivana Ríos Valdés, eds., *Alternativas campesinas: modernización en el agro y movimiento campesino en Centroamérica,* Managua: Latino Editores / CRIES. 243–66.

Leis, Raúl. 1994. "Panamá: movimientos campesinos, transitismo y democracia." In Klaus-Dieter Tangermann and Ivana Ríos Valdés, eds., *Alternati-*

vas campesinas: modernización en el agro y movimiento campesino en Centroamérica, Managua: Latino Editores / CRIES. 95–116.

López Vigil, José Ignacio. 1993. *Las mil y una historias de Radio Venceremos*. San Salvador: UCA Editores.

Neruda, Pablo. [1947] 1980. "La United Fruit Co." In *Poesías escogidas*, Madrid: Aguilar. 442–43.

Ortega, Emiliano. 1992. "Evolution of the Rural Dimension in Latin America and the Caribbean." *CEPAL Review* 47: 115–36.

Rojas Víquez, Marielos. 1994. "Perspectivas del cooperativismo en Centroamérica: algunos elementos para la discusión." In Jolyne Melmed-Sanjak, Carlos E. Santiago, and Alvin Magid, eds., *Centroamérica en la globalización: perspectivas comparativas*, San José: Editorial Porvenir. 145–58.

Román Vega, Isabel. 1994. "Costa Rica: los campesinos también quieren futuro." In Klaus-Dieter Tangermann and Ivana Ríos Valdés, eds., *Alternativas campesinas: modernización en el agro y movimiento campesino en Centroamérica*, Managua: Latino Editores / CRIES. 71–94.

Segovia, Alexander. 1993. "Mercado de alimentos y sistema de banda de precios en Centroamérica." *Cuadernos de Investigación* [Centro de Investigaciones Tecnológicas y Científicas, Dirección de Investigaciones Económicas y Sociales, El Salvador] 4(17): 1–20.

Stahler-Sholk, Richard. 1990. "Ajuste y el sector agropecuario en Nicaragua en los 80: una evaluación preliminar." In Mario Arana, et al. *Políticas de ajuste en Nicaragua*, Managua: CRIES. 63–94.

Stoll, David. 1993. *Between Two Armies in the Ixil Towns of Guatemala*. New York: Columbia University Press.

Thorner, Daniel. 1986. "Chayanov's Concept of Peasant Economy." In A.V. Chayanov, *The Theory of Peasant Economy*, Madison: University of Wisconsin Press. xi–xiii.

Thorpe et al. [Andy Thorpe, Hugo Noé Pino, Pedro Jiménez, Ana Lucía Restrepo, Dagoberto Suazo, and Ramón Salgado]. 1995. *Impacto del ajuste en el agro hondureño*. Tegucigalpa: Postgrado Centroamericano en Economía y Planificación del Desarrollo.

5 ~ ELIZABETH A. SHEEHAN

Class, Gender, and the Rural in James Joyce's "The Dead"

IN 1987, while I was conducting ethnographic research in Dublin, a very urbane university professor explained to me why class, in his opinion, remained a weak basis for political affiliation in Ireland. "The grandparents and great-grandparents of most people in this country were fairly simple country people who huddled in to the church on Sunday," he said, "from whose clothes the odor of turf smoke rose in equal volume." This common rural background, so eloquently evoked, worked against Irish voters' attraction to class-based politics, he believed; furthermore, he explained, "exaggerated language about the injustice of the property-owning class" was distasteful to a people whose nationalist history is closely linked to the struggle for control of land.

In the time since that interview, much has changed in both parts of Ireland, the independent Republic and the British-administered Province of Northern Ireland. In the Republic, my focus in this chapter, discussion of class differences is no longer the domain of liberal academics but has become a commonplace of public discourse, part of the explanation for the dramatic social changes going on in Ireland today. After more than three decades of rapid "modernization," spurred by industrial development, membership in the European Union, and a youthful, well-educated population, the Republic shares with other developed nations an increasing and hardening gap between the economic haves and have-nots. This new reality stands in sharp contrast to both the professor's rustic imagery and the tourist's thatched-cottage fantasy.

Within the wider phenomenon of modernization, one reason for this greater recognition of class is the Republic's coming of age as an urban society. The eastern part of the country, centered in the capital city of Dublin, now contains about forty percent of the population. Urbanism extends throughout the rest of Ireland too, as a cultural reference point and as a shared social experience. Across the Republic, state-built housing projects have expanded into overpopulated and underserviced "new towns," where, as media accounts would have it, restless teenagers are driven to random violence by drugs, boredom, and anger, and where a new and perhaps permanent underclass is being created by a generation of single mothers.

Urbanism's delayed "conquest" of the rural, and the cultural transformations popularly associated with this conquest, thus mark an important shift in the Republic's historic identity as a rural and socially homogeneous country. Whereas in the past class difference in Ireland was often conceptualized in terms of an overarching cultural distinction between Anglo-Irish and Irish Catholic, a distinction that obscured economic differentiation within the majority Irish Catholic population, it has now come to be seen more clearly as an economic marker associated with place: urban squalor in contrast to suburban security. The rural, with its madeleine of turf smoke, seems to be left out of the picture in this dichotomy, perhaps, as this essay suggests, to remain the province of Irish literary criticism and its preoccupation with the rural as the repository of the country's "true," i.e., Gaelic and communal, identity.

In this formulation, the urban remains somehow alien, too much a product of colonial history, and more recently, a product of an acultural transnationalism defined by the mass media and consumerism. Although a younger generation of Irish novelists, notably Roddy Doyle, Dermot Bolger, and Ferdia MacAnna, have won acclaim in recent years for their gritty portrayals of urban working-class life, their accounts may in fact enhance the idealized image of rural, western Ireland for many literary critics. As one such critic, John Wilson Foster, writes of the western regions:

> . . . these [places] have functioned as a kind of otherworld, representations of lonely and barren spaces to which the Irish literary imagination has had frequent recourse. They are places of solitude and retreat (flight and succor), of passion and timelessness, and they exist in the west, in a permanent recess of the Irish psyche. (Foster 1991: 32)

As an anthropologist familiar with the Irish terrain and its history, I find this continued "othering" of the rural West simplistic, if not disingenuous. It denies the long history of urbanism throughout Ireland (Dublin is more than a thousand years old; Galway City at least eight hundred) as well as the permeation of the city by the country, not least by the long march of rural-to-urban migrants. The valorization of ruralism is also the legacy of a conservative political culture that, until the 1970s, successfully exploited the ideology of a classless, Catholic rural society at the expense of social groups, such as the urban poor, who would have benefited from greater attention to issues of social justice. Further, in continuing to assert the primacy of ruralism as the essence of Irish culture, the country's literary specialists reveal their nostalgia for a time when they, as urban cultural critics, could define what Irish ruralism was from the elite perspective of the university and the intellectual journal.

These themes are taken up in this chapter, which addresses the historical relationship between place, class and identity in Ireland through an examination of James Joyce's short story "The Dead." The last story in the collection *Dubliners*, published in 1914, "The Dead" explores the ambiguities of the urban/rural relationship, and, as I will discuss, the deeply rooted significance of class as an indicator of urban or rural identity in Ireland. The story conducts this exploration by creating an apparently oppositional relationship between Dublin, on Ireland's East coast, and Galway, the regional center of the western and most "Gaelic" countryside. As such, "The Dead" seems at first to affirm urban and rural identity as determined by place, yet a closer reading of the story easily dismantles this premise.

This distinction of place is further embodied in "The Dead's" central characters, Gabriel and Gretta Conroy, who in standard interpretations are counterpoised as symbols of their respective origins: Gabriel the sophisticated Dubliner and Gretta his provincial, Galway-born wife. Here I suggest an alternate reading that sees Gretta's identity, as Joyce has described it, to be both western *and* urban. Gretta's character therefore exposes a contradiction in the Irish urban/rural divide, one which is perhaps discomfiting to the Dubliners depicted in "The Dead" but potentially devastating to Gretta herself.

"The Dead's" use of the urban/rural dichotomy, grounded in the east/west distinction, also encloses other parallel oppositions: English/Gaelic, male/female, and, most problematically, dead/alive. My analysis of the story considers how Joyce undermines these presumed oppositions to reveal their history of interaction in both urban and rural Ireland. That Joyce presents this revelation most subtly through a fascinating gender-role reversal speaks to the truly transgressive nature of his critique of early-twentieth-century Ireland. The fact that this reversal—made evident in the story's turning point—has drawn so little attention from Irish literary specialists may speak to their reluctance to abandon a cultural hierarchy that in celebrating the rural also affirms their essentialized view of it.

IS FEMALE TO MALE AS RURAL IS TO URBAN?

Like all of Joyce's fiction, "The Dead" provides a wealth of Irish geographic detail as well as an almost ethnographic account of the story's time and place. Although grounded in the geographic and social reality of 1904 Dublin (the year in which the story is set), "The Dead" covers an imaginative terrain that extends eastward toward Europe and westward to Ireland's Atlantic shores. Consequently, the story lends itself ideally to exploration of the urban/rural, English/Gaelic, and Europe/Ireland distinctions that were especially charged during the nationalist period when Joyce was writing.

This standard approach positions Dublin, a colonized capital, as the midpoint on an urban-rural continuum that begins on the Continent and ends in the far reaches of Ireland's Connacht. This continuum parallels a cultural hierarchy moving from Europe's urban-based "Great Tradition" to the "Little Tradition" of the Irish peasantry, with Dublin poised uncomfortably in-between. However, too great a focus on this explicit urban-rural trajectory may obscure recognition of the story's more subtle continuum. The latter charts a path of relative urbanism starting with the European cities mentioned in "The Dead" (London, Paris and Milan), proceeding to Dublin, and then out to Galway City. Indeed, analysts have paid little attention to the fact that Galway *is* a city, and that the space between it and its surrounding rural region is shaped by sociocultural differences that greatly influence the meaning of the tragic story that lies at the heart of "The Dead."[1]

One reason for this inattention may be the understandable emphasis that interpreters place on the story's male protagonist, Gabriel Conroy, a Dubliner and the only character in "The Dead" whose thoughts we are privy to. Gabriel's western-born wife, Gretta, is, of course, critical to the story and to Gabriel's epiphany at its conclusion. Yet despite a wealth of discussion of what Gretta's Galway background might mean to her husband—his slight embarrassment by her rural origins as well as his eventual turn toward the West—Gretta herself often remains in these interpretations a rather one-dimensional, if appealing, catalyst for Gabriel's transformation.

For example, Ingersoll's (1992) discussion of the gendered implications of travel in "The Dead" suggests that Gabriel's final (although ambivalent) acquiescence to the West, to Gaelic Ireland, and ultimately to death demonstrates his attainment of true "masculine" status through his resigned embrace of the "feminine" signified by Gretta and her rustic origins. In this way, Gretta and rural Ireland are projected, albeit with Lacanian sophistication, as an undifferentiated other, and not surprisingly a female other, given the familiar characterization of Ireland as woman—seduced, raped, or triumphant.

Such imagery clearly draws upon the country's colonial history, as well as the cultural revivalist's idea of a "hidden Ireland" to be found in its noble but embattled Gaelic traditions (Corkery 1925). The former association between place and gender rationalizes the conqueror's rule as both necessary and benign, while the latter—imagining the "female" native culture as awaiting discovery—positions the conquered (male) subject as protector as well as potential exploiter of his country's deepest traditions. Both associations contain clear erotic elements, as Blunt and Rose note: "The construction of a 'sexual space' paralleled the construction of space to be colonized, and the desire for colonial control was often expressed in terms of sexual control" (1994: 10). Gabriel's intense desire for Gretta near the end of "The Dead" (which in Joyce's description is suggestive of marital rape) can be seen not only as a rekindling of their earlier erotic relationship and a reassurance to Gabriel that he actually lives, but also as a way of overcoming the uncomfortable self-awareness the events in the story have aroused in him. Gretta, his beloved wife but also his property, is for Gabriel an identifiable point—a rural, and therefore weaker one—in a wider landscape of power that leaves Gabriel otherwise uncertain of his own position.

However, Gabriel's perspective tells us little of Gretta's own identity and its relationship to rural Ireland. When we read "The Dead" to reconstruct Gretta's earlier life in Galway, it becomes clear that she need not be viewed only in rural opposition to Gabriel's cosmopolitan complexity. Nor is her tragic romance meant to identify her even more closely with the "conquered" but also more authentic Irish country-side. On the contrary, Joyce provides enough information about Gretta to allow the reader to consider the locally meaningful nuances of geography and social class that have shaped her identity as a westerner, but which are effaced by her rustic ascription in the Dublin setting.

In what follows I will provide a brief background to "The Dead" and then trace the story's two main narrative trajectories: the more familiar Dublin-based one that follows Gabriel's symbolic movement from the urban east to the rural west, and a second, less traveled one that reveals Gretta's more ambiguous and unresolved transit across the Irish landscape. In the latter effort my goal, following Johnson and Cairns (1991), is not simply to deconstruct the text, much less distort it to fit my thesis, but to reconstruct it in a way that restores historical specificity to Gretta's identity and to the role class has played in shaping it.

BACKGROUND TO "THE DEAD"

Joyce's original outline of *Dubliners* did not include "The Dead," which was written in 1907, three years after he had begun the collection's other stories (Ellmann 1959).[2] Even without knowing this, the reader can sense that there is something disjunctive about "The Dead" in relation to the book's previous stories. The author's voice here is more omniscient yet more tender; further, "The Dead" links the capital city to the rest of Ireland in a manner distinct from the rest of the collection. The progression from childhood to adulthood that is *Dubliners'* organizing principle is extended in "The Dead" to a consideration of the future as well. Gabriel Conroy can be seen to some extent as Joyce himself had he stayed in Ireland and become, like Gabriel, a teacher. Instead, in 1904, Joyce and his partner, Nora Barnacle, took the mailboat to London and thence to the continent to join a long tradition of self-exiled and homesick Irish.

Nora too is an important presence in "The Dead," although in Joyce's telling her story looks backward to her early life in western

Ireland. Like Gretta, Nora Barnacle was a middle class girl from Galway City. She too had a relationship with a young man there who died of lung disease.[3] Like Gretta, Nora was viewed warily by her husband's family as a sly opportunist, "country cute,"[4] and a drag on her husband's social prospects. Yet Nora's biographer, Brenda Maddox, describes Nora as "irretrievably urban—not a barefoot peasant from the moorland . . . but a city girl, with a ribbon in her hair, a sharp tongue in her head, and an uncle in the civil service" (Maddox 1988: 11). Nonetheless, Nora's western background and down-to-earth manner allowed her to serve as Joyce's "portable Ireland" throughout their lives together, and it is an episode from her girlhood that provided the idea for "The Dead."

In 1904, when "The Dead" is set, Ireland was still part of the United Kingdom, created by the Act of Union in 1800 to solidify British control over Ireland. The eastern part of the country, encompassing Dublin, had been Anglicized since the Tudor period, but as a colonial capital Dublin emerged as a culturally vibrant city in the 1700s. With the Act of Union, Ireland's political administration was transferred to London, and many of Dublin's Anglo-Irish writers and raconteurs followed. This exodus diminished the city's cosmopolitan status but provided space for nationalist and cultural revival movements to gain force in the second half of the nineteenth century. The Ireland depicted in "The Dead" is between two political generations: that of the failed Parnellite movement of the 1880s, and that of the Easter Rising of 1916, which began the process that ultimately created the Republic of Ireland, declared fully independent in 1949.

Although no single interpretation can suffice to explain "The Dead," the dominant reading of the story sees it as Joyce's critique of Ireland's psychological "paralysis" in this latent period, revealed through an examination of artistic but socially insecure Dubliners gathered at a wintertime party. The story's title evokes many parallel meanings: the living death that pervades the Irish Catholic middle classes; Dublin as a city of the dead; the decline of native Irish culture; Gretta's deceased lover, Michael Furey; and the association between Ireland's Western Isles and the site of Tir na nOg, the Gaelic afterlife.

The story's place names play even more explicitly on the theme of a fatal stasis, often conveyed throughout *Dubliners* by an association between celibacy and death (Cowart 1989). Gretta's childhood home is Nuns' Island in Galway City,[5] while as a married woman she lives with Gabriel in Monkstown, a suburb east of Dublin.[6] Gabriel's aunts live on Usher's Island in Dublin City, the actual site of Joyce's aunts' home, but also a place name evoking Poe's tale of a family's horrific destruction. Through his use of such names in both the eastern and western settings of "The Dead," Joyce draws attention to the paradox of a cultural revival movement based on a declining, indeed almost dead, Gaelic language and way of life. Conversely, Joyce dismisses any notion of *life* being truer or more fully realized in the symbolic frameworks of either pure urbanity or pure rusticity. One expression of this complication is Gabriel's longing to escape the party described in the story so he can walk in Phoenix Park, a pastoral oasis in the city but also the home of Britain's administrator of Ireland.

In rejecting the equation between "rustic" Gaelicism and cultural authenticity, Joyce contrasts vividly (and for some earlier readers, disturbingly) with the Celtic Twilight writers of the generation that preceded him: J. M. Synge, Lady Gregory, and William Butler Yeats, all of whom celebrated a Gaelic tradition seen as surviving in western Ireland despite the impact of English language and culture. Instead, Joyce's views of Irish culture are always situated along a continuum of distinction: authentic, native, "true" in relation to what? In *A Portrait of the Artist as a Young Man* (1916), Joyce's alter ego, Stephen Dedalus, muses on a conversation with his English-born professor: "The language in which we are speaking is his before it is mine. . . . His language, so familiar and so foreign, will always be for me an acquired speech. I have not made or accepted its words."

Stephen, the non-nationalist, the would-be cosmopolitan, still realizes his subjugation to an imposed culture that he must live within but cannot fully master. As such, he will always remain "mere Irish," i.e., primitive and symbolically speechless, to the English colonizer, an identity he can escape only by moving to the Continent. Yet Stephen, like Joyce, finds the valorization of Gaelic culture, as reconstructed by urban intellectuals, to be short-sighted and sterile. Escape from one's past may be impossible ("History is a nightmare from which I am trying to awake," Stephen says in *Ulysses*), but embracing a rural identity which falsifies his experience is intolerable. In "The Dead," Joyce offers an earlier exploration of this theme of cultural displacement, using the images of the "male" urban and the "female" rural to reveal the complication of these categories.

GABRIEL'S JOURNEY

The story told in "The Dead" is apparently a simple one. Gabriel and Gretta Conroy, a middle-class Catholic couple, attend an annual party given by Gabriel's aunts, Julia and Kate Morkan, and their niece, Mary Jane. The actual date of the event has been the subject of some literary debate (Dilworth 1986). It is after Christmas, but still holiday time, perhaps January 5, the eve of the Epiphany. This date allows for Gabriel's own epiphany—a critical moment of self-realization in Joyce's philosophy—to take place in the early hours of the sixth, a chronologically satisfying interpretation.[7]

The story portrays two actual journeys and many imagined or remembered ones. In each, the axes of urban-rural, east-west and life-death are evoked and challenged. The first journey takes Gabriel and Gretta westward from their home in Monkstown to the Morkans' home in Dublin. Monkstown is one of a series of suburbs located along the southern side of Dublin Bay, an area which, at the time "The Dead" is set, was associated with the Anglo-Irish gentry. Thus early on Joyce suggests that urban location alone does not guarantee social prestige, as the Conroys' suburban residence suggests a preference for a more "cosmopolitan" English environment than the "provincial" Irish Catholic, although urban, one in which the Morkans live.

The elite connotation of these suburbs is made clear also in the story's reference to the fact that many of Mary Jane Morkan's students, also guests at the party, come from "better-class families on the Kingstown and Dalkey [railroad] line." Kingstown (now Dun Laoghaire) and Dalkey are east of Monkstown, and the former is a port from which ferries depart each day for the British mainland (landing, however, on another part of the Celtic Fringe, Holyhead in Wales) as well as France. Looking eastward across Dublin Bay from this coast, one faces the British Isles and Europe. As the Atlantic is the western peasant's avenue of escape to the new world, so is Dublin Bay the eastern sophisticate's avenue of escape, or return, to the old.

To arrive at the Morkans' dance, the Conroys have travelled past the center of Dublin, marked by Sackville (now O'Connell) Street, to Usher's Island, a commercial section of the quay along the River Liffey, another east-west trajectory. At Usher's Island, the Conroys are no longer in the Anglicized heart of the capital, but west of it in the semi-industrial area near Guinness's Brewery and the Liberties, a working class district. The Morkans live over the offices of a grain merchant, from whom they rent their space. Thus their home, like their general social milieu, is respectable but not particularly desirable.

Torchiana (1986) has pointed out that the Morkan and Conroy families display clear signs of social climbing. Gabriel's grandfather (the father of Aunts Julia and Kate, as well as Gabriel's mother) owned a starch mill and lived in Stoneybatter, a Dublin street that forms part of Ireland's oldest road. That road led to Tara, the ancient seat of Ireland's high-kings. In moving out of their father's home and taking up careers in music, the Morkans have distanced themselves both from their mercantile background and, symbolically, from the heart of rural, pre-colonial Ireland. But Gabriel's mother exceeded them by marrying and settling in fashionable Monkstown, in the house Gretta and Gabriel still live in. By traveling back to Usher's Island, Gabriel is returning part way to his family's earlier class and regional affiliations.

Once at the party, a significant imagined journey is evoked when Gabriel dances with the nationalist Miss Ivors, who invites him to join a group of friends who will spend part of the summer in the Aran Islands, off the Galway coast. Gabriel's wife comes from the west; wouldn't she also enjoy the stay? Gabriel answers irritably that Gretta's "people" come from there, presumably implying her distance from the Irish peasantry, and that he prefers to spend his vacations on the continent where he can brush up on his European languages. "And haven't you your own land to visit," asks Miss Ivors, "that you know nothing of, your own people, and your own country?" "O, to tell you the truth," Gabriel replies, "I'm sick of my own country, sick of it!" Miss Ivors leans close and insults Gabriel by calling him a West Briton, a term still used to denigrate Irish people whose allegiances are viewed as more English than Irish.

Gabriel moves from this unsettling encounter to a parallel conversation with the aged Mrs. Malins, who, although Irish, lives with a married daughter in Glasgow. She bores Gabriel with an account of her recent holiday in the Scottish highlands, another Gaelic region. For her as well, the thought of visiting her "own country" seems remote. Mrs. Malins, along with the elderly Aunt Julia, represents the nearness of death to life at this somehow wake-like party, a theme that surfaces in other guests' imagined journeys.[8] While some of these journeys, such as Gabriel's recollection of a railroad trip with Gretta, evoke a connection between travel and life, others associate distance from Dublin with premonitions of death. At the dinner table, for example, Mrs. Malins' alcoholic son Freddy speaks of his upcoming journey to a rest cure at Mount Melleray, southwest of Dublin in County Waterford, where the monks sleep in their coffins "to remind them of their final end."

Other journeys that take place during the evening are to the past, to youth, and to an imagined better time. At dinner, Aunt Kate recalls an English tenor whom she heard sing as a young woman, the only one who could "please" her, but whose name—Parkinson—is unfamiliar to the rest of the party.[9] Her recollection is part of a general discussion of Dublin's second-class status in relation to England and Europe. The guests at the party are "cultured" enough to appreciate the arts and to bemoan their inferior state in contemporary Dublin, now an afterthought of Europe and Empire. Their references to the great voices are not only to those of dead singers, but in the case of living singers, to those of London, Paris and Milan. When Gabriel gives the after dinner speech, he praises his hosts and Irish hospitality, but also mourns the more "spacious days" of the past when Ireland could claim "those dead and gone great ones."

As Dilworth (1986) suggests, Gabriel's nostalgic words may be what encourages Bartell D'Arcy, another guest, to sing the Irish song that inspires "The Dead's" most powerful imagined journey. This is "The Lass of Aughrim," a ballad that tells of a poor Irish woman abandoned and left to die by her aristocratic lover.[10] The ballad's story reveals another dimension of the urban-rural hierarchy: the sexually exploitative relationship between lord and peasant. Gabriel is downstairs at the time collecting his coat; he can barely hear this distant music but to his urbane ear it seems to be "in the old Irish tonality," a vague association for him with both the rural and the past. He looks up and sees Gretta frozen on the stairs in a reverie, the significance of which he learns only later in their hotel room. As they leave the party, Gabriel embarks on his own reverie, thinking of his and Gretta's sex life and anticipating his intimacy with her later that night.

The Conroys' second actual journey, the return eastward at the end of the party, fails to parallel the outgoing one in that it does not bring them home. By choosing to spend the night at the Gresham, the Conroys delay their full return to the east by stopping at a hotel in the dead center of the city, on Sackville Street, Dublin's east-west dividing line. It is here, in this liminal space between urban and rural, that Gretta reveals to Gabriel that "The Lass of Aughrim" reminded her of someone she knew in Galway, Michael Furey, a young man with whom she'd had a teenage flirtation. Already ill, Michael had died after coming to visit Gretta on the rainy night before she was to leave Galway to attend school in Dublin.

Gabriel is dismayed by the revelation, forced to concede how little he may know of his wife and how pallid his own feelings are compared to the passion Gretta's romance suggests. But as the story ends, Gabriel moves beyond these concerns to consider his own communion with death and the inevitability of his return "home" to the rural west. In "The Dead's" famous closing passage, Gabriel lies awake, facing the window, as his thoughts travel across the Irish landscape:

> The time had come for him to set out on his journey westward. Yes, the newspapers were right: snow was general all over Ireland. . . . His soul

swooned slowly as he heard the snow falling faintly through the universe and faintly falling, like the descent of their last end, upon all the living and the dead.

Thus it is Gretta's story, the deeper significance of which he cannot grasp, that finally turns Gabriel toward the West and rural Ireland. It is logical for him, as a Dublin intellectual, to view this place as an "otherworld," for him a fatal one. Attention to Gretta's experience, however, reveals the limits of Gabriel's comprehension of his future and Gretta's past.

GRETTA'S JOURNEY

Gretta Conroy is the female figure floating across the Irish landscape in "The Dead." Her rural origins and natural beauty would suggest on one level that she is a variation on Kathleen ni Houlihan, a symbol of Gaelic Ireland freed from the yoke of English tyranny.[11] To her husband's family and friends, Gretta appears a less ennobled version of this figure, "a still guileless West of Ireland woman," as Torchiana (1986: 241) describes her; inaccurately, I believe. Whether heroic or humble, Gretta's identity is persistently defined in terms of place by her Dublin acquaintances. Gabriel's efforts to distance her from this place, Galway and the rural West, serve only to emphasize her cultural homelessness. But as the following analysis suggests, to view Gretta as a displaced peasant denies the social complexity Joyce has granted her.

Although Gabriel recalls his mother's early hostility to Gretta, his wife now appears to be well-accepted, perhaps even loved, by Gabriel's aunts. (Gabriel's mother, a strong influence on his cosmopolitan strivings, is dead by the time the story takes place.) Gretta is more at ease in this social gathering than Gabriel, a reminder that the hospitality celebrated in "The Dead" is not uniquely a Dublin quality. I would suggest also that Gretta's "womanly" social skills reflect the fact that in a colonized country, the native must maintain the subtle balance between being both host and guest of the foreign power. Gretta is in three ways colonized, being Irish, "rural," and female. Unlike Gabriel, she recognizes her fluid social status and has developed the flexibility necessary for survival in this state.

Gretta feels free to gently mock Gabriel's affectation for things European, such as the guttapercha galoshes he has made her wear so that she will not catch cold on this snowy night ("Gabriel says everyone wears them on the continent").[12] While still in love with Gabriel, she has gained some distance from her early admiration of his cosmopolitan veneer. Nonetheless, the abrasive Miss Ivors—a university graduate and very likely a Dubliner—seems to cast Gretta as a countrywoman, perhaps one held back from realizing her "true" self due to Gabriel's rejection of Gaelicism. Thus the urban intellectual romanticizes and patronizes a rural other who cannot speak for herself.

Yet Gretta does indeed express irritation at Gabriel's dismissal of the idea of a trip to the Aran Islands. Her response—"There's a nice husband for you, Mrs. Malins"—may also convey her general dissatisfaction with the constraints marriage has placed upon her, especially since it is clear that Gabriel's jaunts in Europe do not include her. Gretta is trapped, allowed neither to return to the West nor to travel abroad, assigned to a cultural limbo.

By viewing Gretta as a naive countrywoman, "The Dead's" Dublin-born characters may affirm their sense of urbane superiority in the face of their actually quite constricted social milieu. When we turn to examine the facts of Gretta's background, however, another picture of this woman emerges. Far from being a rustic, Gretta was born in Galway City, the urban center of the western Connacht region. Thus her identity disconcertingly merges the urban and the rural, and as such, it is a potential threat to the identity of the party's other guests, who do not want to acknowledge the parallel implication: that their assumed urbanism overlies centuries of rural affiliation. Even the long-term Dubliners at the party must recognize that the capital city, for all its artistic strivings, remains hostage at this time to a politicized image of Ireland as a rural and Gaelic nation. In this context, Dublin and Galway can be seen as more alike than different, neither able to claim the cultural sophistication of a London, Paris or Milan.

Further, Galway's diminished status in turn-of-the-century Ireland does not justify erasure of this city's historical significance, especially its role in colonial and economic development. Galway dates to at least the twelfth century and was the seat of the Burke family, an Anglo-Norman (and thus European in origin) dynasty.[13] By the end of the fourteenth century, Galway City was under direct English rule and was a major port with links to Spain. This commercial activity suggests that Galway's place in the world system was well established at a time when Dublin was still a relative backwater.[14] By the seventeenth century, Galway was one of Ireland's wealthiest towns, but it suffered under assaults by Cromwell and later William of Orange. The Great Famine of the 1840s further eroded Galway's economic and political strength, but the city's decline and isolation during this period allowed Gaelic language and culture to survive there well into the nineteenth century (Rynne 1989). Galway's dual identity as both colonial center and Gaelic outpost in itself reveals the difficulty of separating rural from urban, Irish from English, across the terrain of history.

If Gabriel's symbolic journey home takes place after hearing Gretta's story, for Gretta the point of departure arrives earlier when she hears "The Lass of Aughrim" being sung. Arguably, this is a more profound experience than Gabriel's later epiphany, because it brings Gretta directly back to her own past, to a remembered rather than projected self. It is appropriate that she be standing on the stairs as she listens to the song; she is figuratively between two places: the Dublin night that awaits her and Gabriel, and the Galway night when Michael came to visit her for the last time. In this position, she also acts as the filter through which Gabriel hears the old Gaelic tune, but as we come to understand, the song is not hers but Michael Furey's.

It is in Gretta's relationship with Michael that we see the most profound challenge to an essentialist construction of rural Ireland. As "The Dead" reveals, much of the pathos of Gretta's story derives from the fact that, like Gabriel's early relationship with her, her romance with Michael Furey is socially undesirable. In part, this is because Gretta is a city girl, certainly more urbane than Michael, who comes from Oughterard, a town about fifteen miles northwest of Galway City.

In the regional context, this distinction is important, marking one point on an ever-broadening cultural gulf between urban and rural as the city gives way to the countryside with its remote villages and bleak landscapes.

The geographic distance between Gretta's and Michael's origins is matched by their class differences, which have set different limits on their life opportunities. Michael is employed in the gasworks, an extremely unpleasant and dangerous place (and no doubt an environment contributing to his early death from consumption). At seventeen, his schooling is over, and his prospects for upward mobility are slim. By contrast, Gretta is on her way "up to Dublin" to attend a convent school, a form of girls' education that even today is associated with Ireland's more prosperous classes. It is possible that Gretta's family viewed her further schooling, much more than most young Irish women received at the time, as a way to remove her from the threat of such inappropriate romantic ties. Gretta refers to the fact that she and Michael "used to go out together, walking, you know, Gabriel, like the way they do in the country," although most of their meetings must have taken place in or near Galway City. In this way also, she suggests her social distance from her lover's rural background, as well as, in her turn of phrase, its influence upon her.

Most tellingly, Gretta speaks of Michael Furey's "people" as having brought him back to be buried in his local churchyard at Oughterard, the one Gabriel imagines at the conclusion of "The Dead." This phrasing parallels Gabriel's brusque acknowledgement to Miss Ivors earlier in the story that Gretta's "people" come from the West; again, rurality is relative (the latter in both senses: comparatively and through family origin). Gretta uses the term "people" to emphasize Michael's familial connections and restore him to his authentically rural home, while Gabriel has used it to distance Gretta from her family and her putatively rural origins. Michael returns through death to a fixed point, while Gretta remains alienated, not just from western Ireland, but from a city and from an earlier life that Gabriel barely acknowledges.

Gabriel's determined ignorance of western Ireland is made clear in "The Dead," as is his failure to recognize "The Lass of Aughrim." Thus

Gabriel cannot know that the song's lyrics contain the key to understanding the painful complexity of Gretta's identity. In the ballad, as
Nora Barnacle knew it, the lord challenges the seduced peasant
woman to prove she is his mistress:

> If you'll be the lass of Aughrim
> As I am taking you mean to be
> Tell me the first token
> That passed between you and me.

The young woman describes their earlier tryst, then begs for her
lover's compassion:

> The rain falls on my yellow locks
> And the dew it wets my skin;
> My babe lies cold within my arms:
> Lord Gregory, let me in.[15]

He does not, and the girl and her baby both die.

The misrepresentation, indeed silencing, of Gretta's history in the
mainstream reading of "The Dead" is for me summed up in the role
commentators continue to ascribe to Gretta in "The Lass of Aughrim,"
notwithstanding their access, unlike Gabriel, to the song's lyrics.
Having established Gretta as western, rural, and "guileless," these analysts assume that she must also be the victimized women described in
the ballad. Benstock (1994: 26) writes that "it is Gretta as the Lass of
Aughrim" who, by telling Gabriel about Michael, derails the former's
effort to bring his erotic narrative to fulfillment.

However, given Gretta's *own* relationship to the song, it is much
more likely that she sees herself as the seducer in the ballad, the noble-
man who denies his love in favor of class interests. It was Michael who
sang that song, not she, and Michael who came to her window, shiver-
ing in the rain, the night before she "abandoned" him for Dublin.
Further, while Gretta's guilt about Michael is evident ("I think he died
for me"), it does not seem tempered by secret pleasure in her romantic
past. This too suggests the imbalance in their statuses. I would agree
with Cowart's (1989) interpretation that the phrases used by Gretta

to describe Michael indicate that she did not take him seriously as a suitor, however warmly she felt toward him. She has good reason to regret her ladylike farewell to him, which spurred his final visit: "I wrote a letter to him saying I was going up to Dublin and would be back in the summer and hoping he would be better then." It is only later, first when she learns in Dublin that he is dead, and even more so when she hears "The Lass of Aughrim" being sung after so many years, that the loss in her life—not so much of Michael, but of youth and the other choices she might have made—becomes most painful.

To see Gretta as the lord and not the lass challenges much of what we think we know about Gretta, based on Gabriel's view of her and her status within his social circles. It reveals Gretta, in her unthinking youth and beauty, as powerful, privileged, and capable of movement that is denied Michael. Her family background and her own aspirations, modest as these may have been, mark her as a city girl with a future, an outsider (or interloper?) to Michael's rural Ireland. The irony, of course, is that Gretta's flight—away from Michael, but more generally away from the disaster of a hypogamous romance if she remains in Galway—is halted by her marriage to Gabriel, a social achievement her parents probably viewed with approval.[16] Thus it is as Gabriel's wife and "portable Ireland" that Gretta becomes in Dublin what in Galway she was not: The Lass of Aughrim, the rural victim.

NOTES

I would like to thank Patrick Otte, Barbara Ching, and Gerald Creed for their helpful comments on this chapter, as well as my colleague at American University, William Leap, whose work on space and place has influenced my thinking.

1. For example, Bidwell and Heffer (1982) do not include any discussion of Galway City, although they do include Cork City, where an episode in *A Portrait of the Artist as a Young Man* (1916) is set.

2. Ellmann (1959: 239) writes that in adding "The Dead" to *Dubliners*, Joyce was able to present a more sympathetic view of his native country, and particularly its hospitality, than is found in the earlier stories.

3. Nora actually had two Galway boyfriends who died: Michael Feeney,

who died at sixteen of pneumonia, and Michael Bodkin, who died at twenty of tuberculosis (Maddox 1988: 15–17). The character of Michael Furey probably combines elements of both young men.

4. In the story, Gabriel recalls his mother using this term to disparage Gretta. Jackson and McGinley (1993: 167) note that the complete expression is "country cute and city clever."

5. Nora Barnacle's family lived on Nuns' Island.

6. Torchiana (1986: 242–47) notes that Nuns' Island, Monkstown, and Usher's Island were all sites of religious foundations, as was Phoenix Park.

7. However, Kelleher (1965) uses internal evidence to date the party as beginning on January 6th.

8. A mysterious guest at the party, Mr. Browne, is viewed by most analysts as a symbol of death. He pronounces Aunt Julia his "latest discovery" and, at the end of the evening, he follows Mrs. Malins into a hansom cab.

9. The paralysis theme emerges again with this name, although Gifford (1982: 121) notes the existence of an English singer named Parkinson, a musical comedy artist, who performed around the time being recalled.

10. This song is a western Irish version of a Scottish ballad. Aughrim is a small village about thirty miles east of Galway City. See Gifford 1982: 123.

11. Kathleen ni Houlihan urges young men to sacrifice their lives for Ireland, if necessary, just as Gretta may appear to have hastened Michael's death.

12. The galoshes may be viewed also as a sign of Gabriel's smothering protectiveness of Gretta (Ingersoll 1992: 44) as well as an erotic device both hiding and fetishizing Gretta's feet. The prophylactic nature of these "rubbers" is evident as well.

13. Galway was ruled by fourteen "tribes," families that controlled the region's merchant economy. Among these were the Joyces, after whom an area in County Galway is named. Thus, the "Joyce Country" (as it is called) is rural Galway as well as Dublin City.

14. Historical evidence suggests that one of the great symbols of east-west linkage, Christopher Columbus, visited Galway City two decades before setting sail for the new world.

15. These stanzas are found in Ellmann (1959: 295) and repeated with annotation in Gifford (1982: 124).

16. Nora Barnacle's own mother married below her, to a man she eventually left. The danger of such alliances, which destroyed a woman's one chance for security and respectability, would have been a constant concern for middle class parents in turn-of-the-century Ireland.

REFERENCES

Benstock, Bernard. 1994. *Narrative Con/Texts in "Dubliners."* Urbana: University of Illinois Press.

Bidwell, Bruce, and Linda Heffer. 1982. *The Joycean Way: A Topographic Guide to "Dubliners" and "A Portrait of the Artist as a Young Man."* Baltimore: Johns Hopkins University Press.

Blunt, Alison, and Gillian Rose. 1994. "Introduction: Women's Colonial and Postcolonial Geographies." In *Writing Women and Space: Colonial and Postcolonial Geographies,* edited by Alison Blunt and Gillian Rose. New York: The Guilford Press.

Corkery, Daniel. 1925. *The Hidden Ireland: A Study of Gaelic Muenster in the Eighteenth Century.* Dublin: M. H. Gill and Son, Ltd.

Cowart, David. 1989. "From Nuns' Island to Monkstown: Celibacy, Concupiscence, and Sterility in 'The Dead.'" *James Joyce Quarterly* 26: 499–504.

Dilworth, Thomas. 1986. "Sex and Politics in 'The Dead.'" *James Joyce Quarterly* 23: 157–171.

Ellmann, Richard. 1959. *James Joyce.* New York: Oxford University Press.

Foster, John Wilson. 1991. "The Geography of Irish Fiction." In *Colonial Consequences: Essays in Irish Literature and Culture.* Dublin: The Lilliput Press.

Gifford, Don. 1982. *Joyce Annotated: Notes for "Dubliners" and "A Portrait of the Artist as a Young Man."* Berkeley: University of California Press.

Ingersoll, Earl G. 1992. "The Gender of Travel in 'The Dead.'" *James Joyce Quarterly* 30: 41–50.

Jackson, John Wyse, and Bernard McGinley, eds. 1993. *James Joyce's Dubliners: An Illustrated Edition, with Annotations.* New York: St. Martin's Press.

Johnson, Tony O'Brien, and David Cairns. 1991. "Introduction." In *Gender in Irish Writing,* edited by Tony O'Brien Johnson and David Cairns. Philadelphia: Open University Press.

Joyce, James. 1914. *Dubliners.* New York: Viking Press, 1972.

———. 1916. *A Portrait of the Artist as a Young Man.* New York: Viking Press, 1969.

———. 1922. *Ulysses.* New York: Vintage Books, 1986.

Kelleher, John V. 1965. "Irish History and Mythology in James Joyce's 'The Dead.'" *Review of Politics* 27: 414–35.

Maddox, Deirdre. 1988. *Nora: The Real Life of Molly Bloom.* Boston: Houghton-Mifflin.

Rynne, Etienne. 1989. *Tourist Trail of Old Galway.* Galway: Ireland West Tourism.

Torchiana, Donald T. 1986. *Backgrounds for Joyce's "Dubliners."* Boston: Allen & Unwin.

6 ~ BEATRICE GUENTHER

The *Roman du Terroir au Féminin* in Quebec

Guèvremont's and Blais' Re-visioning of a Rural Tradition

IN *Postmodernism, or the Cultural Logic of Late Capitalism*, Fredric Jameson notes that "our psychic experience, our cultural languages are today dominated by categories of space rather than by categories of time" (1991: 16). A study of cultural hierarchies that sets its sights on reconsidering the status of rural culture might seem, then, to locate itself squarely in a Jamesonian project centered on a spatial poetics. Curiously, Jameson's concept only identifies a postmodern, purely urban space, and in this space, the latest mutation ends up "transcending the capacities of the individual human body to locate itself, to organize its immediate surroundings perceptually and cognitively. . ." (Jameson 1991: 44). (The Los Angeles Bonaventura Hotel helps to exemplify this crisis of location.) Jameson goes on to posit that spatial disorientation accompanies and even helps to generate political disempowerment.[1]

In this analysis of postmodernism, the crisis of mapping constitutes one important way of conceptualizing the break with earlier forms of representation. That crisis responds to the bankruptcy, or at least inadequacy, of value systems that draw on antitheses such as surface and deep meanings, or, for that matter, on the opposition of "nature" and "culture," or better: agrarian and industrial domains. Indeed for Jameson, concepts such as "Nature" no longer obtain, having been displaced by the multinational capitalist expansion into precapitalist regions.

The disorienting complexity meant to distinguish postmodernism can, surprisingly, be rediscovered in modern depictions of rural space within the Québécois tradition of the "novel of the soil" (*roman du terroir*). Actually, some of the more famous depictions of rural life seem to fit Jameson's description of a presumably urban "postmodern hyperspace" resistant to mapping. In the early twentieth-century novel *Maria Chapdelaine* (1916) by Louis Hémon, the description of space fluctuates between the colonizing need to mark the frontier and the corresponding anxiety of misreading one's map in the limitless natural expanse. Germaine Guèvremont, writing in the forties, does provide some almost idyllic accounts of a carefully plotted-out landscape. Still, even in her text, "place" (and, by implication, the patriarchal legacy) begins to be redefined in more complex, less spatially-anchored terms. Finally, Marie-Claire Blais' works, spanning the 1960's and 80's, de-contextualize the novel of the soil by avoiding any pastoral, even descriptive, scenes. Indeed, in Blais' 1965 text, the landscape has become indecipherable. The characters can no longer apply the language of geography and astronomy to their space; instead, these traditional means of orienting oneself spatially are pastiched in order to show both the shortcomings of educated and uneducated characters alike. What underlies the pastiche is, in effect, a scepticism that implicitly calls into question the adequacy of conventional forms of cartography. The characters experience the landscapes, both rural and urban, as nightmarish, surrealistically fragmented scenes. Geographical and culturally significant points of reference are replaced by subjectively distorted images that end up bewildering the reader.

It would seem, then, that the postmodern phenomenon of disorientation, created in part by the dismantling of familiar oppositions, does not necessarily mark as clean a break between modern and postmodern forms of representation as Jameson's analysis might suggest. In addition, we shouldn't lose sight of the recognition that such spatial confusion can also still be yoked to agenda that are nationalist and/or (subversively) *engagé*. In point of fact, all three Québécois writers are able to harness the crisis of mapping one's place in order to construct diverging fictions of cultural identity, meant to reform or even to transform their social communities.

By examining how Hémon, Guèvremont, and Blais define rural culture in their *romans du terroir*, I will attempt to isolate the significant cultural resonances accompanying representations of country life in Québec. Even conventional depictions of country landscapes go beyond the evocation of a familiar, unproblematic, physical place, as we shall see in Hémon's text. But it is the works of Germaine Guèvremont and Marie-Claire Blais that help to highlight the dynamics of gender-determined power underpinning the nostalgically pastoral *roman du terroir*—that tradition, which had, after all, been key in establishing Quebec's literary specificity. The feminist reshaping of this form unmasks how cultural norms validate country life by restricting gender (here, in particular, women's) roles. In this study, then, I will attempt to sketch what is at stake in Guèvremont's and Blais' rewritings of the Québécois literary canon in order to explore the impact of these revisionings on a poetics that conventionally has linked identity with place.

In 1912–13, a Frenchman named Louis Hémon wrote a novel that after his death would become the lodestar for those Québécois writers subscribing to the tradition of the *roman du terroir*.[2] In Hémon's *Maria Chapdelaine*, the motherless protagonist renounces her passion for the trapper of the woods, François Paradis, in addition to refusing the life of ease offered her by an émigré Québécois now settled in

Massachusetts. Instead, she marries the unassuming, almost brotherly farmer, Eutrope Gagnon. Maria's unlikely choice is ordained by the intervention of an almost divine "voice of Quebec," a voice characterized as:

> à moitié un chant de femme et à moitié un sermon de prêtre. . . . Car en vérité tout ce qui fait l'âme de la province tenait dans cette voix: la solennité chère du vieux culte, la douceur de la vieille langue jalousement gardée, la splendeur et la force barbare du pays neuf où une racine ancienne a retrouvé son adolescence.

> [half woman's song and half priest's sermon. . . . For in truth all that makes up the soul of the province was present in this voice: the dear solemnity of the old religion, the sweetness of the old language jealously guarded, the splendor and barbarous form of the new country where an ancient root had rediscovered its adolescence (my translation)].[3]

It is in part the intervention of this divine voice that explains why Hémon's novel became a "cultural artifact" in Quebec. His construction of the *roman du terroir* sprang forth from this blend of local color, which through the ideology of sacred identity implicitly privileged a rural way of life over the city dweller's or even the woodsman's existence. (The almost legendary *coureur du bois*, or woodsman, refused to integrate himself into the rural community, preferring the more native lifestyle of roaming vast areas and accepting a more precarious life supported through diverse, temporary tasks in order to preserve his personal freedom.) In the novel, the supernatural voice of Quebec, which calls on the Québécois to continue in the footsteps of their forefathers and to refuse any change (196) is validated by the Catholic church's equation of French Catholic identity with the "glorious" task of carving out and working more land. By appealing to the sacred register, Hémon's novel reinforces how rusticity is central to (true) Québécois identity.[4]

Rural existence, which in Hémon's account seems simpler, purer, more authentic, in short, more "Québécois," is represented through accounts that foreground land, but even this symbol is no less culturally determined than ("sacred") identity is. If we look again at the intervention of the poetic language—meant to conflate national identity and organic growth with legitimate, even consecrated rural life, we can note: it emerges at a critical point in the novel. "Québec" speaks at the moment when Maria must choose the "proper" suitor—when, in effect, she must agree to submit her body both to the labor of the land and the labor of childbirth. The equation of earth and the female body is not localized and, of course, it is not innocent. The feminized depiction of the land helps to mask the violence accompanying the marking and appropriating of "virgin terrain." Maria's willing sacrifice of her body and energy emblemizes the tacit "natural" connection between Québécois land and Québécois *habitants* (pioneer settlers). Not only is the countryside itself described as "offering itself up with the abandon of a wife" (MC: 54), the work of clearing the land is staged as a form of delivery while the act of preparing the ground for planting is named "faire de la terre" (MC: 54)—making earth.

One consequence of representing land through images of motherhood is the dismantling of the opposition between colonizer and colonized. In order to make the landscape familiar, Hémon projects the image of a colonizing Francophone woman onto the role of willingly exploited nature[5]—and this anthropomorphic projection, meant to assert and legitimate Québécois mastery, in turn becomes an enslaving symbol of Québécois identity. Both Québécois and Québécoises become identified with (and through) the land they work. In this sense, while Hémon's novel may have provided a voice for Québécois experience, especially by granting an idealized resonance to physical hardship, it also helped to reinforce a new, equally troubling, antithesis—one that separated Canadians into urban Anglophone colonizers (with a monopoly on political power) and rural Francophones. Within the Canadian hierarchy, the Francophone rejection of urban life marked them as backward, second-class citizens, and their Catholicism with its strong Maria cult, reinforced their connection to both rusticity and "femininity."[6] Indeed, Hémon's novel encourages the rejection of city life by making explicit the danger of urban existence for the Québécois: life in the city means wealth but also the loss of one's language and (Catholic) community. In short, for Hémon urbanization means both assimilation into the "enemy" culture and the abandonment of a sacred duty—the (French) colonizing and peopling of North America. By yoking identity and place together so absolutely—even though he does draw on powerful symbols such as sacred duty and female fertility—Hémon thus ends up simultaneously establishing an important literary tradition for the Québécois and helping to imprison them within it.

Louis Hémon's *Maria Chapdelaine* helped to spark the imaginations of many Québécois novelists. Germaine Guèvremont, writing in the forties, and Marie-Claire Blais, writing twenty years later, also adopt the tradition of the *terroir*, but they do so by redefining it. For them, the equation of cultural identity, labor of the land, and motherhood cannot be couched in as blithely positive a way as it is for Hémon. In short, they reappropriate the space represented by the term *terroir*, which conventionally had glorified the patriarchal lineage. In Guèvremont's reworking of the Québécois tradition, for instance, she turns her lens on young motherhood in order to show how its inflated, even mythical status must be debunked.

In the second novel of her never-completed trilogy, *Marie-Didace* (1947), Guèvremont begins by shifting attention away from the primary term—the working of the land—in order to focus on the experiences of individuals, primarily women, within a rural community. Her account demystifies the experience of motherhood within the farming village context. Although this demystification highlights the protagonist's (Phonsine's) inability to fulfill completely the role of maternal center of a household—thus ironically reaffirming the general importance of such a function—the novel also grants Phonsine's perspective a certain "tragic" validation. Instead of dwelling only on Phonsine's sacred mission *manqué*, Guèvremont shows how the young woman's own early orphaned state, as well as her later difficulty in conceiving, effectively marginalize her status within the family-oriented community. Thus, the cult of motherhood shows some rifts in Guèvremont's account: motherhood is no longer represented as instinctual in each woman. At the same time, the oppressive burden of such a cult on individual women is thrown into relief.

Guèvremont also de-naturalizes the maternal bond. Once Phonsine finally does give birth to a child, her daughter seeks out other, substitute mothers. Two consequences emerge from this refashioning of a familiar story. Phonsine's attempt to assume fully the proper role of mother only alienates her further within the community. Even more significantly, the maternal body no longer circumscribes the represented experience of the Québécois women. The substitute mothers that Phonsine's daughter prefers over her own mother do not bear children themselves. They become adoptive mothers, better able to provide nurture and comfort to the small child than her own birth mother.

It has already been pointed out by other critics, notably Patricia Smart, that Guèvremont also transforms the Québécois novel by decentering the text. No single narrative perspective acts as primary filter—certainly not that of the aging patriarch, whose lineage will only continue through his sickly, infantile son and his energetic, married daughter, who, by marrying, has entered into a new family line. The multiplying of narrative voices can be read in two ways. On the one hand, it does appear to be somewhat revolutionary by fragmenting the text, thus destabilizing the authority of any one position.

There is more, however. When one reads the beginning section of the novel—during which Phonsine explores the effects of her pregnancy—against the text's conclusion, it becomes clear that Guèvremont—while not shattering the tradition of the *terroir* completely—still reforms that heritage. By granting another protagonist, the unmarried, physically handicapped Angélina Desmarais, the final word, Guèvremont legitimates, even valorizes what conventionally was to have no voice or future. Angélina's own name points to the significance of her role. On the one hand, she is connected to the angelical. More significantly, she is a woman "of the marshes"—an area that conventionally belongs to the infertile margins of rural community. Still, this space also does boast its own tradition of the "jardin maraîcher": the cultivation of fruits and vegetables. In short, this character who acts as a focal point for usually marginalized qualities and experiences helps, precisely, to revitalize those elements. In fact, Angélina's self-appointed task is to protect the spirit of her community—by arranging funeral masses for the two separate "strangers" she had befriended and, more importantly, by accepting the responsibility for Phonsine's abandoned child. It is Angélina—and implicitly the values she represents—that guarantees, in effect, the survival and expansion of a community whose exposed vulnerabilities in turn make problematic a rhetoric of conquest and domination.

The representation of the land is also affected by Guèvremont's redefinition of community. Through the filter of Angélina's consciousness, laboring over the earth is disassociated from images of mastering it; working the land is instead transformed into an image of "nurturing." The detail of ". . . her hands [that] mimed the maternal gesture of placing a plant under shelter"[7] is, finally, the symbol that stands out most clearly at the end of the novel. In short, by refusing to equate motherhood only with the physical act of giving birth, the concept can be redefined as the act of protecting and nurturing life—that of children or of plants, and, by extension, of the land itself.

Guèvremont's *roman du terroir* takes as its context a rural setting and highlights the motif of motherhood, inherited from Hémon's literary tradition. And yet, instead of reproducing faithfully the "necessary" connection—that would equate land and female body—in order to legitimate the specificity of Québécois experience and community, Guèvremont's text retains those key symbols but underplays the values of "rootedness" and "possession" in favor of a rhetoric of nurturing. Belonging to the community, while continuing to play a central role, is now defined in terms of a responsibility—both to the fellow villagers and to the land. The pioneer anxiety of claiming the land in order to determine one's place and to hew one's identity has ceded its place to the vision of motherhood and labor as *functions*. The child and the land are no longer figured as possessions or as ciphers pointing to an overarching scheme (whether this be greater cultural power or competition with the Anglophones and their value systems). More importantly, motherhood and the construction of a rural community are no longer equated with a rigidly defined, essentialized mission. In short, in order to move beyond the limitations of Hémon's poetics of the land, Guèvremont underscores primarily the inclusiveness, flexibility, and (potential) freedom to define one's own role within her fictional Québécois community.

Thanks in part to Guèvremont's refusal to perpetuate the symbolic equation between land and the female body, the *roman du terroir* itself appeared to lose vitality. An equally significant factor contributing to the apparent obsolescence of the *terroir* tradition is the "Quiet Revolution"[8] that acts as the backdrop to Marie-Claire Blais' 1965 *Une saison dans la vie d'Emmanuel* [*A Season in the Life of Emmanuel*]. The Quebec of the sixties is marked by dissatisfaction with the traditional values that had foregrounded, among other elements, the Catholic faith, suspicion of any secularized education, and, in particular, the sanctity of rural life. Marie-Claire Blais contributes to Quebec's "Quiet Revolution" by systematically parodying the various facets of the cult that had blended religion with rusticity in order to make the acceptance of rural hardships a sacred duty. During this decade of secularization and urbanization, Marie-Claire Blais focuses explicitly and bitingly on the bankruptcy of a way of life in which mothers (portrayed as mechanical brood-mares) as well as physically and intellectually stunted children are both sacrificed to the Church's doctrine of Francophone colonization through reproduction, the policy of "survivance" (or cultural survival through intense procreation).

Blais' most bitter attack continues Guèvremont's refusal to transform Québécois children into political or cultural symbols. She satirizes, in particular, the churchmen, by foregrounding their carelessness, even sadism, which kills off her novel's first protagonist: an irreligious eleven-year-old boy, Jean le Maigre [the Scrawny One], endowed with an irrepressible poetic gift. The boy's literary impulse helps to provide poetry with a political charge: his fantasy even sets its sights on capturing his own fading consciousness, that is, his own death—accelerated by the churchmen's oppression of him. The hopelessness of Jean's life in the rural villages, overrun with children, cannot block the power of his poetic energy; even his own hopelessness and decline can be transformed self-consciously into art. Jean le Maigre's creativity helps to underscore both the loss to the culture of a poet and the abuses of an institution originally glorified by the *terroir* tradition.

Equally scathing is Blais' depiction of the ineffectual educators in the rural world she represents. One teacher struggles vainly with the intricate mutations of the verb "absoudre" [to absolve]—an example that shows more than the obvious fact that education in *Une saison* is overshadowed by religion. Those teaching the Church's doctrine are even incapable of mastering the grammatical form, not to mention the presumably key concepts associated with the Christian faith. Here again, the debunking of the Church's role (its outdated and ineffectual impact on the education of "its" youth) is central to the writer's agenda to revise the *terroir* novel. Blais also sets out to demystify another Québécois icon in the novel; she shows the practical consequences of a policy that takes literally Hémon's glorification of "natural" Québécois motherhood by demanding that women reproduce continuously. In the country, the overabundant children have no food, no warmth or shelter, and receive no attention, not to mention useful education. Indeed, in Jean le Maigre's case, there isn't even any protection from religious abuse, even when this abuse culminates in the boy's death. Blais' portrayal of the "body-locked," unconsciously reproducing, silent mother shows how both mother and child have been victimized. Here the rhetoric of working the land no longer defines rural existence; that rhetoric has been eclipsed by the colonization of both the maternal body and the future generations it produces. The brutally literal representation of the effects of too frequent childbirth calls into question a rhetoric that posits a natural, transparent link between country living, frequent reproduction, and cultural (consecrated) identity. In short, Blais throws into relief the flawed aspects of Hémon's *Maria Chapdelaine*, where it is only the abstract potential of reproduction that is extolled through idealistic hyperbole.

In this novel, where the bastions of rural community are systematically dismantled, Blais does not fall into the trap of simply reversing the hierarchy of values. Where rural life can no longer be sacred, life in the city does not automatically become sanctified, or even affirmed. The author positions herself carefully—and this is nowhere clearer than in her parody of the cult of the Virgin Mary. When, in the second half of the novel, Blais plots the trajectory of the now-deceased Jean le Maigre's older sister, she conflates Héloïse's experience of mysticism with her discovery of sensuality. The Christian rhetoric of the "metaphorical Spouse" prepares Héloïse's repeated seduction by the convent's priest. And through the novel's careful parallel structure, Héloïse's earlier confusion of mysticism and sexuality is echoed during her migration to the city where she eventually becomes a prostitute.

Blais denounces, then, the mystifying rhetoric of Catholicism by showing how indistinguishable the sacred and profane can be. Héloïse's room is decorated with both porn and a crucifix; the brothel's madam replaces the Mother Superior, and Héloïse perceives her granting of sexual favors as the means to console, even "save" her clients. But the contamination of the two poles "sacred" and "profane" as the means to discredit key elements of the *roman du terroir* constitutes only one, perhaps even (too) familiar, narrative strategy. More interesting is the insight that Héloïse's fluctuation between the cult of the Virgin and the cult of the Harlot facilitates her continued manipulation by others. Her prostitution in the city can be read as the logical counterpart of the "sacrifice" of her body, offered to the rural priest of her convent.

This connection is hardly limited to Héloïse's individual experience. By representing a collage of newspaper ads—in which the various employment opportunities open to urban Québécois women are detailed, Blais shows that the abuse of the female body is certainly not unique to a rural setting. The excerpted classifieds call for a "Jeune personne responsable demandée pour vieillard ayant perdu la raison... une infirmière de grandeur moyenne yeux bleus. Une personne seule souffrant d'amnésie.... Pour garder enfants de un à huit ans et animaux également en bas âge. Femme cinquante ans au moins. Un veuf impatient" ["Young person who will be responsible for an old man having lost his reason," "a nurse of medium height with blue eyes to take care of an amnesiac," and "a fifty-year old woman prepared to watch over the young children and animals of an impatient widower"].[9] The urban space represents no new, promising place, unmarked by rural customs; it only serves to continue the colonization of women's bodies. In *Une saison*, then, traditional Québécois values (which had often been portrayed as being under siege to more modern, urban Anglophone values) are parodied. Blais' satire leads, in short, to a refusal of a cultural identity couched simply in terms of rusticity. Most interestingly, however, her novel calls into question even the validity of establishing a rural/urban antithesis.

It might seem that not much is left to the *roman du terroir* in Quebec after Blais' bitter parody of Francophone rural existence in *Une saison*, and a cursory glance at her later novel, *Visions d'Anna ou le vertige* (1982) seems to bear out this assumption, since its setting appears to be predominantly urban. In addition, this more postmodern text might also seem to support Jameson's elision of rusticity (or nature) in his vision of late capitalist reality. The meanderings of several consciousnesses that intersect without overlapping might appear to devalue the realist or even nationalist project of establishing geographical differences—whether these be Québécois, Canadian, rural or urban. The point seems to be, as Jacqueline Viswanathan writes, "a multiple focus, where the character only exists by constantly interacting with other consciences."[10]

And yet, even in this later text, spatial references—not to mention evocations of nature—are not completely suppressed. In fact, it is especially the memories anchored to specific places (such as highways, city parks, backyards or quiet rivers) that help to define the characters. One of the more centered, lesbian characters, Liliane, chooses solitary immersion in a fiery (because star-filled) river in order to meditate upon alternatives to a (as she puts it) burlesque "T.V. culture that smiles frivolously upon the responsibility of living": ". . . l'Amérique du Nord aurait ses abris nucléaires, en Inde, ils périraient par milliers, pensait Liliane, c'était cela, la justice de la société actuelle. . ." ["North America would have its nuclear shelters, in India, they would perish by the thousands, thought Liliane, that was it, the justice of current society. . . . "[11] It is significant that Liliane's retreat to the river away from crowded, polluted spaces coincides with her ecological *prise de conscience* (or political awareness). This scene, which in contrast to *Une saison*, conjures up an (albeit unnamed) place, does more, however, than characterize Liliane and her personal or political agenda. The evocation of space—that is neither purely urban nor agrarian—seems to point to the need to re-map, in fact, to reclaim culturally overdetermined terrain. The spatially-anchored scenes, such as the one by the river, are carefully decontextualized: "Couchée dans l'herbe, les mains repliées sous sa tête, Liliane regardait ce ciel qui annonçait l'orage . . . [Lying in the grass, her hands folded under her head, Liliane looked at this sky which announced the storm. . . (A: 195)]. By refusing to provide the reader with geographical coordinates, Blais steps back from furnishing local color in her novel—nor does she promote a narrowly-defined nationalist agenda. As we shall see, this move is not limited to one scene in the text.

In contrast to *Une saison*, where the interweaving of city and country life primarily focuses on the different characters' economic exploitation, in *Visions d'Anna*, landscapes assume more personal symbolic associations—without sacrificing, nonetheless, political relevance. The privileging of such a symbolic reading is hardly clearer than in the overarching frame of the text: the protagonist (Anna) shuts herself up in her own room; she is torn between the world of the marginalized drifters and pushers on the one hand, and the universe of her mother, who works as a therapist and educator for the (almost allegorical) "Correctional Institute." Even here, the oppposition of rural and urban space has been reworked as that separating insiders from outsiders. Highway scenes, while not purely "rural," are peopled with individuals who deliberately distance themselves from urban/e values. Such "outsider" scenes contrast with the bourgeois, urban setting of a professional, at least superficially more sophisticated dinner party.

Marie Couillard proposes one interpretation of this frame (Anna's self-imposed exile) in her article, "*Visions d'Anna* ou l'écriture du vertige de Marie-Claire Blais." She argues that Anna's choice of a *lieu clos* [enclosed space] symbolizes both the desire to abandon the self as well as the refusal to act, since all action seems to be tainted by complicity with omnipresent violence.[12] And yet, what might appear to be the bracketing out of space becomes, paradoxically, the condition for a rather creative redefinition of Anna's relation to settings, both experienced and imagined. Anna's self-imposed captivity leads, namely, to visions triggered by a painting in her room of an Honfleur beach by Boudin (one of Gustave Courbet's associates). Her attempt to retreat before the world helps her, finally, to transcend the walls of her room and to evoke a new space, even if that space cannot elide the (for her) tainted contact with urbanization:

> Les dernières ressources de la terre, les derniers vivants s'égrenaient dans la reproduction de Boudin, pensait Anna, sur ce mur que Raymonde avait jadis peint en rose, toute cette eau, toute cette lumière, pensait-elle, on ne les verra plus, désormais que les tableaux, cette eau, cette lumière, dans un tableau seront nos convalescentes visions d'une autre vie, d'un autre siècle, quand demain nous chercherons enfin la guérison de tous nos maux, sous les empreintes de notre agonie sociale, collective . . . .

> [The last resources of the earth, the last of the living drop off one by one in the reproduction by Boudin, thought Anna, on this wall that Raymonde (her mother) had formerly painted pink, all this water, all this light, she thought, one will henceforth only see them in the painting, this water, this light, our convalescent visions of another life, of another century shall be in a painting, when tomorrow we shall finally search for the cure of all our ills beneath the imprint of our social agony. . . . (A: 204)]

The beaches of Honfleur, by being invaded by the bourgeois bathers of the nineteenth century, do not belong, strictly speaking, either to a rural or to an urban space. And from this scene, which emblemizes implicitly the impossibility of keeping separate two supposedly antithetical realms, springs forth Anna's both anxious and lucid insight into the impossibility of fixing spatial boundaries. One could add: this insight underpins the formal construction of the novel. The inter-weaving of the scenes, in addition to accenting the subjective interaction of the characters, pushes us to recognize the interconnectedness both of the characters' lives and of the rather diverse landscapes. While that interconnectedness (reminiscent of Jameson's spatial disorientation) no longer privileges a nationalist, not to mention province-based, agenda, it still does carry with it a political charge. Indeed, recognizing that interconnection—rather than clinging to the need for cultural or national divisions as the necessary precondition for autonomous identity and political agency—characterizes the radical orientation of *Visions d'Anna*.

The associative logic of the novel reinforces the impression that otherwise distinct spaces are interlocked in several ways. First, the descriptions of the grass in the city park, where Anna remembers meeting her younger friend, ends up being interspersed with even earlier memories of the long freeways along which Anna and her former, delinquent friends trudged. The coexistence of the two images in Anna's consciousness implies parallels. It provides yet another example of her realization that neither space can be classed as fully rural or urban any longer. In both scenes (within and outside the city), images of industrialized and non-industrialized regions are simultaneously present.

The grass in the park triggers another association in Anna's mind, and it is this scene that helps draw attention to the more global impulse in the novel.[13] By emphasizing the connections between different settings, by refusing to privilege only Québécois points of reference, Blais goes beyond the recognition that the sharply defined country/city antithesis has been unsettled. (Her novel clearly also addresses more than purely Canadian consequences of such a deconstruction). What might be at stake in the overlapping of the different settings becomes apparent in an emotionally charged scene, which, significantly, Anna recalls while in the city park. Even the staging of Anna's vision, that is, the juxtaposition of the park scene and Anna's memory of a key moment in a suburban backyard, underscores the reasons for this scepticism about establishing clear boundaries—whether they be between individuals, between urban and rural spaces—or even between "nations."

Anna conjures up a recent encounter with her biological but estranged father, Peter, at his suburban pool. Peter has chosen to construct an enclosed safe space in his verdant backyard in order to protect his youngest daughter (Sylvie), issued from a more recent liaison, and to exclude, here ineffectually, his older daughter, Anna. The scene does more than draw attention to a father's betrayal of his daughter or to the bankruptcy of family values, for that matter. From within this urban, closed-off space springs the awareness that the attempt to cloister oneself, to find refuge in any space is futile:

> Peter avait imaginé le feu, les cendres, la dispersion des corps mutilés, il avait oublié l'existence de ce mince nuage noir, dans le ciel, ce pressentiment de Sylvie, si concret . . . . ce mince nuage noir qui avançait paisiblement vers la terre, doucement, sans bruit, dans un grand silence, et qui, en quelques instants, tuait toute vie.

> [Peter had imagined fire, ashes, the scattering of mutilated bodies, he had forgotten the existence of this thin black cloud in the sky, this so concrete presentiment of Sylvia . . . this thin cloud which advanced peacefully toward the earth, gently, without a noise, in a great silence, and which, in some moments, would kill all life. (A: 195)]

The tension between "making earth" or letting oneself be corrupted by city-dwelling Anglophones dissolves before this much more global insight.

The more complex treatment of space in *Visions d'Anna* marks one way of noting how the *roman du terroir* constitutes a (substantively revised) subtext to the novel. Another important topos carried over from the *roman du terroir* in this quite sophisticated novel is, however, the continued importance of community. Once again, it is the description, if not definition, of motherhood that predominates in the 1982 vision of a possible community. Not surprisingly (when one considers this novel's precursors), the act of giving birth is passed over in this text. Instead, the reconciliation (or *rapprochement*) between Anna and her mother, Raymonde, figures as the central narrative intrigue. Blais highlights the difficult task of repairing these hardly "natural" ties; for Blais, the mother-daughter bond cannot be taken for granted, as is highlighted by the ending, when Anna and Raymonde find their way tenuously to one another—and this almost by accident.

Equally significant in this novel is the spectrum of possible family relations. Divorce, the dissolution and piecing-back together of family ties, the existence of step-families and of homosexual partnerships are all explored in *Visions d'Anna*. But it is particularly through the figure of a homeless mother, "Rita, the woman of/from Asbestos" that Blais challenges most radically the resonances of the tradition of the *terroir*. Here the family, where the father no longer plays any role at all, has been uprooted completely. Moreover, the appropriation of one's own space—rural or urban—is cast as irrelevant to the construction of community. Indeed, even in this mobile, thus undefined class (neither bourgeois, working class, or *paysan*), it is the very attempt to carve out one's own space that seems to evoke patriarchal values and, more troublingly, that calls up the accompanying violence, which threatens to shatter the bonds between mother and child (here Rita and her son, Pierre). Like Raymonde, Rita must struggle against losing her child. And, as is the case for Raymonde, the barrier that separates Rita from her child results mainly from her dependence on others, although for the homeless mother, the stakes are reduced to the search for even miserable shelter:

> . . . le lit du camionneur, c'était cet arrêt au bord du temps, la putréfaction de la cabane abandonnée à midi, le couple inerte, quand dans des fauteuils, les derniers gardiens étaient de nobles chiens errants, affamés mais lucides observant cette décadente race supérieure, celle des hommes, que ne rachetaient plus les gestes de l'amour.

> [. . . the bed of the truck-driver, it was this pause at the edge of time, the putrefaction of the hut abandoned at noon, the inert couple, when in armchairs, the last keepers (of the hut) had been starving, lucid dogs

observing this decadent superior race, that of men, who no longer were redeemed by the gestures of love. (A: 178)]

Rita's dependence on a truck-driver for shelter leads to the abuse of herself and of her children. Only by leaving, only by refusing the measly possessions of the truck-driver, can she begin to reconnect with her son. It should also be noted that Rita's decision at the end of the novel does not replace an oppressive, brutal space with a more idealistic, maternal one. All that is sketched in is Rita's and perhaps the reader's recognition that the project of motherhood still needs to be defined. Also, the possibility of constructing a home—either as a place or, more metaphorically, as a family or community, is left open in the text. After all, Rita's last words in the text are: "viens, mon garçon, dit-elle, on va continuer notre chemin, ce n'est pas encore ici le bout de notre route" ["come, my boy, she said, we will continue on our way, this isn't yet the end of our road" (A: 204)]. Still, through this example we can see how the poetics of space, in part by foregrounding the politics of domestic space, calls into question one of the more fundamental precepts of the *roman du terroir*: the importance of carving out one's own parcel of land in order to establish one's family and, by extension, one's cultural community. In Blais' 1982 novel, which explores the twin issues of community and ecology, the policy of "survivance" is no longer yoked to the purely Québécois crisis of identity; it has become relevant to all readers of her text.

Especially when juxtaposed with Guèvremont's literary remodeling of the rural tradition in Quebec, it is clear that Blais has debunked and transformed key elements of the *roman du terroir*.[14] Rather than searching for ways of identifying the particularity of Québécois experience, Blais sets out to denounce certain (especially religious) policies established in the name of the Québécois ideal—and this is true of *Une saison* as well as of *Visions d'Anna*. Indeed, she takes Guèvremont's work one step further. Rather than only pointing to the split between the "natural" body and the social functions attributed to that (female) body, Blais exaggerates through parody the social discourse that is used to harness the body's energies. And, in *Visions d'Anna*, the concept of motherhood is not only couched in terms of a *function* (rather than an essentialized state of being); it becomes the difficult, central but also intensely personal *project* of mothering. The equation between cultural procreation, the female body, and the land that had grounded Hémon's vision of the Québécois heritage, if not mission, is thus dismantled and demystified. It is no longer through this rhetorical sleight of hand that the call to rural living and to Québécois identity can be legitimated.

And yet, Blais' work, while taking on the Church's doctrine of "survivance francophone," can still be reconciled with the tradition of the soil. Her bitter parody of life in the country does not advocate flight into urban space. Her text, while reinforcing the need to scrutinize sharply the institution of (holy) motherhood, reminds us that more is at stake in the effaced opposition of rural and urban space than Jameson's "schizophrenic" crisis of language, where the relation of signified to signifier has given way to an easily fragmented chain of signifiers. In her account, we are reminded of Raymond Williams' *The Country and the City*, in which Williams notes how the simplistic opposition of agricultural and industrial development masks an almost inextricable, mutually supportive interweaving of the two economic systems (CC: 293). Especially in *Une saison*, that interweaving of economic exploitation takes place through the harnessing and oppression of women's bodies. Rural and urban forms of exploitation mirror rather than oppose one another.

On one level, then, Blais uses the crisis of mapping distinctions between rural and urban space in order to highlight the negotiation of power along gender lines. But it is no longer only the model of exploiting the economically less privileged that unmasks unsettling parallels between rural and urban space. In *Visions d'Anna*, Blais adds the insight that the potentially catastrophic destruction of the earth represents another urgent need to recognize the interweaving of industrialized and non-industrialized spaces. In short, through these re-visionings of the *roman du terroir*, as Kwame A. Appiah might put it, the effacement of a clean break between the rural and the urban does not participate in the game (or Derridean playfulness) of postmodernity (KA: 348). The blurring of boundaries locates itself squarely on a literal and political plane.

Blais—and Guèvremont before her—do not point to apparently unavoidable spatial and political aporia; they both adopt an *engagé* stance. Blais, especially, makes a convincing case for her strong impatience with the abuses she associates with a rural lifestyle and "solid" or "healthy country values." But the revisioning of the *terroir* tradition is not only negative—or reactive, for that matter. Where Guèvremont reforms the patriarchal legacy of the *terroir* by continuing to foreground its pastoral setting (all the while modifying its values), Blais revolutionizes the tradition. What almost outweighs her politically-oriented deconstruction of the rural/urban antithesis is her radical vision of community. Perhaps the most fitting emblem of Blais' revolutionary revisioning of the *roman du terroir* lies in the open-endedness, indeed, the multiplicity as well as the unconventional cast of the familial and community ties she chooses to represent.

NOTES

1. It is important to recognize Jameson's concern over "our faulty representations of some immense communicational and computer network [that] are themselves but a distorted figuration of something even deeper, namely, the whole world system of a present-day multinational capitalism" (Jameson 1991: 37). He calls for a new political art that would strive to overcome our paralysis, an impotence brought on by "spatial as well as social confusion" (1991: 54). Jameson's emphasis on the need to invent and project "a global cognitive mapping, on a social as well as a spatial scale" (1991: 54), leaves unaddressed, perhaps even repressed, the representation of (a more traditional, more "naïve") rural space.

2. In her *Le Québec, un pays, une culture*, Françoise Tétu de Labsade points out that 1846 marks the moment when the tradition of the *terroir* seems to take root in Quebec. She cites as examples Patrice Lacombe's *La Terre paternelle* and Pierre-J.-O. Chauveau's *Charles Guérin*. In addition, the words of a critic, dating from the 1870's, are quoted in order to define the essential traits of the *terroir* novel. This tradition presumably foregrounds "the beauty of detail and downplays worries and tragic incidents. Gentle passions are preferred over violent ones, and domestic and rural bliss becomes the highest

expression of happiness on earth" (413–14, my translation). In contrast, Tétu de Labsade argues, Hémon's novel's own prominence can be explained in part through its historical period, when Europe was beginning to boast of its new colonial possessions, soon to become part of new empires (431).

Patricia Smart, in her *Ecrire dans la maison du père*, highlights another aspect of the novel in order to explain its cultural prominence. According to her, Hémon's choice of a female protagonist gave the novel a double charge. On the one hand, female existence in the *terroir* tradition supposedly had no "story" value; it was limited to the unchanging role of wife and mother. Hémon's decision to put Maria Chapdelaine at the center of his novel explains, then, part of his novel's popular appeal.

And yet, *Maria Chapdelaine* cannot be read as being completely iconoclastic either, since the promise of a unique (female) destiny is gradually undermined, as the novel progresses, until the protagonist is left with the simulacrum of a choice between two equally undesirable suitors. By finally being imprisoned in her domestic world, Maria helps to reinforce the rigidly dualistic code of values which underpins the novel of the *terroir* (112–17). *Maria Chapdelaine* becomes a paradigm, in that it provides both the promise of a scandal about gender roles and then the enactment of containing that potential scandal.

3. Louis Hémon, *Maria Chapdelaine* (Montréal: Fides/ Bibliothèque Québécoise, 1980: 195). All subsequent references to this text will be marked as (MC: page number). All translations from the French are my own.

4. Françoise Tétu de Labsade's cultural history of Quebec helps to explain how the Church took over the State's function after the Conquest of 1763. "Starting from 1830, and even more after 1840, the Church played the role of intellectual leader, especially in the rural parishes (the English, administrators, soldiers, and tradespeople occupied the cities more massively). Keeping the French language alive under English rule, staying Catholic under a Protestant monarchy, this meant reinforcing among the Canadians (that is, the Québécois) the responsibility of not allowing themselves to be marginalized in their own country. The solution was to occupy one's space more massively—through the work traditionally best known to those people—agriculture (62, my translation). This situation is ultimately challenged by the "Révolution Tranquille" of the 1960's (cf. endnote 8).

5. The feminization of the frontier landscape in U.S. literature has been studied in great detail by Annette Kolodny in her *The Land Before Her: Fantasy and Experience of the American Frontiers, 1630–1860*.

6. It is interesting to consider Roch Carrier's satirical *La Guerre, Yes sir!* (1968), which exploits these associations, in part to parody the stereotypes. In

Carrier's novel, however, the Anglophone/Francophone antithesis is constructed in order to satirize both poles.

7. Germaine Guèvremont, *Marie-Didace* (Paris: Librairie Plon, 1947: 236, my translation).

8. The *Révolution Tranquille* occurred after Québec's Premier, Maurice Duplessis, died in 1959. The sixties brought important social reforms, piloted by Jean Lesage, such as the secularization of education and a general turn away from the Catholic Church. In her *Writing in the Feminine: Feminism and Experimental Writing in Quebec*, Karen Gould notes: "In 1964, a new Ministry of Education was created in Quebec whose progressive reforms included the important move to coeducational public schools, the right of free access to a high school education, and the abolition of the *écoles ménagères* that had traditionally prepared many young Quebec women to become "good" homemakers rather than working professionals" (8). She also cites "the creation of the *cégeps* (a state-supported junior college system) along with the various campuses of the new Université du Québec" (8).

The term "quiet" or "tranquil" refers to the general lack of violence and turmoil accompanying the period of change. It should also be noted that this era sparked an overarching re-evaluation of and break with many traditional values considered to be quintessentially Québécois. Gould points to the rapidly declining birth rate after World War II and emphasizes how the church lost control over women's sexuality and their attitudes about sexual practice. She goes on to argue: "[these changes] brought about important modifications and, for some women, radical transformations in the relationships they had previously maintained with fathers, husbands, employers, politicians, and clergymen, figures who had traditionally represented the political, economic, cultural, and sexual power of male authority in Quebec" (6–7).

9. Marie-Claire Blais, *Une saison dans la vie d'Emmanuel* (Québec: Stanké, 1980: 147, my translation).

10. Jacqueline Viswanathan, "'Cette danse au fond des coeurs': Transparence des consciences dans *Le Sourd dans la ville* et *Visions d'Anna*," *Canadian Literature* 111 (1986: 93).

11. Marie-Claire Blais, *Visions d'Anna ou le vertige* (Montréal: Boréal, 1990: 198, my translation). All further references to this text will be marked (A: page number).

12. Couillard seems more interested in analyzing Anna's *dérive mentale* [mental drift] and uses this motif in order to emphasize the importance of the multiple meanings behind the word "vision:" seeing, the mental reconstruction of what one has seen, the link with the supernatural, hallucinations, illusions, dreams, and, finally, obsessions.

Marie Couillard, "*Visions d'Anna* ou l'écriture du vertige de Marie-Claire Blais," *Québec Studies* 17 (1994): 117, 120.

13. Couillard lists the many examples from Blais' 1982 novel that bear witness to the impulse toward universalism. There are references (among others) to Denmark, Japan, Paris, New York, Prague, Miami, and Portland. See Couillard, 120.

14. After completing this paper, I discovered Lori Saint-Martin's article on the *roman de la terre au féminin*. I was struck by her analysis of what might constitute a feminist revising of this Québécois tradition. In her study, she targets in particular the relationship that is usually silenced either through non-representation or even more commonly through scenes of death: the relationship between mothers and daughters. Her thesis that (novelist) Nicole Houde's decision to throw into relief women's (especially mothers') sufferings over the years—thereby forcing a critical reevaluation of Québécois history—constitutes writing *au féminin*, certainly holds true for the three novels under scrutiny here.

While Saint-Martin's analysis of rural space in Houde's novel centers primarily on how women are fenced in (through the analogy of repressive home and psychiatric hospital [191]), her remarks on the consequences of feminist revisionism upon language itself are quite thought-provoking. She notes how in *La Maison du remous* the "shackles of traditional realism" and the "system of representation" (191) begin to be undermined; in the 1986 text, women are either unable or unwilling to use language "correctly." Their other acts of disobedience or of unconventional behavior help to lay bare how women's "madness" carries the potential of evading a referential language oppressive to women:

> "Enfermée à son tour, Laetitia dit se nommer Louise, le nom qu'elle donnait, petite fille, à sa jumelle imaginaire, plus libre et plus heureuse qu'elle; se conserve ainsi, entière, l'image du bonheur. Selon cette lecture féministe, la folie traduirait l'évasion des femmes, leur abandon du langage référentiel, et leur recherche d'un nouveau discours qu'il faudrait entendre autrement."

> ["Locked up in her turn, Laetitia names herself Louise, the name she had given as a young girl to her imaginary twin, freer and happier than herself; thus an image of happiness is wholly preserved. According to this feminist reading, madness would translate the escape of women, their abandonment of a referential language and their search for a new discourse that would have to be understood differently" (196, my translation)]. Lori Saint-Martin, "*La Maison du remous* de Nicole Houde, ou le roman de la terre au féminin," *Québec Studies* 17 (1994): 187–199.

REFERENCES

Appia, Kwame Anthony. 1991. "Is the Post- in Postmodernism the Post- in Postcolonial?" *Critical Inquiry* 17: 336–57.

Blais, Marie-Claire. 1980. *Une saison dans la vie d'Emmanuel*. Québec: Stanké.

————. 1990. *Visions d'Anna ou le vertige*. Montréal: Boréal.

Carrier, Roch. 1968. *La Guerre, yes sir!* Montréal: Stanké.

Couillard, Marie. 1994. "*Visions d'Anna* ou l'écriture du vertige de Marie-Claire Blais," *Québec Studies* 17: 117–24.

Gould, Karen. 1990. *Writing in the Feminine: Feminism and Experimental Writing in Quebec*. Carbondale: Southern Illinois University Press.

Guèvremont, Germaine. 1947. *Marie-Didace*. Paris: Librairie Plon.

————. 1990. *Le Survenant*. Montréal: Bibliothèque Québécoise.

Hémon, Louis. 1980. *Marie Chapdelaine*. Montréal: Fides (Bibliothèque Québécoise).

Jameson, Fredric. 1991. *Postmodernism, or the Cultural Logic of Late Capitalism*. Durham: Duke University Press.

Kolodny, Annette. 1984. *The Land Before Her: Fantasy and Experience of the American Frontiers, 1630–1860*. Chapel Hill: University of North Carolina Press.

Saint-Martin, Lori. 1994. "*La Maison du remous* de Nicole Houde, ou le roman de la terre au féminin," *Québec Studies* 17: 187–199.

Smart, Patricia. 1990. *Ecrire dans la maison du père*. Montréal: Editions Québec/Amérique.

Tétu de Labsade, Françoise. 1990. *Le Québec, un pays, une culture*. Louiseville: Boréal (Imprimerie Gagnée Ltée).

Viswanathan, Jacqueline. 1986. "'Cette danse au fond des coeurs': Transparence des consciences dans *Le Sourd dans la ville* et *Visions d'Anna* de Marie-Claire Blais," *Canadian Literature* 111: 86–99.

Williams, Raymond. 1973. *The Country and the City*. New York: Oxford University Press.

7 ~ DAVID MAYNARD

Rurality, Rusticity, and Contested Identity Politics in Brittany

COMPETING ideologies surrounding the representation of rural identity are heavily politicized in contemporary Brittany (western France). While images of rural life in the region have been manipulated over time by French intellectual elites to stigmatize and/or romanticize peasants in the provinces, Breton ethnic nationalists in the late twentieth century have struggled to appropriate, redefine, and contest these representations as part of ethnoregionalist political mobilization. Yet Breton ethnic activists disagree about how rurality and rusticity should be employed—or denied—in the problematization and politicization of Breton identity. This chapter examines how and why ethnic activists in Brittany simultaneously embrace and reject symbols of rurality and rusticity by analyzing these processes in three specific domains: 1) discourse among activists about two contrasting summer folk festivals in Brittany (the Festival de Cornauille and the Festival Interceltique, respectively "traditional" and "modern" expressions of Breton cultural production); 2) political and literary debates surrounding Hélias' romanticized 1975 ethnography *The Horse of Pride*; and 3) contrasting representations of folklore and daily life in three museums (the Musée de Bretagne and the Ecomusée du Pays de Rennes, both in Rennes, and the Musée National des Arts et Traditions Populaires in Paris). The analysis focuses on the ambiguity of the rural in constructions of Breton political struggle and associated contradictions of rurality and modernity. This case demonstrates that ethnoregionalist identities and their associated identity politics cannot be fully understood without paying attention to place and the cultural hierarchies of rural/urban difference.

BACKGROUND ON THE BRETON MOVEMENT

The Breton movement is a multi-party ethnoregionalist social movement in Brittany (western France), a region where significant minorities claim a distinctively Celtic ethnic identity and/or speak Breton as a second language. The movement consists of a set of unstable micro-parties, cultural associations, coalitions and factions whose total membership numbers somewhere between two thousand to five thousand "militants." These militants tend to be male, fairly young (thirty to forty years old, on average), urban-dwelling, university-educated, and employed as middle-class salaried professionals. A large proportion work in educational institutions (lycées, universities) so "middle-class intellectual" is not an inappropriate label. As a group they generally share a leftist ideological position emphasizing resistance to what they perceive as the linguistic and cultural domination of the region by the French state or, less often, to economic arrangements, such as the domination of Brittany and Breton workers by externally owned (Paris-based or transnational) capitalist enterprises or by the inequality producing effects of European Union (EU) and state policy. While the majority of Breton militants speak Breton, they frequently speak an intellectual form of the language not well understood by less educated rural speakers of "popular" Breton. Finally, the movement is a classic example of a "weak" ethnoregionalist political formation (see Gourevitch 1979) which does not possess widespread legitimacy or support in Brittany.

While there are many ideological and political paradoxes in Breton militancy, the symbolic role of rurality and rusticity in Breton ethnic political struggle is perhaps most problematic. In essence, the paradox is this: while rural agricultural life (a cultural concept of "rurality") is privileged ideologically as the most profound and authentic expression of Breton cultural identity in militant circles (see Kuter 1985, McDonald 1989), that same rural life—especially through its cultural dimension of "rusticity"— is despised and rejected by militants as an archaic obstacle to the construction of a distinctively modern Breton society which would appeal to the middle class and largely urban membership of the movement (see the introduction to this volume on the distinction between rurality and rusticity). This, in turn, is closely linked to the most fundamental contradictions apparent in Breton ethnic politics. While the movement represents itself as progressive or radical, it pursues, in both intellectual and class terms, an elitist, exclusionary political agenda. With respect to linguistic issues, Breton militants speak and act for an imaginary constituency—those ten thousand or so neo-Breton speakers and all those non-Breton speaking militants (or would-be militants) who might learn the intellectual form of the Breton language—not for the interests of the 600 thousand or so living speakers of popular Breton in rural lower Brittany. Very few peasants belong to the Breton political movement. On economic issues, Breton militants largely speak and act for their own class interests while on the surface claiming to speak for the Breton people or nation.

THE AMBIGUITY OF MODERNITY: FOLK FESTIVALS, POPULAR LITERATURE, AND THE PARADOXICAL POSITION OF BRETON CULTURE IN THE BRETON MOVEMENT

Ethnoregionalist movements like those in Brittany appropriate, transform, and deploy complex sets of politicized symbols as a key dimension of struggles in identity politics. Jacqueline Urla argues that ethnic nationalist movements symbolically appropriate modernity as one form of cultural resistance (Urla 1990). This works in two ways. First, the appropriation of modernity by nationalist movements refutes widely held assumptions that modernization inevitably entails the decline of difference through processes of cultural homogenization. Second, this same appropriation challenges the hegemonic view that ethnic cultures and languages are relics of an archaic and traditional past. One important way to appropriate modernity is to make ethnic minority language and cultural expression more "modern", especially in the realms of the sciences and the arts. Thus linguistic reform in Brittany has long sought to create and promote a modern scientific and technical vocabulary in Breton—and is targeted at specific occupational groups like architects, engineers, and health care professionals. In addition, nearly all Breton militants stress the importance of creating novels, plays, films, and television programs in Breton as a way of removing Breton language and culture from the stigmatized ghetto of the rural past and thereby, of course, making Breton language and culture modern, urbane, and sophisticated.

Although the Breton movement has been in organizational decline and disarray since 1981, "Breton cultural nationalism is probably running stronger today than at any other time this century" (Riding 1991). Cultural movements in Brittany—those groups devoted to the preservation and performance of traditional or neo-traditional costume, dance, music, and sports—are far larger and more active than the Breton movement itself. Moreover, there is little overlap between the two. By some estimates, as many as 100 thousand people are presently involved in such cultural associations. To some extent, the growth of these cultural associations is linked to the commodification of Breton culture in the context of tourism, but it is also accurate to say that the groups represent a largely depoliticized expression of cultural difference. In other words, wearing the costumes, dancing the dances, and performing the music are not necessarily accompanied by explicit nationalist political demands.

But an alternative reading of these cultural associations is also possible. On my most recent visit to Brittany (July 1995), I attended a joint session of Basque and Breton performers presenting traditional popular songs and dances from their respective regions in the large public space in front of the Rennes city hall. The performance was organized by the Celtic Circle of Rennes (recently listed among the best performance ensembles in Brittany) with the support of the city government. The setting was dramatic: a stage in front of the Hotel de Ville, a building covered with over one hundred French flags, but with the emblems of Brittany and a Basque flag also clearly visible just behind the stage. On a pleasant Tuesday evening from 9:00 to 11:00 p.m., a crowd of perhaps three hundred people watched first the large Basque ensemble perform their dances with numerous colorful costume changes, then the smaller Breton group, then the Basques again, and finally both groups together as they joined the audience in a closing traditional dance. Without a program or any explanation from the master of ceremonies for the evening, it was impossible for me and, no doubt for most of the audience, to interpret the cultural symbolism of the music or the dances.

How then can we theorize about presentations of regional "traditional" culture which are heavily marked ideologically as linked to the rural and rustic past? For many in the crowd of urban-bourgeoisified Rennais, the dance no doubt served as semi-exotic and partially commodified performance art, but it is also rural/rustic performance art, and thus it exists in a larger political context. Two of these contexts are worth elaborating in more detail.

The Breton movement, and its participants, are "marginal" in any number of contexts—from the region, to France, to the European Union generally. This marginality is certainly political, but it has social and cultural dimensions as well (see Maynard 1992). Anna Tsing (1993) has argued that marginal groups—those that are beyond the peripheries of state power and which lack the institutional means to actively contest hegemonic ideas about representations of their own culture— resort to a variety of ritual and discourse forms to assert the existence of a "human community that deserves autonomy and respect" (Tsing 1993: 101). Popular dance and music—ideologically indexed as both rural and rustic and as traditional as well—represent precisely an assertion of cultural identity within a heavily constrained autonomous space and therefore operate as a form of cultural resistance and empowerment for marginal groups. In this ethnographic example, the setting is particularly relevant since the cultural performance takes place at an urban regional center of French state symbolic and political power, although it should be noted that the long-serving Socialist Party mayor of Rennes has been a sympathetic supporter of Breton cultural production within the city.

A second political context that needs to be explored here involves the multistranded connections between Basque and Breton ethnic politics. There has long been an ideology of solidarity between the various ethnoregionalist social movements which oppose their respective central governments in western Europe, but this ideology is also sometimes transformed into political practice. Beginning in 1991 and continuing through the fall of 1994, the French authorities have arrested about one hundred people in Brittany on suspicion of sheltering and aiding Basque nationalists from ETA (literally "Basque Homeland and Freedom"—a formation that employs violent strategies in political struggle against the Spanish state and has been the target of equally violent state repression). But, "no one has yet been brought to trial, no Basque has been arrested in Brittany nor have any arms or explosives been found which could justify an accusation of collusion with the ETA guerillas . . . it seems that the French judge L. LeVert, in charge of anti-terrorist activities, is intent on proving that there is a pro-ETA network in Brittany" (Heusaff 1994: 8). After an impressive organizing and lobbying effort culminated in a large and peaceful protest in Lannion on September 17, 1994, those Bretons suspected of sheltering Basques from ETA who were among the most recently arrested and jailed were released pending possible future legal action by the French state. The French and Spanish governments actively cooperate in the surveillance and repression of Basque nationalist groups like ETA. For its part, the political Breton movement in general falls somewhat short of active unequivocal condemnation of violence in ethnoregionalist political struggles in the Basque region, and claims ideological solidarity with other oppressed ethnic minorities. So it is not particularly surprising that parallel forms of solidarity would emerge at the level of cultural performance groups. Cultural production in Brittany— in this instance the preservation, creative reconstitution, and performance of rural folkloric dance, music, and costume—is therefore highly politicized and must be understood in a larger political context even though the performances themselves may not entail any explicit ethnoregionalist political discourse, claims, assertions, or demands.

Breton militants have at best an ambivalent view of the cultural movements. One militant, speaking of the largest annual folk festival—the Festival de Cornouaille held every summer at Quimper—said wearily, "Oh, you know, it's like Africans dancing for the white tourists," and he went on to laud the virtues of the Festival Interceltique held at Lorient—a more "modern" expression of Breton culture. Given the weakness of the Breton movement, they have difficulty disavowing any potential allies, and my informant's comment reflects the ambiguities and contradictions militants encounter in the symbolism of "traditional" and "modern" culture. The mostly urban character of the contemporary Breton movement helps explain the ambivalence as well as the cynicism of my informant.

While it is perhaps true that folk festivals in Brittany can be described as either "traditional" or "modern," the boundaries between the two are increasingly blurred. In the 1995 Festival de Cornouaille (July 17–23), traditional Breton and Celtic music and costume were well represented, but then again so were more contemporary forms including performances by Dan ar Braz and Celtic world music groups. The twenty-fifth edition of the Festival Interceltique (August 4–13, 1995) featured numerous performances of traditional songs and dances as well as keynote concerts by popular artists like Simple Minds and Alan Stivell. Even the festival most closely linked to Breton militant politics—the Gouel Broadel ar Brezhoneg (or National Festival of the Breton Language)—held on June 3–4, 1995, combined traditional music, dance, costume, and sports with such modern expressions of Breton culture as the rock groups EV and Stone Age. The most likely explanation for this blurring of boundaries revolves precisely around the continued strength and popularity of performance groups like Celtic Circles and the continued weakness and marginality of Breton militant politics: Breton political activists need and seek out any allies they can find.

A second arena where these contradictory ideas about rurality are played out is the literary debate surrounding Hélias' 1975 book *The Horse of Pride*. The volume is a romanticized, sentimental, and nostalgic ethnographic/autobiographical account of rural agricultural life in the Pays Bigouden (western Brittany) in the early twentieth century. Hélias' goal was "to recreate a Breton-speaking civilization which had almost no contact with French civilization" (348), but, as he laments, "nothing is left of my early civilization but wreckage" (334). While the book achieved great popularity in both France and the United States, it was less popular among Breton militants. For Xavier Grall—whose 1977 response is entitled *Le Cheval Couché* ("The Lying Down Horse")— Hélias represents Brittany as a dead civilization of rural cultivators embedded in some folkloric, archaic vacuum of France's eternal antiquity. Grall, a Breton writer, journalist, and poet, accuses Hélias of shedding crocodile tears for a lost Breton civilization (56), while simultaneously arguing that Hélias himself is a victim of Parisian cultural elitism producing work which appeals primarily to Parisians with second homes in the region; Parisians for whom Bretons are ethnological and archaeological curiosities—the Indians of the Hexagon, as it were. Grall believes that Brittany remains a living culture and society but admits that it could yet perish if Bretons are unable to rid themselves of French ideologies which threaten to make Breton culture exist only in dusty books or museum collections (230).

BRETON RURALITY AS REPRESENTED IN
ETHNOLOGICAL MUSEUMS

A final example of these processes pertains precisely to museum representations of rural Breton culture. In Paris, the Musée National des Arts et Traditions Populaires takes many of its exhibits from the "folkloric periphery" of Brittany—especially *coiffes* (lace headdresses traditionally worn by Breton women) and agricultural implements—and presents them in a timeless, decontextualized format. The Musée de Bretagne, located in Rennes and directed until recently by a Breton militant, represents rurality in a form more consistent with militant than hexagonal ideologies. Their exhibits depicting the late nineteenth and twentieth centuries stress economic change, attempts to overcome economic underdevelopment by diversification and political protest—a far different representation of the periphery. Another museum, located just to the south of Rennes—the Ecomusée du Pays de Rennes—is a "living reconstruction" of rural agricultural life situated primarily in the late nineteenth century, and presents still more complex and ambiguous views of rurality.

The Musée National des Arts et Traditions Populaires (ATP) was originally founded in 1937 by the French ethnologist Georges Henri Rivière as a celebration of France's ancient artisanal and peasant civilization. Located since the early 1970s in the Bois de Boulogne, the ATP is both a museum and a center of research focusing on the ethnology of France. My analysis here focuses only on the "cultural gallery"—a space of roughly 2350 square meters with aproximately five thousand objects on display that is open to the general public.

The ATP is somewhat off the beaten track, a relatively shabby and not much frequented museum that is not even listed in many of the standard tourist guides for Paris. The panel at the entrance to the Cultural Gallery informs the visitor that "more than four thousand objects presented in the context of their use evoke the techniques, customs, beliefs, practices, institutions, and the production of rural society in preindustrial France." There are two kinds of exhibits in the Cultural Gallery. The first is an attempt to reconstruct particular cultural moments—a fishing boat, a kitchen in Brittany, a woodworking shop from the Maine, a barrel making shop (again from Brittany)—with accompanying audio programs designed to evoke and explicate particular productive and social activities. The second type of exhibit presents neutral, austere displays of objects grouped according to topical themes: economic activities, social customs, the life cycle, ritual. In the latter form of exhibit, objects from different French regions and time periods are displayed together, usually with a general text describing the overall theme of the panel. Virtually all of the exhibits are identifiably rural in origin. The objects are nearly always positioned in time and space and are contextualized in terms of *use* but not in reference to how they fit into daily social life at any particular historical moment.

Considerations of time and space are of great significance in the ATPs representations of rurality. Although there appears to be a conscious attempt to include most rural regions of France, some of the largest and most prominent displays—pottery manufacture, a kitchen from Finistère, a barrel making shop, beekeeping—are from Brittany. This suggests that Brittany (and especially Finistére for reasons that I will explain shortly) occupies a large space in the imagination of rural France by the French ethnologists who have constructed these museum representations. Other mythologized folkloric rural peripheries—Basque areas, the Pyrénées, Auverge, Aveyron—are also over-represented in the exhibits on display in July 1995. While the exhibits themselves are changed periodically, this pattern was also visible in my visits to the museum throughout the 1980s. Different regions therefore occupy equivalent yet hierarchically prioritized spaces in the French academic imagination of rurality. These exhibits are frozen in the preindustrial time of France's "traditional society" (generally somewhere between the end of the *ancien régime* and the rural modernization of the 1950s, but some exhibits extend the cultural continuity much further back in time) in the sense that little or no attention is paid to historical transformations of rural life—a trope that thus mirrors Lévi-Strauss' "cold societies" or Fernand Braudel's *"longue durée."*

The ATP's exhibits make an important partial and problematic exception to the decontextualized, timeless, and homogenized representations of rurality, namely the reconstruction of a "common room" from a house in the village of Goulien (Finistère, Lower Brittany), circa 1930. The exhibit contains furniture and household objects—tables, an armoire, a fireplace, an enclosed bed, cooking and eating ware, and a pair of *sabots*, or wooden clogs (shoes that mark both rural and rustic cultural identity and function in militant circles as politicized objects representing past linguistic repression in the region). Items are authentically arranged and daily life is effectively evoked by an accompanying audio program. Yet although the history of the house is described from the time of its initial construction in 1852 to its sale—one would imagine to some Parisians purchasing a second home, but in fact to local people—in the 1960s through the lives of the three generations of Bretons who lived there, the notions of time employed in the texts which accompany the room remain problematic.

Two notions of time and historicity appear in the textual representations of this exhibit. The first involves the assertion of essentialist timelessness: the viewer is assured that even though the exhibit is set around 1930 (before electricity and running water), it "carries the imprint of a manner of living that was characteristic of the nineteenth century in Goulien" and, at another point, that "daily contact with that distant past [going back to pre-Roman times], geographical isolation, and an agricultural economy contributed to the conservation of a traditional lifestyle and the local people seem to have long resisted change." The second notion of time implicated in this exhibit follows the tropes of French ethnological writing on rural France in general and on Brittany—and especially Finistère—in particular (Cuisenier and Segalen 1993; Morin 1970); namely, the trope of modernization theory. In the narratives of French rural ethnography, change has often been understood as a succession of technological innovations—including new agricultural technology and new consumer goods—in the lives of peasants. The museum discussion of change in the Goulien village room conforms to this generalization. The introduction of oil lamps, a wood furnace, a cement floor, electricity, and running water receive privileged attention in the texts accompanying the exhibit. These changes are also connected in a less-than-subtle way to moral commentaries on the disappearance of rural society. In the audio program, the narrator nostalgically laments the loss of traditional "rural" cultures with their strong senses of family, community, and cultural meaning and their replacement by the homogenized and sterile consumer cultures of television and huge supermarkets. It is often the case, however, that urban middle class intellectuals are far more romantically sentimental about the demise of rural farm life than the older Breton farmers to whom I've spoken over the years, who don't particularly regret the passing of rural poverty and economic hardship, but still highly value family and community ties. The story of the room as told by the museum curators at the ATP, then, mirrors the French ethnographic trope of the modernization story (a story frequently told as well by Anglophone anthropologists and historians of western Europe; see Cole 1977; Weber 1976) and is a good example of ethnographic ideas and assumptions being superimposed on museum material culture. This modernization trope, once again, is found in perhaps its most prototypical textual form in the ethnography of Brittany and specifically in Edgar Morin's work on Finistère (1970).

In summary, the ethnological exhibits in this Paris museum tend to treat rural cultures—most notably those of Brittany—in a decontextualized, homogenous, and essentially timeless manner, or alternatively, as part of a rural village modernization story. The relevant questions then become: how exactly do museums in the "periphery" of Brittany represent their own region's rural culture, how do these representations differ from metropolitan versions constructed by French ethnologists in Paris, and how are these representations linked to political discourse and action among militants in Brittany?

The Musée de Bretagne is located in an imposing building in the heart of the city of Rennes. Its displays are organized chronologically from the earliest prehistory of the region to the late twentieth century, and the thematic foci are the history, geography, ethnology, and sociology of Brittany. Although the chronological framework elides any perception of timelessness, rural life—in a region that was primarily rural until the middle of the twentieth century—receives uneven and ambiguous attention and, in general, urban and elite cultures are privileged in the museum's narrative of Brittany's past. Three examples of this privileging of urban elite culture are particularly significant. First, in the room depicting the Middle Ages, the museum curators have this to tell the visitor about rural life:

The outline of a history. . . . Land clearing, often instigated by monks, seems to have stopped towards the XIIIth century. In this rural world, production was mainly for direct consumption. Cereals (rye, wheat and oats) were cultivated, livestock included pigs, cattle and sheep, and bees were kept. . . . Vines covered the slopes east of a line from Lamballe to Vannes.

A marked contrast developed between the interiors of Brittany and the relatively wealthy seaboard. Serfdom disappeared for the most part in the XIth century, and the majority of the peasants turned to the cultivation of new land. Little is known about the activities of the rural world at this time. The XIth century saw the emergence of the small market town, a new form of settlement confined to rural areas. In the XIVth and XVth centuries the cultivation and weaving of hemp and flax contributed to enrich the parishes and encourage outside contacts.

This text is the only detailed explanation of rural life for the Middle Ages part of the exhibit and although plows, grain measuring bowls linked to feudal extraction of surplus, and models of farming villages from the period are on display in this room, much more space is devoted to the cultural production of high art, including numerous texts and a thirteen minute slide show about sculpture and art in Brittany's churches. The overwhelming emphasis is on international trade, urban-based political power, and bigger political events related to autonomous state formation in Brittany (a topic of considerable political significance within the contemporary Breton movement which will be discussed later).

A still more conspicuous example of the privileging of the urban in this regional museum is found in the "Brittany of the *Ancien Régime*— 1532–1789" section. This very large room contains period drawings, maps, texts, and material culture representing the political and social stuctures of the time, but with a highly visible prioritizing of urban places and of intellectual, political, and cultural elites. For example, in the display depicting the bourgeoisie, a detailed text on the commercial wealth, social and political influence, and cultural production of this urban group is accompanied by an astonishing array of objects: four portraits, maps of three principal port cities (Lorient, St.-Malo, Nantes), three books, ceramics from India, porcelain from the Indies, tea boxes from China, silver candlesticks, a silver wine taster, a platter and pitcher in pewter, and a number of other objects. In sharp contrast, however, the section on the peasantry during the *ancien régime* has only one small and nearly hidden text panel describing the exploitation and poverty of rural cultivators with virtually no associated material culture except for a 1785 armoire from the Cornouaille area, loaned to the museum by, ironically enough, the ATP. Since it is not directly linked to the text on the peasantry, the visitor might conclude from its ornate character that this piece of furniture belonged to the "minority of rich cultivators" mentioned in the text. Overall, the aspects of Brittany's historical past marked as rural and rustic remain invisible and unnoticed among the far more central displays of the wealth, cultural production, and power of urban elites. A clearly symbolized hierarchy of place emerges in this part of the museum despite some minor ambiguities such as the caption on a die stamp used by the bourgeoisie to mark bolts of cloth which notes that "the cloth industry, principally domestic and rural, furnished the only important export" (and hence a significant source of elite wealth) prior to the industry's collapse in the seventeenth century due to foreign competition. Here, then, the rural foundations of Breton regional culture are submerged in a narrative stressing the political and cultural power of urban elites, while history is told as a particular form of politicized discourse.

The third key representation of rurality in the Musée de Bretagne is found in the "Modern Brittany" (1789–1914) displays. This large, well-lighted room further complicates the analysis as the displays focus primarily on rural life: agricultural technology, rural artisanal production (metal working), household objects (including yet another set of armoires, this time accompanied by a caption explaining how furniture constituted a form of peasant investment) and, most spectacularly, a collection of colorful everyday and ritual costumes from the various regions (*pays*) which make up Brittany. Unlike the ATP, this museum is careful to show intra-regional, gender and superficial functional variation in costume, but as in the view from Paris, there is no explanation of how any of the objects were used. While this room focuses on technology, cultural creativity, and distinctive regional variation in rural Brittany during the late nineteenth century, and is moreover in sharp contrast to the differential treatment of rural versus urban culture in the preceeding *"Ancien Régime"* exhibit, the costumes convey a contemporary folkloric reconstruction commodified for tourism. In the utter absence of any elaborate textual explanation of their symbolism or function, the costumes appear colorful but lifeless, exotically folkloric but clearly not "modern" and therefore very similar to the hierarchically devalued representations of rurality seen in the rest of the museum. As of July 1995, the room on "Contemporary Brittany" was closed for renovation (actually for furniture storage) but my previous visits to the museum suggest that regional industrial development and forms of worker protest received treatment nearly equal to that of the perhaps more significant transformations in agriculture and forms of peasant protest. The absence of a contemporary Brittany in the museum's current displays, however, might lead visitors to believe that the region's history and culture effectively end around 1914. I return now to the issue of how Breton militants tell their own version of regional history and how these narratives affect the positioning of rurality in the region's identity politics.

HISTORICAL CONSCIOUSNESS AND
ETHNOREGIONALIST IDEOLOGY

Eugen Weber, in his monumental work *Peasants Into Frenchmen* (1976), writes:

> City dwellers, who often (as in the colonial cities of Brittany) did not understand the rural language, despised the peasants, exaggerated their savagery, insisted on the more picturesque—hence backward—aspects of their activities, and sometimes compared them unfavorably with other colonial peoples in North Africa and the New World. In nineteenth century Brest it was not unusual to hear the surrounding countryside

described as "the bush": *brousse* or *cambrousse*. But colonial parallels
were little needed when the armory of prejudice was so well stocked:
"Potatoes for the pigs, the peels for the Bretons." (1976: 6)

Brittany's association with a colonial metaphor is of great significance
to an ethnographic and historical understanding of Breton ethnoregionalist political struggle. Since 1970, Breton intellectuals have produced histories of Brittany which represent five hundred years of
French-Breton relations as colonial domination. While these revision-
ist accounts are essentially "historically accurate," their political significance lies elsewhere. Breton activists use their accounts as counter-
hegemonic discourse in opposition to French nation-state ideologies
stressing the civilizing influence of Paris over the provinces. This
attempt to show how a history of forced cultural assimilation and
internal colonialism adversely affects all Bretons today is a key symbolic basis for contemporary ethnic political action.

In *The Invention of Tradition*, Eric Hobsbawm writes that "all
invented traditions, so far as possible, use history as a legitimator of
action and cement of social cohesion" (1983: 12). Breton militants organize both their consciousness of everyday life and their political struggle around intertwined notions of the history of collective repression
experienced by the Breton people and personal memory of cultural or
economic discrimination. In applying the term "invented tradition" to
a Breton construction of French-Breton history, I recognize that all histories—including "official national histories," of course—are invented
to some degree, and are intrinsically no more and no less invented
("ideological constructions of the nation-state") than versions offered
by social movements opposing the French state.

Two of the most prominent loci of the production of Breton historical knowledge are Skol Vreizh ("Breton School") and Dalc'homp Sonj
(literally, "let us remember," also referred to as the Breton Historical
Association). Skol Vreizh consists of a team of twenty historians, mainly instructors and researchers from the Universities of Rennes and
Brest, but also teachers from high schools throughout Brittany. Since
1970 Skol Vreizh has produced a five volume *History of Brittany and*

the Celtic Nations, ranging from prehistory to the present. Originally intended for secondary school students, these books are now targeted for an adult reading public. They are widely available in bookstores throughout Brittany, and have sold over 100 thousand copies. Dalc' homp Sonj consists of over 350 members divided into thirteen local committees whose general goal is to popularize and disseminate the history of Brittany. In 1983, the association began publishing a glossy quarterly historical review by the same name.

While these publications span a wide range of topics, three points clearly emerge. First, many current and former Breton militants are active as researchers and writers in both groups. Second, an avowed goal of Skol Vreizh and Dalc' homp Sonj is to present Breton history to a wide audience since the history of Brittany is largely ignored in French schools. As Jean-Jacques Monnier (Skol Vreizh) put it, "one could very well have followed with passion French history in school without ever having heard of the history of Brittany." Monnier is also an important figure in the largest Breton political party, the Democratic Breton Union. Here, the political agenda is to demonstrate that Brittany and the Breton people have a history and identity distinct from that of France. Third, much of the content of these publications deals precisely with the chronicle of oppression and resistance, both recent and not so recent, so vital to the symbolic construction of Breton political struggle. So these histories have a fundamental political function in much the same way that Hobsbawm suggests.

During my fieldwork in 1987, a two volume work on *The Breton State in the Fourteenth and Fifthteenth Centuries: Dukes, Money and Men*, written by Jean Kerhervé of Skol Vreizh and the University at Brest, appeared. It is primarily a detailed description of fiscal and administrative structures in Brittany prior to the French annexation of the region. I was initially puzzled by the attention such a weighty historical tome generated in the Breton militant press. But by the end of my fieldwork, its significance was clear: Brittany was portrayed as a prosperous, autonomous, well-functioning, and well-organized entity conquered by the expanding French monarchy. Such an understanding of the historical past is an all-important ideological underpinning of the Breton ethnonationalism of the present (for another perspective focusing on archaeological research, see Dietler 1994). If there is a French nation-state hegemonic ideology, it would be one glorifying the inevitable, natural, and beneficial expansion of French language, culture, and civilization throughout the hexagon, and indeed throughout France's colonial possessions as well; thus the production of Breton historical knowledge functions here as a form of counter-hegemony.

But this knowledge is a particular kind of counter-hegemony—as the museum representations demonstrate, "rural" and "urban" dimensions of regional history are hierarchically segmented with urban places, elites, cultural production, and state formation processes receiving privileged attention while the rural places and peasants, though not completely ignored, are marginalized by comparison or, alternatively, decontextualized and removed from their historical connections. This hierarchical segmentation of historical knowledge is closely related to the prinicipal contradictions of tradition and modernity discussed at the beginning of this essay, but it is also an outcome of the political culture of Breton militants—a culture in which the largely middle class, highly educated activists are themselves products of French education, language, and culture which share, at least implicitly, some of the values alluded to by Eugen Weber. More generally, militant beliefs—in a historical Breton state and civilization subjected to French conquest and, in some militant ideologies, the possibility of recreating an autonomous independent Breton state through political struggle—lead activists to specific forms of historical narrative which stress independent state formation, multiple forms of oppression experienced historically and at present by the Breton people, resistance to the expansion of French influence in Brittany, and indigenous expressions of cultural creativity and achievement. These forms of historical consciousness, in turn, tend to deny and devalue rurality as being marginal—indeed incidental—to these processes.

MORE RECENT MUSEUM REPRESENTATIONS OF RURALITY
IN BRITTANY (WHERE MODERNITY AND RURALITY FINALLY
INTERSECT WITH COMFORT)

Walking south from the rapidly gentrifying old center of Rennes with its commercial centers, boutiques, bars, and restaurants, one passes by some older residential quarters, by the women's prison, then by some newer housing developments, high-rise apartments, a shopping mall. Eventually, over the expressways which circle the city until, barely five kilometers from an urban and bourgeois starting point, one discovers a rural looking countryside, complete with fields and cows. It is here that a tourist or ethnographer will find the Ecomusée du Pays de Rennes. Developed in the 1980s and opened in June 1987, this fifteen-hectare site is a working farm/plant and animal conservatory/ historical theme park and museum principally devoted to representing and explaining rural farm life in the latter half of the nineteenth century although the exhibits trace the farm's history back to its origins in the 13th century.

This is a very different sort of museum. Using a combination of audio visual programs, demonstrations of rural production practices such as cider making, displays of artifacts, technology, and costumes, and an amazing wealth of accompanying explanatory text, the curators have done some interesting cultural work presenting and validating rurality. Some of the text is worth translating in detail:

> From big market town to regional capital. In 1842, Rennes was only a big market town in the middle of the countryside and it had a population of 35 thousand. At the end of the twentieth century, the rural space was reduced to a zone to the northwest in a city that has nearly 200 thousand inhabitants. Several facts will help in understanding this transformation.

The panel, in the now too familiar story line of modernization, goes on to give a chronology of changes including railroads, a water system, urban development, and industrial implantation.

Rennes—a rural commune from 1856 to 1986. 333 farms, 495 if one includes those of agricultural day laborers, such is the face of Rennes in 1856, one year before the arrival of the railroad. In 1986, there remained around fifty farms, especially in the northwest zone reserved for agricultural activities. The rapidity of this transformation in the third quarter of the twentieth century has been spectacular.

And above the entrance to the exhibits on the third floor:

Living in the region of Rennes. How did the men and women use to live? Their life circumstances, clothing, food, language reveal their social milieu. One can see the longstanding difference between rural and urban milieus despite their proximity and the frequent exchanges between city and countryside. The special character of rural life is found above all in the rhythm of daily life regulated by the unfolding of the seasons and the succession of agricultural work.

This is a frequently revisited theme in the Ecomusée: that the past is really not so distant from the present, and that rurality and the urban are, indeed, close neighbors in both time and space. Another theme is the attempt to give the earlier owners and inhabitants of the farm—by detailing their business deals, inheritances, marriages, and shifting fortunes—names, faces, voices, personalities, and humanity. This is a far more personalized and nuanced view of rurality. While the museum is quite large and complicated in its structure, several significant points of contrast can be developed between this site and the others previously described in this chapter.

Overall, the Ecomusée is a *living* museum of rurality (necessarily so since it still operates as a farm in a limited and specific way, and its ongoing activities make the museum especially popular with groups of school children) which stresses the following themes:

1) social and economic transformations over various time frames using modernization as a trope;

2) a rural world which has only recently been transformed and which, indeed, changed very slowly until the early to mid-twentieth century;

3) a rural world whose inhabitants are personalized, individual-
ized and humanized rather than categorized, homogenized, and symbolically decontextualized;

4) the connections between the agricultural past and the agricultural present through the functions of the museum as working farm
and genetic conservatory of domesticated crops and livestock; and
finally

5) the existence of social class as well as historical variation in this
recently transformed rural world of the late nineteenth and early
twentieth centuries (a theme conspicuously absent in the representations of rurality in the other museums discussed).

In presenting these themes, the museum evokes quite effectively
the lived experience of daily rural life: work, food, and rituals are all
presented in ways that are not static, symbolically empty, or monolithic through a heavy reliance on multi-media forms of communication.
Nevertheless, the gendered audiovisual presentations of older women
describing traditional and regionally distinctive cooking recipes and
older men describing traditional farming and agricultural processing
techniques convincingly construct the image of this world as belonging to the time of the *grandmères* and *grandpères* of, if not exactly the
children visiting the museum, then certainly those of their parents.

CONCLUSION

One complicated and puzzling issue raised by the Ecomusée is that
one of the people behind its creation—Jean-Yves Veillard—is also
heavily involved in the Musée de Bretagne, and was one of the original
founders of the largest Breton political party, the Democratic Breton
Union. The ambiguity of the categories "rural" and "traditional" in
militant constructions of Breton cultural identity once again becomes
apparent.

These ambiguities are manifested in still other forms. In Brittany,
there are "neo-ruralists"—back to the land, counter-cultural militants
who practice organic farming and speak their newly learned Breton to
their livestock much to the bewilderment and cynical amusement of

older Breton-speaking farmers. In Brittany, it is common for adults in militant-sponsored Breton language classes to spend time working on a farm with popular Breton speakers for both linguistic practice and to try to get in touch with the "authentic" culture and language of the Breton "people." For various reasons—mostly having to do with linguistic competence and comfort—these encounters between the rural and urban speakers tend to be frustrating and exhausting for both parties. Yet the underlying reality of Breton ethnic politics remains: the movement is primarily urban, intellectual, and middle class in form, and its militants have come to rely on certain sets of symbols (principally of linguistic, cultural, and economic oppression) in their not always successful attempts at political mobilization. Given the ideological association between rurality and tradition discussed earler in this essay, and the militant need for distinctively "modern" (and urban) Breton culture exhibited in its core constituency, it is not surprising that "rurality" would occupy an ambivalent, ambiguous, and marginalized space in militant constructions of Breton identity. It is also probable that the current trend toward incorporation of "traditional" and "rural" cultural elements into Breton ethnoregionalist discourse and practice is a product of the continued—and perhaps greater—political weakness of the movement over the past decade, since it is clear that cultural associations are more popular in the region than Breton autonomist political parties.

While rurality (and in the popular and academic French imaginations, rusticity) lies at the historical core of Breton identity, the largely urban, middle class, and intellectual social form of the Breton movement leads to an ambiguous embracing and (mostly) denying of those powerful symbols. While Breton language and culture are highly associated in the French (and Breton as well) popular imaginations with an historically indeterminate, folkloric rural, and rustic past, the cultural and political contradictions of the Breton movement—most particularly the militant imperative to create modern and urban forms of Breton culture and language—lead those militants, while ideologically and rhetorically prioritizing rurality as profound cultural authenticity, to in fact marginalize images of the rural in their constructions of regional identity and history. These potentially powerful symbolic codes are therefore largely elided from militant discourse and practice even though they could well be deployed to make ethnoregionalism a more broad-based political force in Brittany since they appeal to a far larger segment of the region's population. Contradictions like these explain, in part, the limited efficacy of the Breton political agenda in the late twentieth century.

NOTE

My research was supported financially by the Council for European Studies, the Ph.D. Program in Anthropology of the City University of New York, and Sigma Xi. Numerous people have made useful comments on this work: Barbara Ching, Gerald Creed, Michèle D. Dominy, Karen Frojen, Edward Hansen, Donna Kerner, Aisha Khan, Chris Leonard, Allyson Purpura, Susan Carol Rogers, Jane Schneider, Malve von Hassell, and Eric Wolf. I thank all of them for their help.

REFERENCES

Cole, John W. 1977. "Anthropology Comes Part-Way Home: Community Studies in Europe." *Annual Review of Anthropology* 6: 349–78.

Cuisenier, Jean, and Martine Segalen. 1993. *Ethnologie de la France*. Presses Universitaires de France.

Dietler, Michael. 1994. "'Our Ancestors the Gauls': Archaeology, Ethnic Nationalism, and the Manipulation of Celtic Identity in Modern Europe." *American Anthropologist* 96: 584–605.

Gourevitch, Peter A. 1979. "The Re-emergence of 'Peripheral Nationalisms': Some Comparative Speculations on the Spatial Distribution of Political Leadership and Economic Growth." *Comparative Studies in Society and History* 21: 302–22.

Grall, Xavier. 1977. *Le Cheval Couché: Réponse au Cheval d'orgueil*. Librairie Hachette.

Hélias, Pierre-Jakez. 1978. *The Horse of Pride: Life in a Breton Village*. New Haven: Yale University Press.

Heusaff, Alan. 1994. "Repression of Breton-Basque Solidarity." *Carn* 88: 8.

Hobsbawm, Eric. 1983. "Introduction." In Eric Hobsbawm and Terence Ranger, eds., *The Invention of Tradition*. New York: Cambridge University Press.

Kerhervé, Jean. *L'état Breton aux 14e et 15e siècles: Les ducs, l'argent et les hommes*. St.-Malo: Maloire, 1987.

Kuter, Lois. 1985. "Labeling People: Who Are the Bretons?" *Anthropological Quarterly* 58: 13–29.

Maynard, David. 1992. "Ideology, Collective Action and Cultural Identity in the Breton Movement." Ph.D. Dissertation, City University of New York.

McDonald, Maryon. 1989. *"We Are Not French!": Language, Culture, and Identity in Brittany*. New York: Routledge.

Morin, Edgar. 1970. *The Red and the White: Report From a French Village*. New York: Random House.

Riding, Alan. 1991. "Celts and Proud of It (Even if They are French)." *The New York Times*, August 2.

Tsing, Anna Lowenhaupt. 1993. *In the Realm of the Diamond Queen: Marginality in an Out-of-the-Way Place*. Princeton, NJ: Princeton University Press.

Urla, Jacqueline. 1990. "Contesting Modernities: The Resistance in Ethnic Minority Cultural Politics." Paper presented at the Annual Meetings of the American Anthropological Association, New Orleans.

Weber, Eugen. 1976. *Peasants Into Frenchmen: The Modernization of Rural France 1870–1914*. Stanford: Stanford University Press.

The Rise and Fall of "Peasantry" as a Culturally Constructed National Elite in Israel

ISRAEL has had a unique opportunity to invent and establish a culture for itself. In the span of about a half a century, a whole array of culture—language, dress, customs, rituals, meanings, and values—was created for and by an immigrant population whose immediate origins were mainly Eastern and Western European, North African, and Western Asian. The process by which this occurred has been written about fairly extensively;[1] I shall only address a part of it, the emergence of a culturally constructed "peasantry" as an elite class, and its subsequent decline from moral as well as political power. Occurring within the last fifty years, the Israeli trajectory provides a concentrated instance of rural devaluation often more protracted elsewhere. As such, it may provide special insights into the factors affecting this development. Towards that goal, I attempt to account for the declining value of rural identity within Israeli national identity.

THE PEASANT-PIONEER IMAGE

The historical significance of this culturally constructed peasantry is derived from its incorporation into the ideology of Zionist Socialism in the early years of this century by what is known as the "Second Aliya," the wave of Jewish immigrants to Israel of that period. These were the principal architects of the contemporary State of Israel and its social foundations. The underlying idea is as follows: the Jews had fallen into a state of pitiable degeneracy and weakness through their dependency on urban capitalism, alienated from nature and their own bodies. This critique applied not only to the Jewish businessman, filthied by money and the exploitation of others' labor, but also to the traditional orthodox religious scholars, supported by charity. Both were objects of contempt for Zionist radicals.

To save themselves, Jews had to engage in manual labor, to learn to support themselves by their own efforts, particularly through farming.[2] At the same time, the land of Israel also required salvation: in the north, malarial swamps had made sites of Biblical fame uninhabitable, while elsewhere, overgrazing had produced deserts where there had once been forests and farms. The "new" Jews would save themselves and the land at once, by farming—draining the swamps and greening the desert, *with their own hands*. What Jews were told to leave behind was urban: the ghetto and the little Jewish town (shtetl). What they were told to embrace was rural: the farms that would spring from their restoration of the ruined land and which would provide their material sustenance.

The image of the Jewish rural population at the time of the founding of modern Israel is consequently associated in Israeli culture with the heroic notion of "pioneering" and these settlers are frequently referred to as "pioneers." Amos Oz, one of Israel's most distinguished contemporary writers, encapsulates the heroic image of the pioneer perfectly:

They came to a bare and baring land, where the harsh climate and the grinding toil and the loneliness of the whispering nights stripped a man naked of every possible disguise. And each and every one of them was revealed in the nakedness of his soul, without mercy or shade.

Many were broken. They fled from the bleak encampment, or from the Land, or from life. The first generations experienced waves of suicides and scandalous defections of the 'misled' and quiet defections by the dejected and depressed. Some went home to the *shtetl* to mummy and daddy. Others went to 'seek their fortunes' in America or elsewhere.

And those who remained? They seemed to be the product of a Darwinian natural selection: big, strong, powerful, logical, hard as stone statues, tough with themselves and with others. Some became celibate; here and there a disguised fanaticism emerged; you view them with mixed feelings, now they are old.

They were devotedly attached to an idea, the essence of which was a wonderful yet terrible straining towards a superhuman 'purity.' To leap free from the shackles of flesh and blood and to resemble gods or giants of yore. To set up in these bleak places communes of equal partners that would be not only a spearhead of the Zionist enterprise and the Jewish people but also the vanguard of a worldwide transformation, a reform of the world and the individual by means of a radical change in the conditions of life that appeared to be entirely natural and essential for human existence: property, competition, hierarchy, material rewards and punishments. All these were consigned to extinction, so that a new chapter would open. (1995: 122–123)

The rural institution created to implement the pioneer's ideology, to organize the work of establishing a new Jewish presence in Israel, and to build up the infrastructure of farming, was the famous *kibbutz* (pl. *kibbutzim*), a rural commune. Its members ideally owned no private property, shared all work, ate together, raised their children together, recognized no inequality, and depended on the labor of their own hands. Thus, the rural ideal was not a replication of a stereotypical peasant/farmer, but a new way of life in the countryside, a new identity altogether, despite romantic notions about rurality and salvation. Life in the kibbutz has been the subject of fascination by non-Israelis as well as Israelis for many decades, a fascination which has produced a huge literature.[3]

The fact that the kibbutz has held a privileged place in Israeli society and culture has received less attention, at least from outsiders. However, it has been pointed out frequently that while the kibbutz inhabitants never constituted more than ten percent of the Jewish population of modern Israel, they have received subsidies, and have contributed national leaders, far out of proportion to their numbers (Arian 1967). Such privilege makes for a very odd, unusual sort of peasantry indeed.[4] The contribution of the kibbutz to the Israeli leadership in the early days of the State meant that it held special influence in the Israeli Labor Party, which held power until 1977. Consequently, state policies favored the interests of the kibbutz and the rural sector it dominated when the state was founded. Political clout had material benefits as well as social ones. The simplicity of poverty adulated by the founding ideologists imagining a rural life free of urban excesses was, paradoxically, to be undermined by the strength of the kibbutzim during the period of Labor Party power. Sons and daughters of the kibbutz became, disproportionately, members of Israel's "aristocratic elite." Not that kibbutz life actually entailed the urban excesses so repellent to the founders—it did not. But material benefits of political influence—security, prosperity—later became targets of urban resentment and generated a contradictory image of Israeli rurality.

THE NEW PEASANTS: "RELUCTANT PIONEERS"

For a variety of reasons, the founders of the new Israeli state and society felt compelled to reject traditions of Diaspora Jewish society associated with the countries from which immigrants arrived. First, while analysts of the Jewish situation in nineteenth-century Europe understood the role of externalities in the oppression of Jews, many also viewed Jewish customs which had arisen in *shtetl* and *ghetto* society as themselves sources of oppression; such customs thus had to be shed to liberate the Jews.[5] Second, the melding of a new Jewish society for Israel out of immigrants from so many different countries and ethnographic traditions required the creation of commonalities and the rejection of differences. An alternative culture to the multitudes of interpretations of Jewish tradition in the Diaspora was seen as an urgent need for a society of immigrants.

A third element is rarely addressed directly. After the establishment of the State in 1948, large waves of immigrants came from Third World countries, particularly North Africa and the Middle East. If the customs and practices of the *shtetl* and the *ghetto* were regarded as old-fashioned and contemptible by an earlier generation, those of the Jews of the Third World were at least equally disdained in the 1950s by the new Israelis of immediate European origin (Heller 1973, Shama and Iris 1977). By this time, an entire army of "leaders," *madrichim*, had been organized to indoctrinate the new immigrants in the ways of *Israelis*— many of which were in the process of being invented (see Weintraub, et al. 1971, and Willner 1970).

National planners decided to settle many of the new immigrants into rural communities and new towns near the borders of the new nation, in part for reasons of defense, in part for the purpose of spreading economic development geographically. But these planners perceived the now-established kibbutz as an inappropriate form of organization for the Third World immigrants, too radical a departure from their own customs. Instead, those destined for farming were settled in communities which took their form from a less famous early alternative to the kibbutz, the *moshav* (pl. *moshavim*), a kind of socialist cooperative which allowed for private family life and farming activities.

This placement led to the creation of an alternative identity and another type of "peasant" for rural Israel, somewhat less "heroic" than the early kibbutz pioneers but still heroic, still pioneers, and far closer to the traditional conception of a peasant. The moshavnik was not a radical communalist, but a villager with his own donkey (later, a tractor) and little house and small plot of land. Of course, the immigrants had to be *taught* to be peasants of this sort; most had been urban artisans or merchants before immigrating to Israel.

While the first of the moshavim were founded in the 1920's, it was only after the establishment of the state and the decision to settle immigrants from non-European backgrounds (as well as immigrants from European backgrounds) in such communities that the moshavim began to outnumber the kibbutzim, and they remain the predominant form of Jewish rural settlement. In the 1950's and 60's, they were studied and written about fairly extensively by sociologists and anthropologists, but by the late 70's and 80's there was a sharp decline in the number of studies and publications about these communities (Schwartz 1995b). There was never a body of more general literature about the moshav comparable to that about the kibbutz for the wider public.

The newer settlements enjoyed the benefits of the experience of their teachers, infrastructure such as roads and market towns, and institutions such as banks, which were not available to the pioneers. But more importantly, from their perspective, they had the disadvantage not only of being newcomers, but also of having only the land that was left after the pioneers had taken the best land for themselves. The stereotypical rural settler of the 1950's was, in the words of one Israeli anthropologist, a "reluctant pioneer," of North African or Middle Eastern origin, less than fully competent in modern ways, in need of state patronage (Weingrod 1966). Anthropologists documented the newcomers' resistance to the imposition of rural identity as well as rural livelihood upon them; they frequently sought employment in towns. But because the state continued to regard rural settlement as crucial to the well-being of the nation, for reasons of defense, self-sufficiency, and geographic population distribution, this patronage continued—the politically powerful veteran communities received their subsidies, and the much weaker new communities benefitted and received further assistance precisely because they were weak (see Shapiro 1971).

Both types of community saw themselves as serving the interests of the nation. The veteran kibbutzim not only had long records of service defending the frontiers, contributing soldiers who had suffered casualties far out of proportion to their numbers, and long records of service by members to government and paragovernmental agencies, but knew themselves to have been pioneers and creators of Israeli society. The newer communities saw themselves as more exploited, obliged to live in remote areas for the sake of national security, to struggle to create arable land, to live a hard life at great personal sacrifice.

THE DECLINE OF THE PEASANT ELITE

In the 1980's, the image of the rural settler had fallen from grace, as projected in the national media and in the conversations of urban dwellers. Urbanites, some 95 percent of the population, increasingly regarded both moshavim and kibbutzim as unduly privileged. The expression of resentment took the form of criticism of lifestyle and economic irresponsibility at the expense of the wider public.[6] A typical example of media coverage, though more moderate than many, was an article in the English-language *Jerusalem Post* which recounted that

> Living standards and spending habits that were shaped in the get-rich-quick atmosphere of the '70's and early '80's failed to adjust to the sudden change brought on by the austerity plan. As an official of the Settlement Department put it: "A lot of farmers got used to big houses, fancy cars and trips abroad. In the city, people were forced to cut their living standards when things tightened up. On many moshavim, though, the easy money atmosphere still prevailed." (Hoffman 1986: 9)

To understand this mode of disapproval it is important to know that Israelis have described themselves as having a pervasive fear of being taken for "suckers" (in Israel, the Yiddish term *"frier"* is used) (Chafets 1986: 197–223; Kressel 1995). This fear of having been hoodwinked into working for some unworthy person's benefit may be the outcome of Israelis' experiences with socialism—an issue to explore at another time. In any case, the suggestion that rural people were living well and urban people were paying for it was the encapsulation of a kind of anger and resentment characteristic of Israelis at this time.

But the fact that farmers were living well, better than most middle-class Israelis, was hardly adequate to account for their fall from grace in Israeli popular opinion—including, to a certain extent, their own. Rather, this was the outcome of a long and complex process of change, both political and economic, which seriously undermined the power of the rural elite and all it represented.

ECONOMIC CHANGES

1. *Overproduction*: An early step toward change occurred in the early 1960's, when Israel discovered itself more than self-sufficient in basic foodstuffs, and began to limit farm production with quotas dictating the quantities of locally marketed products farming communities could sell at subsidized prices (see Baldwin 1972, for a case study). Veteran communities were privileged in the allocation of subsidies, much to the resentment of new settlers. Newcomers felt that kibbutzniks were selfishly grabbing up most of the resources, with veteran moshavniks not far behind in the competition.

2. *Labor and Ethnicity*: A large leap in the direction of change occurred as a result of the 1967 war, which not only reduced threats along the borders, but created conditions for a huge influx of cheap Arab labor. While settlements were supposed to support themselves by their own labor, small farmers became increasingly dependent upon Arab labor (and to a lesser extent on Jewish labor, primarily Arabic-speaking Jewish immigrants from Third World countries), engaging in the type of exploitation which they were founded to eliminate. The use of Arab labor seriously altered the attitude of moshav dwellers toward farm labor itself; women and children began to avoid farm work in part to avoid association with Arab workers, and male farmers became managers of workers rather than workers themselves (Kressel 1995). Meanwhile, kibbutzim, having shifted to mechanization for their larger-scale field operations, also required little actual farm labor from their members, and turned to factory production as a prime source of income and employment.[7] The hope that manual labor would lead to personal and national salvation had eroded, bit by bit, and with it, an important part of the *ideological* justification for state support of the rural Jewish community.

3. *Prosperity*: Economic conditions had changed fairly radically from the time of the settlement process of the 1950's, bearing testimony to the astonishing success of Israel's development efforts. Farming rapidly became mechanized, reducing dependence upon animal and human labor. Farmers grew steadily more prosperous, and their lifestyles by and large reflected this prosperity. By the 1980's, most were living in accommodations far more pleasant than their urban counterparts, enjoying fresh air, greenery, often lovely community amenities, excellent and spacious housing (unlike the cramped quarters of urban apartment dwellers), and fairly easy access to excellent schools and health care facilities—indeed, easy access to cities and anything they had to offer. This prosperity is owed in part to an economic boom, in part to the "easy money" of an inflationary government economic policy, and in part to a willingness on the part of the rural communities to spend money on improving their standard of living. However, it is hard to appear heroic or peasant-like when you have a community swimming pool and your own air-conditioned car, a three-bedroom ranch-style house, and a big grassy lawn with a flowered border, and you spend your leisure hours tending these bourgeois possessions.

4. *Financial Collapse*: Success in farm production was costly in market terms—worldwide, the same process repeated itself. Farmers, obliged to incur debts to pay for new technology in order to compete in the marketplace, could not bring in sufficient income to pay their debts. High levels of inflation in Israel disguised this basic fact from farmers for a time, but by the early 1980's, the nation was obliged to pursue austerity measures to curb inflation. Farmers' debts mounted. Finally, by 1986, their lending institutions were thrown into bankruptcy (Schwartz 1995a, 1995c). The population at large, by now regarding the farming sector with a jaundiced eye, was reluctant to bail out the farmers again; the rightist Likud Party and its coalition government leaders, unsympathetic to the rural sector in the first place, were not eager to help out, for reasons to be addressed below.

POLITICS

1. *The "Upheaval"*: In 1977, for the first time in national history, the ruling Labor Party was ousted from office. So fundamental a change was this that the election has been termed "the upheaval" in the popular and not-so-popular press. The overthrow of the Labor Party is inseparable from disillusionment with its leaders, the Pioneers and their offspring, the "aristocratic elite" of Israeli society, the sons and daughters of the kibbutzim and the moshavim. And this disillusionment is, more frequently than not, traced to the failed Yom Kippur War of 1973. As journalist Ze'ev Chafets put it,

> For decades the people had abdicated any real responsibility, preferring to rely on the judgement and leadership of the pioneer establishment and their sons. But the war had let a genie out of the bottle. For decades the pioneers had seemed larger than life, and had fostered great expectations. In 1973 these expectations had been disappointed—and now, four years later, the pioneer would have to pay. (Chafets 1985: 48)

2. *Politics of Ethnicity*: The national elections of 1977 dealt a huge blow to the political power of the rural sector (Sherman 1982). The Labor Party had been the mainstay of the kibbutzim, its veteran founders came disproportionately from old kibbutzim, and its ideology was supportive of both kibbutzim and moshavim. The Likud Party had its support in the urban sector, and appealed to the immigrants from Third World countries (and their offspring) who felt disenfranchised by the Labor Party, whose roots and founding members were identified with Eastern and Western Europe. The Likud promised them they would no longer be left out. It offered recognition to the more conservative, particularly religious, elements of society, as well as to the ethnic Jewish minorities. The melting pot was out, cultural diversity was in.

The rage of the Sephardic (mainly Israeli Jews of non-European origin) population was nowhere more evident than in the isolated "development towns." Yael Yishai writes,

The hostility of the development towns to kibbutzim reached its peak during the 1981 general election campaign, when kibbutz members were accused in a campaign advertisement in a local newspaper as being 'bloodthirsty beasts feeding on Kiryat Shmona' (a development town). On the other hand, kibbutzim have claimed that their members are engaged in voluntary work for the benefit of development towns, and that in 1978–79 there were 2,500 of their members engaged in such work in twenty-five development towns. Far from being grateful, many of the urban residents regard such efforts as an unwelcome intrusion under the guise of philanthropic activities; and they were particularly resentful of the part played by such kibbutz volunteers during the election campaign. Oriental Jews see the co-operative settlements, and the Labor party to which they are affiliated, as symbols of economic exploitation, of the affluent 'first Israel', contrasting with the salaried workers employed in the regional enterprises of the kibbutzim. They therefore did not hesitate to express their frustration and resentment by voting against the Labor alignment and for the Likud. This hostility did not fade after the general election. In September 1981, the Prime Minister was reported to have referred in a radio interview to members of kibbutzim as 'arrogant millionaires enjoying their swimming pools.' This accusation led to a vociferous public debate, which exacerbated the existing friction and estrangement. (1982: 237)

3. *Settlement of the Occupied Territories*: The losses of the 1973 war and the subsequent peace settlement with Egypt by the Likud government had special consequences for the rural sector and its image among the population at large. The Likud government promoted settlement of the captured territories, seeing this as an opportunity to channel money from government to political parties which supported it, including the radical religious right. Ze'ev Chafets writes

The emergence of the Gush Emunim movement [a movement of radical religious settlers of the occupied territories] shortly after the Yom Kippur War constituted a double opportunity for the young orthodox sabras [native-born Israelis]: to defend the God-given patrimony and, for the first time, to become centrally involved in the country's political life. Pioneering had always been the key to 'Israeliness,' and Gush Emunim seized the technique and vocabulary of the early Labor Zionist settlers in its efforts to 'create facts' in the disputed territory. (1985: 159–60)

However, while the Sephardic right did not oppose this new settlement movement (Yishai 1982), it did not become very popular; the political left strenuously opposed it, and it was a source of embarrassment and anxiety to the majority of moderates. Much of the money directed toward new settlement, then, was invested in activities which a large proportion of Israelis disapproved of, and in communities whose purpose and ideals, while Zionistic, were in sharp opposition to those of the founding fathers of the nation and its established rural sector. There was considerable public resentment toward subsidies for this type of settlement, but the resentment spread to subsidies for the rural sector in general. Then, when the peace with Egypt was negotiated, settlers who had taken advantage of Likud policy to settle in the Sinai received handsome remuneration from the State for leaving. This policy sparked considerable resentment from the population, who saw the settlers as profiteers. As for the settlers in the West Bank and Gaza, most of the public viewed them similarly, as selfish profiteers, not praiseworthy pioneers; even members of the settlement department of the Jewish Agency saw them this way.[8]

SOCIOCULTURAL CHANGE AND DISILLUSIONMENT WITH SOCIALISM

Meanwhile, the second and third generations on the farm were themselves rejecting the ideology of the founding fathers. While they, like the general public, despaired of the "cynicism" of the younger generation, they also saw themselves as hard realists, and resented having the martyrdom of their forefathers thrust upon them (see Kressel 1995). Farming had become a business rather than a religious calling, and the times, as well as the government, forced businesslike attitudes upon farmers. Of course, these new attitudes entailed a shift of identity for those living in the countryside. The founders were heroes, pioneers; the sons were businessmen. Similarly, the larger public looked at rural people differently. The respect due to a pioneer was gone; rural people had become suburbanites.

After the fiscal collapse of the mid-1980's, moshavim began to disestablish themselves as generalized cooperatives; members thus refused to accept responsibility for one anothers' debts. Fewer made pretenses of being farmers, and, in fact, many let others farm their land outright while they took paying jobs out of the community. Farm women in increasing numbers joined the paid workforce as their urban counterparts had always done. Kibbutzim also became increasingly businesslike out of necessity, and at the same time they altered the form of domestic life to resemble that of the public at large. Communal dining and childrearing, the hallmarks of kibbutz life, quietly disappeared from most kibbutzim.

Many writers have sought to defend this transformation. Amos Oz (1995), for example, writes,

> The kibbutz is developing an organic character. It is a new kind of
> village, containing a few inter-related families and a few principles
> that do not need to be carved on the lintels and recited day and night.
> The kibbutz is no longer an experiment. It is growing in accordance
> with its own inner legitimacy, not according to a rational ideological
> scheme. (131)

As the farming sector came to resemble more and more the rest of the population, the reasons for its leadership in cultural as well as political matters simply evaporated. A home base in a kibbutz or a moshav is no longer prestigious, no longer anything special. The moshavnik or kibbutznik is certainly no longer the leader or repository of knowledge of what it means to be an Israeli. Since Israel is no longer a nation of new immigrants, the veterans are no longer the experts. Nor does the new Israeli culture have to do battle with older traditions, the customs of the shtetl and the ghetto—they are sufficiently distant to admire in museums now.[9]

CONCLUSION

The Israeli case exhibits one version of the manipulation of an image, that of rural identity, through time. In this instance, rural identity became associated first with sacrifice, pioneering, social innovation, and socialism. Then, because of the role the pioneer farmers came to play in the political structure, they and their descendants came to be associated with elitism, aristocracy, and privilege. Targets of resentment at a still later period, they were forced to transform themselves and their identity in a new era dominated by a new ideology; no longer the leaders in a capitalistic society, they were seen as weak businessmen, even parasites of the state. Thus, the (self-) characterization of old European Jews as capitalist parasites who could only be redeemed by a "return to the soil," was turned on its head. Those who lived from the soil became "the parasites" while the urban toilers, businessmen, and capitalists were seen as supporting them in a style they neither earned nor deserved. Although the complex associations of socialism, of pioneering, and of ethnic identity and conflict all serve to make this instance of rural devaluation unique, it can nevertheless serve to motivate a search for similar complexity in other explorations of rural identity and cultural hierarchy.

NOTES

The author conducted field-work in rural Israel during the 1980's with the support of the City University of New York's Research Foundation, and participated in a symposium at the Ben Gurion University of the Negev with that institution's support in 1991; these experiences contributed substantially to the material presented in this chapter.

1. Amos Elon (1981), for example, describes intergenerational differences to show cultural roots and transformations; Liebman and Don-Yehiya (1983) analyze the tension between traditional religion and its role in civil national identity in the new State; Tamar Katriel (1986) uses a sociolinguistic cultural trait, "dugri talk," to explore, rather brilliantly, the meaning of Israeli cultural identity; Virginia Dominguez (1989) takes a postmodern approach to the

construction of culture in Israel; and Alex Weingrod (1990) looks at the process of establishing an Israeli Sephardic identity.

2. Israelis associate this idea with its prominent proponent, A. V. Gordon.

3. Some have speculated that even the social science segment of this literature reflects the ideological and emotional proclivities of its authors, from blindly supportive to bitterly disappointed, depending on the era and the author (see Schwartz 1995b, for a summary review).

4. In fact, situations like this raise questions about the very concept of peasantry. In many respects, the privileges of the Israeli Jewish farming population would seem to exempt them from this category, usually conceived as an oppressed and exploited class (Wolf 1966). Yet many of the elements of the category were there: subordination to a state which absorbed their surplus production, living from agricultural production mainly by their own labor, farming as a "way of life" rather than as a "business," engaging in a market system, absence of wealth in a society where wealth could be and was accumulated by others. In conversation with an official of the Israeli Ministry of Agriculture in the mid-1980's, I heard the official refer to small farmers in cooperative settlements (moshavim—see below) as "peasants." But in Hebrew, farmers are known as "agriculturalists" or by the term describing their type of community—moshav or kibbutz, that is, "moshavnik" or "kibbutznik." It is perhaps inappropriate to apply the term "peasant" to this cultural category in Israel, especially in consideration of the dream of classlessness envisioned by the pioneers. Nevertheless, no other term in English conjures up the image of the hardy farmer who works the land and lives simply that was the goal of the transformation that the Zionist pioneers sought to achieve.

5. The initial dichotomy represented by the kibbutz as a social construct was in reference to shtetl/ghetto society. Stanley Diamond (1957) argues, however, that there are important similarities between the two institutions.

6. For a more scholarly version of the popular press expression of outrage over the irresponsibility of the moshavim at public expense, see Sherman and Schwartz, 1991.

7. Kibbutzim were the most egregious "sinners" in the employment of immigrant Jewish labor. In the early days of the massive Jewish immigration from the Arabic-speaking countries, new immigrants settled in camps awaiting "absorption" would be employed for manual labor in near-by kibbutzim; later, when they were permanently settled in "development towns" far from the main cities, they became workers in the kibbutzim. The hypocrisy of this relationship was cause for fierce resentment (Yishai 1982), a matter which will be explored more below.

8. The source of this information is my own interviews with both West Bank settlers and Jewish Agency functionaries in 1986.

9. In fact, there are not only displays of traditional culture in many of the country's museums, there is also a Museum of the Diaspora in a suburb north of Tel Aviv, devoted to an admiring display of the diversity of Jewish cultures "prior to the ingathering of exiles."

REFERENCES

Arian, A. 1967. "Utopia and Politics: The Case of the Israeli Kibbutz." *Journal of Human Relations* 14: 391–403.

Baldwin, Elaine. 1972. *Differentiation and Cooperation in an Israeli Veteran Moshav*. Manchester: Manchester University Press.

Chafets, Ze'ev. 1986. *Heroes and Hustlers, Hard Hats and Holy Men: Inside the New Israel*. New York: William Morrow & Co.

Diamond, Stanley. 1957. "Kibbutz and Shtetl: The History of an Idea." *Social Problems* 5: 71–99.

Dominguez, Virginia. 1989. *People as Subject, People as Object: Selfhood and Peoplehood in Contemporary Israel*. Madison: University of Wisconsin Press.

Elon, Amos. 1981. *The Israelis, Founders and Sons*. Tel Aviv: Adams Publishers.

Hoffman, Charles. 1986. "At the End of the Line." *Jerusalem Post Magazine*, July 25; 9.

Heller, Lilia. 1973. "The Emerging Consciousness of the Ethnic Problem Among the Jews of Israel." In M. Curtis and M. Chertoff, eds., *Israel: Social and Structural Change*. New Brunswick, NJ: Transaction Books. 313–332.

Katriel, Tamar. 1986. *Talking Straight: Dugri Speech in Israeli Sabra Culture*. Cambridge: Cambridge University Press.

Kressel, Gideon. 1995. "Those Who Stay in Agriculture are not 'Friers': Change in the Moshav Economy Erodes its Work Ethic." In M. Schwartz, S. Lees, and G. Kressel, eds., *Rural Cooperatives in Socialist Utopia*. Westport, CT: Greenwood Press. 155–83.

Liebman, Charles, and Eliezer Dan-Yehiya. 1983. "The Dilemma of Reconciling Traditional Culture and Political Needs: Civil Religion in Israel." *Comparative Politics* 16: 53–66.

Oz, Amos. 1995. *Under this Blazing Light*. Trans. Nicholas de Lange. Cambridge: Cambridge University Press.

Schwartz, Moshe. 1995a. *Unlimited Guarantees: History and Political Economy in Israel's Cooperative Agriculture*. Beer Sheva: Ben Gurion University Press.

———. 1995b. "Moshav and Kibbutz in the Anthropology and Sociology of Israel." In M. Schwartz, S. Lees, and G. Kressel, eds., *Rural Cooperatives in Socialist Utopia*. Westport, CT: Greenwood Press. 3–30.

———. 1995c. "The De-cooperativization of Israel's Moshavim, 1985–1994." In M. Schwartz, S. Lees, and G. Kressel, eds., *Rural Cooperatives in Socialist Utopia*. Westport, Conn: Greenwood Press. 223–43.

Shama, Avraham, and Mark Iris. 1977. *Immigration Without Integration: Third World Jews in Israel*. Cambridge, MA: Schenkman Publishing Co.

Shapiro, Ovadia. 1971. *Rural Settlements of New Immigrants in Israel: Development Problems of New Rural Communities*. Rehovot: Settlement Study Center.

Sherman, Neal. 1982. "From Government to Opposition: The Rural Settlement Movement of the Israel Labor Party in the Wake of the Election of 1977." *International Journal of Middle East Studies* 14: 53–69.

Sherman, Neal, and Moshe Schwartz. 1991. "The Effect of Public Financial Assistance on Moshav Economic Affairs." *Human Organization* 50: 163–72.

Weingrod, Alex. 1966. *Reluctant Pioneers: Village Development in Israel*. Ithaca: Cornell University Press.

———. 1990. *The Saint of Beer Sheba*. Albany: State University of New York Press.

Weintraub, Dov, *et al.* 1971. *Immigration and Social Change: Agricultural Settlements of New Immigrants in Israel*. Manchester: Manchester University Press.

Willner, Dorothy. 1970. *Nation Building and Community in Israel*. Princeton: Princeton University Press.

Wolf, Eric. 1966. *Peasants*. Englewood Cliffs, NJ: Prentice-Hall.

Yishai, Yael. 1982. "Israel's Right-Wing Jewish Proletariat." *The Jewish Journal of Sociology* 24: 87–97.

9 ~ MICHÈLE D. DOMINY

The Alpine Landscape in Australian Mythologies of Ecology and Nation

CONTEMPORARY Australian nationalism developed out of Aboriginal and European peoples' changing relationship to a special and vast landscape of alpine country and outback called "the bush." Since European settlement, the cultural meaning of the alpine landscape as "high" has shifted from pastoral frontier, a site for rural identity, to remote wilderness, a site for urban-based identities located in ecological paradigms. Nature conservation legislation creates national parks and wilderness areas, thus endangering the survival of alpine rural culture as high country cattlemen lose their value to the national economy. They become culturally "low" while at the same time traditional rurality is erased and its representations appropriated by urbanity as historically "high." This metaphoric reversal of high/low afflicts other alpine communities in Appalachia and the United States west,[1] and on the South Island of New Zealand.

Allen Batteau's *The Invention of Appalachia* provides an appropriate backdrop for an analysis of rural identity both geographically (where else is the divide in United States culture between urban/rural and high/low more extreme?) and theoretically, as Batteau explores sets of distinctions established by the image of Appalachia in semantic and narrative space. Not only is Appalachia propagated as a literary invention through symbolic forms and processes, such as myth-making, sacrifice, social drama, pilgrimage, and commodity—some of which the contributors to this volume are examining in other rural and national contexts—but transnationally rural cultures are also "creatures of the urban imagination," as they are defined and redefined, and culturally elaborated within the nation state context as (in Batteau's words) "different groups seek to impose their will on others" (1990: 199). Likewise Richard Handler notes that the terms "high/low" "encompass or can be made to stand for an array of distinctions and dichotomies we draw concerning elite and popular culture, urban and rural culture, class and mass culture" (1994: 1).

My ethnographic work in New Zealand focuses on alpine pastoralist families whose rural elite status as settler descendants has faded. I have examined the place high country people occupy in New Zealand's changing mythologies of nationalism both as an image of antipodean pastoralism and as an image of resistance to modernism (Dominy 1993a; 1993b). These images represent an Arcadian "ideal society" in which New Zealand is characterized as a country of abundant natural resources and an ordered egalitarian social structure (Fairburn 1989). However, in the current contest for control of key cultural images, urban folk often erase high country inhabitants from the landscape (1993a) and declare the tussock grasslands to be in ecological danger. They claim this territory as a visual icon that can exist as the reified "natural," unmediated by culture. Consequently, as South Island high country pastoralists have moved to the nation's economic and political margins, they have begun to elaborate the symbolic dimension of their lives as part of a process of contestation over whose rights to, and con-

ceptions of, land prevail. They face persistent external economic challenges and political pressures from those with competing interests in
public lands. Theirs is a contest for habitation, a localized version of
identity construction within the nation state context. To these rural-
identified New Zealanders, the mystique attached to the high country
and an urban-based sense of visual ownership seem to be external
constructions imposed on a landscape that is being commodified as
scenery and as recreational sites in ways that impede pastoral sheep
farming. Issues of access and land use, of ownership and control, of
power and privilege prompt negative sentiment toward high country
people and the mystique their habitation embodies.

Such an array of distinctions emerges in my cultural analysis of
linked ethnographic and textual materials focusing on dichotomous
refractions of the countryside in the Australian Alps. Competing spatial discourses suggest metaphoric representations of alpine space as
frontier legacy on the one hand, and as reclaimed wilderness on the
other.[2] These discourses are simultaneously dialogic and conflictual.
Like other contributors I critique not only the distinction, but more
importantly the implied false fixity and closure of the rural, a fixity
that Marilyn Strathern (1982: 249) has described for Elmdon, Essex as
"a village in the mind." In our cases the divides are the result of complex cultural legacies—including the internalization of other peoples'
tropes—and political processes. Similarly, Lawrence Levine (1988: 8)
asserts that our categories of culture, as ideological products, are "per-
meable and shifting rather than fixed and immutable." In my analysis,
the cultural category of wilderness, derived from urban-based nationalisms linked to ecology, displaces the cultural category of the frontier
and marginalizes its rural occupants.

DECONSTRUCTING "THE ENVIRONMENT"

In the Australian Alps, these issues emerge in spatial debates over
the removal of high country cattlemen from public lands for the establishment of an alpine national park and the designation of wilderness
areas. National parks preserve scenery and natural features, plant and

animal communities, historic features, and opportunities for recreation. Wilderness areas are defined as extensive "essentially undisturbed" natural areas in which "ecological processes are virtually free of human interference"; areas with high scientific and ecological value, and areas that feel remote and isolated (National Parks and Wildlife Service 1988: 50). I focus on the alpine site of the "Man from Snowy River," made famous in "Banjo" Paterson's epic poem (1891) and more recently in George Miller's film "The Man from Snowy River" (Fox, Australia 1982) to examine alpine hinterlands and their placement within the cultural hierarchies of the nation state. Here too settler descendants' rural status as contemporary pioneers has faded. As the landscape of the nineteenth-century peopled frontier recedes, that of the twentieth-century unpeopled wilderness advances while continuing, as in the past, to preserve and redefine the former in legend. The transformation of rural mountain ecosystems and their socioeconomic aspects includes the ideological creation of the rural environment by recreationists and tourists. As Linda Graber (1976: 114) has argued, the wilderness ethic is an urban phenomenon that intensifies with the degree of separation of urban people from rural modes of production and ways of life; in the alps these are the very aspects of rurality that wilderness erases.

In these mountains, known as the Snowies, these processes are part of the contentious debate over natural and cultural resource management in the Alpine National Park; in New South Wales the debate derives from the aftermath of the removal of grazing in Kosciusko National Park between 1943 and 1969;[3] in Victoria it derives from threats to remove the remaining cattlemen from Victorian public lands. At issue is the dialectical interplay between alpine and Australian cultural heritage and their relationship to the formation of a national ethos embedded in ideas about the singularity of the environment. Providing an instance from Australia in which urban and rural are strategically opposed, I suggest that what is at stake politically in these "rewritings of tradition" are competing models of biodiversity and ecologically sustainable development, models that could be reconciled with the integration of natural and cultural resources, and scientific and local knowledges, in a bioregional model. Such a model defines geographical boundaries not so much in terms of natural features but in terms of human use and perception—in terms of people's use of a place through time and their feelings about an area. It values the local and the regional (Alexander 1990: 168, Parsons 1985: 4), opening up the possibility of rural and urban interaction in the national park context.

Sue Hodges (1992) has argued that images and tales of mountain cattlemen remain a significant part of the European cultural heritage, known widely in Australia and recognized as part of the Australian ethos. Nevertheless, wilderness conservation proponents and the Parks Service often aim to remove cattlemen and the imprint of their historical presence on the landscape such as stockmen's huts and stock routes. At the same time, as Roger Good (1992: 148) notes, without limits, increasing numbers of visitors to the alpine zones pose similar ecological problems to those of stock grazing.[4] As the conservationist[5] replaces the pioneer, ambivalence persists in the perceptions urban folk have of the place of rural folk in these mountains. For example, mountain cattlemen find themselves part of a process of rural peripheralization in which Grenier's (1992) alpine vision (embracing human habitation in the frontier) and his Australian vision (linking Australian identity to a vast wilderness empty of human habitation and needing protection) collide. Many New South Wales cattlemen shared with me their sadness and anger in being "closed out" of the park: "we are locked out" of that country, "we don't have the [gate] key to that country"; forbidden to take their horses onto the old stock routes in the areas of the park[6] that they know, they say they cannot pass on a knowledge of place to their children without breaking the law and bringing out the surveillance helicopters to "be hunted like animals." They feel displaced in a park that has become a "rangers' playground," a place that urban bushwalkers know better than they. A retired park employee who had worked with graziers in the early days of the park's formation said sympathetically: "To run a park you have to switch on [listen] to all the social values that are there."

Geographer Nicholas Gill and historians Tom Griffiths and Sue Hodges provide valuable interpretive analyses that are attentive to the divisions in cultural politics about definitions of environment and the meaning of landscape in Australian national park lands.[7] For instance, Griffiths (1991) documents not only the dominance of an ecological scientific paradigm in determining environmental value, but illustrates its influence in two powerful popular processes of rural land definition— the wilderness movement and the culture of park management. Gill points to the importance of attending to pluralities of meaning attached to environment in his study of conflicts over bushfire management between a rural farming community and the National Parks and Wildlife Service on Kangaroo Island in South Australia. Like Griffiths (1991: 101), he makes the case for attending to local histories of fire in order to understand indigenous cultural systems. He notes that global perspectives on the environment and on resource management have eclipsed local knowledge (1994: 237). Correctly I think, he notes that "inneraction [sic] with nature refers to the relation of society with nature as inherent within its everyday practices. In this relation nature is a subject of social action, not simply an objectified backdrop to human affairs" (1994: 226). His statement is not an idle nod to cultural constructivism; it suggests that when the nation considers nature in its biophysical sense, or the monolithic concept of "the" environment or "wilderness," the prevailing paradigm is one of reification and reductive absolutism.[8] Also the aboriginal is conflated conceptually with "the natural." In contrast, Deborah Bird Rose says that because the Dreaming[9] is everywhere, there is no such place as wilderness; conceptualized in European terms, wilderness suggests an egocentric view of landscape in which we see nothing unless we see marks of self there (Rose 1995). Tom Griffiths (1991: 92) argues that wilderness is also a Eurocentric notion that tends to "naturalize" aborigines. Bruce Kapferer (1988: 142–143) discusses the metaphor of the bush as an urban symbolic fantasy, and suggests an overlay of bushman and aboriginal in mythologies of nationalism; these constructions, he argues, are part of a white Australian imagination. And anthropology invites us to elicit competing ethnoecologies for alpine environments by simultaneously providing the space to include the particularity of grazier knowledge of place, and challenging park managers to acknowledge that their version of ecology is indeed a situated ethnoecology, an ethnocentric ecology, rather than "scientific" fact. As Mulvaney argues in his introduction to an alpine cultural heritage symposium, "cultural landscapes cannot be defined always in the 'objective' manner demanded by science, industry and administration" (1992: 14). This dialectical construction of rural and urban ethnoecologies deriving from "place"-based distinctions invites us to analyze their cultural significance without unthinkingly privileging the urban perspective (see Creed and Ching, this volume).

Indeed, an interpretive science can be useful to ecology. Timothy Flannery's ecological history of Australia documents the difficult relationship between humans and the environment as it recounts a "great ongoing saga of fire, rainforest and fauna" (1994: 387; see Pyne 1991). Flannery's reading is not particularistic and omits specific readings of localized niches like the alpine and subalpine.[10] He argues that all of Australia is already a profoundly modified landscape and that the role of fire and the relationship of herbivorous creatures to fire is complex and dynamic (1994: 228). His reading of the Australian stockman's relationship to particular ecological niches links the cattleman with grasslands now deprived of large herbivores[11] whose extinction left fodder for fires until the coming of European grazing; he relates this aspect of fire to the pattern of other frontier societies with a stockman culture (1994: 392–93). Little about the condition of any Australian lands, he suggests, is static or unmodified over time.[12] Furthermore, from a high country perspective, habitation includes both that of humans and domesticated animals (Hodges 1993: 79).

Flannery cites the International Union for the Conservation of Nature's (IUCN) definition of "Wilderness Areas" as:

> large areas of unmodified or slightly modified land, or land and water
> retaining their natural character and influence, without permanent or
> significant habitation, which are protected and managed so as to
> preserve their natural condition. (1994: 378)

and he states without hesitation that the IUCN's definition of wilderness "simply does not exist in Australia" (1994: 379). He responds to the inadequacy of such definitions and to the inadequacy of a system of reserved lands for preserving biodiversity by suggesting instead that better conservation would occur if Australian policy allowed for "exploitation of *all* of our biotic heritage, provided that it all be done in *a sustainable manner*" including the use of endangered species and rainforests (1994: 402). Flannery's direction is apparent within UNESCO, whose Director-General, Federico Mayor, in addressing Australia International Council of Monuments and Sites (ICOMOS) on the topic of "World Heritage Convention and Cultural Landscapes," said our ideas about biodiversity have been mistaken. We have been wrong to exclude humans from an ecosystem where man and "nature" are inseparable; sustainability, he notes, must only be expressed in human terms. He attributes our mistakes to ecosystem decisions that are city-based (Mayor 1995). This shift in thinking was clearly expressed in the third annual report to the United Nations Commission on Sustainable Development (April 1995) in its recognition of mountain ecosystems and environments as "rich and unique centres of biological and cultural diversity, water stores and sources of minerals," and in its recommendation that the economic and political marginalization of mountain communities be reversed; in particular it calls for the empowerment of "mountain communities to exercise large control over local resource management and conservation" and the "recognition of their knowledge . . . as an integral part of sustainable development."

Indigenous knowledge can be used not only to document cultural heritage and preserve it in particular historical sites but also to sustain aspects of that heritage in the present.[13] Such knowledge can provide insight into the cultural values of Australian mountain cattlemen at a moment when cultural and traditional land use issues are at stake, and the conflicts over the management of public mountain lands seem endless and irreconcilable.[14] Environmental regulatory policymakers clearly must consider the changing symbiotic relation of mountain environments and human populations as well as human impact on mountains. Policy often "neglects the perceptions and experience of the rural population, the people most closely linked to the land," and reflects "an elitist [corporate] urban perception" of conservation and wilderness (Gomez-Pompa and Kaus 1992: 271). Cultural, environmental, and socioeconomic systems are powerfully interactive, shaping and influencing each other, and within this interaction, constituencies compete in mountain areas; none of these systems, including the ecosystem, are static. We need to examine the different environmental understandings of those who engage in extractive or consumptive activities (forestry and range management) and those who engage in preservation and certain types of recreation (conservationists).[15] Especially acute in the area of park management, the differences are most frequently voiced with respect to fire management, the impact of cattle on vegetation, and the control of blackberries and brumbies (wild horses). Graziers draw on experience; the Parks Service on scientific research. These different environmental understandings need to be interpreted, not assumed nor oppositionalized. Hodges identifies the primacy of aesthetics, which she calls "metaphors of sight" that privilege spectacular wilderness scenery, in shaping national park land management policies (1992: 121). She concludes that such metaphors, when employed in an unpeopled, "untouched" wilderness, have real consequences, not only because they impede the preservation of historic sites of (especially Anglo-Australian) human habitation, but also because they exclude the associative value of these landscapes for rural families.[16] Again the local rural voice, or eye, is subordinated to that of the national and/or continental, and by extension transnational, and the protection of cultural resources is subordinated to that of natural resources.

ETHNOGRAPHY AND LEGEND

Against the construction of the urban legend of the "Man from Snowy River," I juxtapose exploratory fieldwork with high country "rural" mountain cattlemen, and urban-based alpine ecologists. As Ellen Badone has argued for Brittany and Quebec, "intellectuals idealize the language of the rural folk, in highly similar terms" and rural peoples often "find themselves objectified and valorized for the very features of their existence that they are seeking to abandon. . ." in the present (1992: 807). Stockmen's huts are one such feature. As one ecologist reminded me, "the huts were incredible hovels with snakes and rats," having little to do with high country identity. Former employee stockmen told me that they endured the harsh climate and living conditions "in a hard slog" while owners were absent. Urban-based groups like the Kosciusko Huts Association have worked hard to preserve these huts and collect oral "hut histories," and bushwalkers, often against the will of the Parks Service, have sneaked building supplies into restricted areas to prop up the buildings so that they qualify for preservation status. Similarly now, many old stockmen reminisce nostalgically about particular stockmen's huts and their remote sitings, and grazier descendants reconstruct a history of the huts, seeking the fence posts of old stockyards and the markers of shepherds' graves; one woman who grew up in what is now Kosciusko Park included me in two expeditions she led to her childhood home, now restored within the park as a heritage site—one for some descendents of Australia's First Fleet, and one for a grazier descendant who works in tourism. Legend, oral tradition, and historical site preservation substitute for the preservation of living culture while simultaneously defining what it was.

I went "up top" to the snow lease area on a Victorian station twice in the autumn of 1995, the first time for the weekly salting of the cattle with the manager. We drove up by Toyota Landcruiser with a favored cattledog, ate a bushmeal of chops, potatoes, and carrots by the old stockman's hut, and slept in our swags under the snowgums; in the night we heard brumbies. The next morning we drove through the eucalyptus bush to replenish each of the salt licks and to call "come here cattle," and the manager told me how he had reestablished the licks, learning from a neighbor how best to position them. When he first took over the station, no cattle had been put on the adjoining 93 thousand acres of leasehold country for many years, and he had never taken cattle out into the high country before; he was worried that they would "scatter into the bush," and that he would lose them; but in the first autumn muster (roundup), "the cattle were there." He reestablished a high country tradition on a property with a recent history of outside ownership.

In April, my second trip "up top" took place, for the autumn cattle muster, with a late twentieth-century twist. This year, the manager and two local stockmen went on the muster accompanied by the owner and four of his Sydney-based friends, a television producer and her cameraman who were doing a promotional spot for a special in October celebrating a "Banjo" Paterson centennial, and myself as anthropologist. The urban construction of the most traditional of high country secular rituals, the muster, predominated both in terms of its visual construction for a television audience where eggs cooking on the fire, saddles resting on the fence yards, and stockmen in Akubras and oilers (raincoats) were featured in filming as components of heritage—and in terms of its value as a trailriding and camping experience for urban businessmen. The media define the image, turning it into a mythic landscape. Reflexively, the group joked together about the possibility of my doing a semiotic analysis of the array of woolen sweaters before the campfire—an Aran, a Guernsey, and a merino Toorallie from the Monaro Plains; the owner and the anthropologist were less "upmarket" in their serviceable bushshirts, and the manager wore a basic navy sweater. The "authenticity" of this experience was highlighted all the more for me when we failed to find any cattle; most had worked their way down after the first snow two weeks before, and those that remained were on two more remote snow leases, both of which were beyond the riding capacities of those of us who were not locals. This station is not typical of the remaining leasehold properties in Victoria, many of which are still in continuous family ownership, but it shares some of their features, most especially, as I will discuss in the case of Tom Groggin Station, the definition of the high country legend externally imposed by tourists and recreationists. One member of our party repeatedly noted the "fantastic" vistas and panoramas, illustrating the primacy of the metaphor of sight. The locals focused on where the cattle might be, on the brumbies whose tracks they followed along the contour lines, and on the skills of their horses in maintaining secure footing, not tripping, handling steep descents with a smooth walk, and negotiating their way through closely spaced trees without grazing their riders' legs, thus mediating their relationship to the landscape in terms of domestic stock, both their horses and cattle. Stockmen told me that if someone were lost ("geographically misplaced" or "geographically embarrassed" bushwalkers would say) he "would trust his horse to steer him right"; "the horse will remember which way it came"; "it can lead you home if you are lost"; "you don't get lost although you might spend an extra night out," especially when fog and rain move in. Cattle too "know the way if they've been out there before." Similarly, in the New Zealand high country, sheep and working dogs mediate the way in which place is known.

Unlike the urban sightseer's, the cattleman's relationship to the high country of Victoria and New South Wales is not primarily visual or panoramic but is rooted in social experience, in culture as the embodiment of knowledge, and in practical use; in daily practice, this relationship resists the idyllic representations and pastoral nostalgia that characterize literature, art, and media portraits of peripheral zones. In this sense, landscape is not characterized as scenery, a commodifying process which Allen Batteau (1990) has analyzed in national park formation in the Appalachians as "appropriating nature." Now as Australian cattlemen begin to participate in the commodification of their own heritage, they too participate in the construction of their own legends. We need to ask therefore: what about nonmetaphoric rusticity? Can we find it? When a rural population reclaims their folk culture, is this less metaphoric than ethno-regionalist or nationalist constructions of identity as rural? It is useful to think of Anthony Cohen's point when he reminds us to focus on the particularity of the experience of one kind of Scotsman.

> A man's awareness of himself as a Scotsman may have little to do with the Jacobite wars, or with Burns, or with the poor state of the housing stock in Glasgow. It has to do with his particular experience as a farmer in Aberdeenshire, as a member of a particular village or of a particular group of kin within his village. (1982: 13)

This is a cogent reminder that while resisting the temptation (in Handler's words) to "romance the low," we must remember the rural folk, not solely as representations of urban elites (ourselves included) but as social actors simultaneously transformed, reified, and constructed by and against larger political processes. Let me turn again to Batteau for evidence:

> In every province of meaning, whether Appalachia or ethnography, the elements of reality, the rules of meaning, and the tension and motivation of consciousness of one set of texts become imposed on other texts, other performances. Even in the seemingly most basic reality, the negotiations of face-to-face encounters, one participates with preconceptions of the other's identity, of the language being spoken, and of the purposes of the encounter. Face-to-face experience is no more real than any other text (1990: 10).

He would, I suspect, argue that all rusticity is in fact metaphoric, although his perspective is slanted no doubt by literarily derived, rather than ethnographically derived, materials.

In Australia the urban voice has constructed rurality metaphorically through legend and through a tourist industry built on the preservation and commodification of legend. Russel Ward's history of the nineteenth-century evolution of Australian national identity places its origins in the "brute facts of Australian geography," of "scanty rainfall and great distances"; this is the geography of the frontier, of the outback, of the bush (Ward 1958: 11). Ward's bush was a generic bush—it could be the rainforest or the desert, the mountains or the outback.[17] An up-country ethos or bush ethos was popularized in the influential Sydney newspaper, the *Bulletin*, and Ward writes that the bushman became the "homespun folk-hero," and "from 1881 the presiding deity of Australian literature"; he cites the publication figures for "Banjo" Paterson's *The Man from Snowy River and Other Verses*, first published in 1895, and reprinted three times in the next twenty-nine years with over one hundred thousand copies sold (Ward 1958: 223). This was a search, Ward claims, for a folk-hero to symbolize the nation, and "the Man" was part of a cult of the noble frontiersman, rooted in European imperialism (Ward 1958: 253).[18] Hodges calls it "the lynchpin [sic] of legends" (1992: 111). Then, as now, the bush legend was "a construction of urban writers, artists, critics and the *Bulletin*, in fact, a mouthpiece for the liberal urban bourgeois against the interests of rural pastoralists" (Schaffer 1988: 29). The bush was as pure and natural, as "wholesome as the wattle" (White 1981: 116–17). From Lines's (1991: 185) perspective it was a "facile" countryside "contrived" by a majority urban population, and it "did not evoke any sense of relatedness between humans and the non-human world." Similarly, Michael Taussig examines the creation of the image of the bushman as a product of the culture of nationalism (1992: 71).[19] Taussig takes on Russel Ward's "Australian legend," and the "genetic heritage" of outback life that celebrates the "elemental bond between man and frontier" in the bush (conceptualized doubly as outback and alpine) to uncover Australian nationalism's investment in a mythology of war. Taussig's "Man" whom he calls an "Australian hero" has become the ANZAC soldier and a "testimony to the persuasiveness of imperialist poetics" (Taussig 1992: 71).[20] While Taussig's reading of legend carries critical bite, John Hepworth's (1987: 137) reading as a journalist reflects the opiate qualities of the legend particularly as it pertains to war; in an account of the Victorian Mountain Cattleman's annual Get Together, he sees the young men in "caped coats and broadbrimmed hats tending their horses" and claims, "suddenly I saw what they really were—the living ghosts of splendid young men who 70 years ago stood side by side, looking up the parapet of Gallipoli."

Although "Banjo" Paterson acknowledged that "the Man" was a composite character, towns on the perimeter in two different states (New South Wales and Victoria) compete to identify him and claim him as their own. Hodges writes that "the Man," reputed by many to be Jack Riley, who was manager of Tom Groggin station, is a "living monument" (1992: 113); in this sense, he is analogous to the historic huts preserved as interpretive sites throughout Kosciusko as a reminder of past grazing days. Communities commodify the "Man" with rodeos, mountain musters, and trail riding expeditions that follow brumby trails and old stock routes; some properties promote adventure and heritage tourism and take visitors up to the lease country on the annual muster or to salt the cattle. The legend was translated into film in the mid 1980s with the making of the "The Man from Snowy River," and the film site of its sequel, a cooperative effort with the local Victorian community where it was shot, is now a major tourist destination. Communities like Jindabyne in New South Wales in the east, and Mansfield and Corryong in Victoria[21] in the west, are participating in processes of self-commodification, as they recognize an opportunity to "sell their heritage." The locals say they have to be the ones to define who they are, and some events, such as the annual Man from Snowy River Awards in Jindabyne, tend to be attended by residents rather than tourists. East and West compete to claim the Man, battling over authenticity and selling their heritage when identity and market value are at stake. The intensity of the legend (as political capital) corresponds to the intensity of the threats to the leases (as vital to economic survival),[22] as the mountain cattlemen and their descendants market their culture and make it desirable to city people.

Even alpine indigenes, settler descendants whose livelihood was (and in Victoria is) based on a leasehold grazing economy, accept and promote the urban construction of alpine cultural heritage. Nowhere is this more evident than in the case of one of the most celebrated of high country stations, Tom Groggin, in the Murray headwaters on the border of New South Wales and Victoria. The famed Jack Riley was manager here for many years at the turn of the century. He is commemorated each year on Riley's ride, conducted by a commercial trailriding operation based at the station, as people follow the difficult bridle track from Groggin to Corryong (commemorating the arduous attempt to move a dying Riley from his hut to the local hospital). Nearby Corryong features a museum celebrating the Man from Snowy River Country, and guide signs direct tourists to Riley's gravesite.

Groggin won an important court ruling in 1992 against the Victorian Minister for Conservation and Environment that preserved the right to graze cattle on four licenses. The Minister had sought to use the occasion of a lease transfer from an urban family corporation to the director of a public investment company to declare a wilderness zone, but the judge found his method wrong. The claimant's use of the legend may have helped the case, and Groggin's survival as a leasehold property has ensured the perpetuation of grazing on its alpine leases as stockmen continue to ride their horses on the brumby tracks. The case was won on a technicality and the details are not important to my argument,[23] but it is significant that the Supreme Court judge began his ruling with the statement that cattle grazing at Groggin has a place in Australian literature. Acknowledging its scenic value and the commercial connotations of the matter, he cites "Banjo" Paterson: "I bought a run a while ago/On country rough and ridgy . . . "; the owner "knew that they had the day" as soon as the judge began to read his judgement. Rurality at Groggin is valorized by the local community and the courts in a rural legend that sustains its farming practice.

At the Man from Snowy River Awards ceremony in Jindabyne on Australia Day 1995, one descendant of a mountain cattleman family urged residents to keep "a corner of our heritage alive and available for the public to see." He urged a plan and a coordinated effort "to put it together before it dies." In conversation he said that "chardonnay socialists in four wheel drives" come to seek clean mountain air and "the wildflower thing," but have difficulty specifying what the Man from Snowy River represents. Often he is reduced to yahoo status, risking his horse in an unrestrained chase after brumbies, as in the legend. In practice, though, stockmen manage their resources more carefully. On one alpine muster we had three sightings of brumby mobs including a beautiful black foal with a blaze on its forehead. One young stockman explained his pursuit to me: when he chases them his "adrenaline takes over and I can't help myself"; he wants the "challenge of seeing where you could take it," so "the steeper the better," a thrill he compared to driving the 'dozer when he was logging; but he curtails the chase rather than risk his horse, a particularly skilled bush horse "who takes care of her rider," and "knows how to chase." The stockman may be living the legend, but not the legend repeated by urban sightseers.

The Snowy Mountain descendant's "Man" is a "real stockman"; his self image rests in the understated abilities of elderly drovers, honored each year with community awards for stockmanship skills, for their knowledge of the mountains and for community service. A real "bushie," a top bushman, has an "uncanny knack of knowing where to go, and when to go, and how to go." He is a quiet achiever who does his job with confidence. This is the "real" bushman "at home in the bush," standing in stark contrast to urban mimicry in Akubra hats and Dryzabone raincoats. He said that what they have is what "Banjo" Paterson saw and illustrated by writing the poem, but the community is in danger of outside interests defining it for them, as developers create resorts and build ski fields in the national parks, and urban buyers purchase old station properties as weekend homes and trailriding operations. For locals, the "Man" is the "Man" because of the detailed knowledge of place he has; Hancock in 1972 recognized this and stressed the need for testimony on the mountains based on local knowledge. In the absence of ethnographic studies and perceived consultation with the locals on the part of the parks, such testimony is lacking; perhaps purposefully so, as alpine images are appropriated for homogenized nationalist rhetoric.[24]

A NATIONALIST ECOLOGY

By the late 1940s the bushman was replaced by the Snowy Mountains Hydro-Electric Scheme as the dominant image of development in Australian life (White 1981: 165). Begun in 1949, the scheme diverted the easterly flowing headwaters of the Snowy, Eucumbene, and Upper Murrumbidgee Rivers westward through the Alps via dams and series of tunnels providing irrigation to the Murray and Murrumbidgee basin and electricity to three of the nation's major cities, Melbourne, Sydney, and Canberra (Gare 1992: 207, 209).[25] William Lines writes: "In straightening the rivers—making them run as they should—the Snowy Mountains Scheme represented the rational, methodical, development of Australia's natural resources" (1991: 200). As an icon of Kosciusko, the Snowy Mountains Hydro-Electric Scheme is also an urban construction and reconstruction of the mountains, both figuratively and literally. From its beginning, when it fostered a high powered public relations project to elicit support and provided coach tours to the public, it has been a tourist attraction (Gare 1992: 221). Like "the Man," the Snowy (as it is elliptically called) has passed into the folklore of the nation, as Hodges argues, in part because of the success of the Scheme in presenting itself "in synchrony with the natural environment" with workers "portrayed as a new bree[d] [*sic*] of "'mountain men'" (Hodges 1992: 115).

The story of the creation of the Snowy Mountain landscape as both provider of electricity and irrigation schemes, and as national park is a familiar metanarrative. Batteau describes how family land in the southern mountain region of the United States was drawn into the continental economy as Nature was transformed into commodity either in the name of resource development or wilderness conservation (1990: 87). Batteau's argument that Appalachia as a symbol "has always contained some highly charged images of American national identity," parallels the construction of Australian national identity. The image of the Man from Snowy River also celebrates Australian ingenuity and vision as does the engineering effort involved in building the massive Snowy River Hydro-Electric Scheme, a scheme resembling that of the Tennessee Valley Authority.

As one park official said, "the Snowy tore the mountains to bits." A grazier son recalled the expression of Adaminaby residents in a photograph taken as the Scheme was about to blast the original town under the hydrowaters: "I couldn't think what it reminded me of until I realized it was the faces of highland New Guinea people when they saw their first plane, a look of stunned shock." With its network of roads and dams, the Scheme opened up the country and its surrounding towns to tourism, recreation, and immigration; one ecologist noted that the Snowy might have engineered a wilderness for four-wheel drives. Optimistic locals noted, "the sons of the first Monaro graziers married the daughters of the Snowy workers," as marriages linked country to city, and brought multiculturalism to the communities fringing the alps.

CONCLUSION

Embedded in discussions of the Australian Alps is a binary array of salient matched oppositions, condensed in competing imageries and definitions of wilderness and postpioneer landscapes. The salient components of a "high" urban/Australian vision and a "low" rural/alpine vision of landscape follow:

Australian vision	alpine vision
called "bush"	called "country"
remote wilderness	inhabited frontier
natural resources/values	cultural resources/values
unmanaged	managed [fire and grazing]
conservationist	extractive/productive
preserved/static	sustainable/evolving
uncommodified/nonproductive	material commodification/productive
vegetative focus	domestic stock focus
botanist	cattleman
walking tracks	bridle tracks/stock routes
bushwalker	horseman
aesthetic/visual/scenery	activity-based/associative/resource
natural beauty	living culture
national park	family farm lease
public values/nation	mateship
aboriginal landscape	European landscape
urban-based	rural-based (in practice)
	urban-based (in legend)
pre/post imperial	imperial [formative nationalism]
anthropocentric/eurocentric	local/rurocentric
metaphors of sight	metaphors of stock
reifies nature	praises heritage/sites

Theorists often do not ask whose sets of distinctions these are, and yet clearly what Grenier calls the ("high") Australian vision represents an urban-based cultural hierarchy that defines and incorporates the ("low") alpine vision. Urban-based legislative power and land management agencies define the Australian vision as authentic, apolitical, and driven by environmentally sensitive scientific ideology; the alpine vision is seen as a rhetorical construction of the present political moment and is excluded from these dialogues as sentimental and false. The Australian vision suggests the dominance of an ecological rhetoric rather than a bioregional rhetoric that could be based instead in what Alexander (1990: 171) has called "local geographical identification," a sense of being "at home." The incorporation of local and regional voices is valued in a bioregional model that recognizes the necessity to revitalize places as composites of biotic and cultural processes.[26] Local knowledge based on long term association with place must be tapped, as in the New Zealand high country, where farmers are embracing and defining sustainability while creating computer programs for measuring it.[27]

When I returned to New Zealand in May of 1993 to participate in a symposium of the East Asia-Pacific Mountain Association, I learned that the High Country Committee had responded to an emergent language of "resource management," "multiple use," "sustainable development," and "landscape" by producing a new kind of high-country coffee table volume, large enough in size, according to the present chair, to make it difficult to shelve. Called "Spirit of the High Country: The Search for Wise Land Use" (1992), the twenty-six page, glossy, photographic essay makes the richness of cultural heritage and affinity for the land explicit (and desirable) by stressing the mutuality of production and conservation. The Committee writes in its direct, distinctive, practical high-country prose, "Like most things in life, it is a matter of getting alongside other people to see where they are coming from. We hope that this publication helps to achieve that" (1992: 1).[28] Their title "Spirit of the High Country" taps both notions of farming resilience and fortitude through challenging climatic and political circumstances, as well as notions of the symbolic power of mountains and the mystique they carry in New Zealand's images of itself as a nation. A concern that New Zealand high country land rapidly is being alienated by foreign buyers with an interest in its commodification for tourism has begun to unite the constituencies of city and country, recreation/conservation groups and farmers in new coalitions (Ansley 1994, 1995). Not only is land at stake, but the sale of a shared national heritage as well. The link the Committee makes in this avowedly public relations effort is both strategic and sincere, as well as proactively self-defining in a context where formulations of local and national identities both use the high country as symbolic template. The Committee takes on some of the key questions that have defined our analysis in this volume.

In sum, Batteau (1990: 199) urges interpretive scientists to explore these mythical images and historical realities together with the "hard facts of economics and politics . . . not as competing views of reality but as different faces of common underlying processes." We must continue to ask: How do rural peoples respond to the increasing peripheralization of rural culture as others appropriate their most significant political symbols of identity, in the cases of the New Zealand and Australian Alps, the landscape they inhabit? How do the views of competing constituencies with an interest in land management change over time, and how are they expressed and codified in social institutions, cultural practices and political movements? Transnationally, as Creed and Ching have suggested to us, cultural elaborations of the distinctions between countryside and city, and I would add, as refractions of countryside—wilderness and postfrontier—contribute in complex ways to ecological and economic crises. We ought to identify common processes as we continue to ask these kinds of questions comparatively and as part of a collective endeavor. Our next comparative step should be to engage in carefully systematic ethnographic studies of parallel kinds of cultural hierarchies, such as those suggested here, to meet this challenge.

NOTES

The Australian research builds comparatively upon long term ethnographic work in the New Zealand high country with sheep station families (Dominy 1993a, 1993b, 1995); it was conducted while I was a Visiting Research Scholar at the Cultural Heritage Management Center, University of Canberra (January–May 1995). My thanks to Brian Egloff of the Center, to John Harris of Applied Science, and to Roger Good of the National Parks and Wildlife Service of New South Wales for arranging my visit to the university and for sharing their personal libraries with me. The University of Canberra's Visiting Scholars Program and Bard College contributed grant monies towards the research. The National Library of Australia provided not only reading materials but a quiet desk in the Petherick Reading Room. I would like to thank especially Yola and Rob Cox, Bernie Sheather and Pam Byrne, Neville and Kate Locker, Dean Turner, Ruth and Jim Nicholas, Sue Hodges, Neville Gare, Tom Barry, Sandy Blair, Juliet Ramsay, Angie McGowan, Simon Cubit, David and Linda Young, Jeannette Hope, Alec Costin, and Neen Pendergast for hospitality and conversation about cultural heritage issues in the Alps. Daniel Berthold-Bond, Jonathan Kahn, and Mark Lytle at Bard led me to helpful U.S. references.

1. See especially Donald Worster (1992) on the contested sacred space of the Black Hills, and Richard White's (1991) "The Imagined West" for examples of this kind of analysis.

2. See David Maynard (this volume) for a discussion of "metaphoric rusticity."

3. See especially Helms (1893), King (1959), and Edgar (1969) for critical reports on grazing on Kosciusko. For a summary of current political tensions, see Clark (1992).

4. For example, in Kosciusko National Park unsightly steel walkways have been installed to protect the flora.

5. I use the term to refer to a variety of urban-based ecological perspectives. See Frawley (1992) for a typology that does not collapse the range of variation in the categories of Australian conservation and environmentalism.

6. These are areas designated by the park management plan as those of Outstanding natural resources, Natural values and/or Special scientific values (National Parks and Wildlife Service 1988: 57).

7. The interpretive lead was provided by D. J. Mulvaney in his production of an occasional papers volume for the Australian Academy of Humanities in which Griffiths's paper appears. For Mulvaney's perspective, see his introduction to the symposium on cultural heritage of the Australian Alps

(1992). He is distressed by the ranked dichotomy between natural and historical heritage and the dominance given to the natural. Mulvaney (1992: 14) notes that an earlier conference on the "Scientific Significance of the Australian Alps" in 1988 was intended to consider cultural significance and yet revealed a limited understanding of the meaning of culture in the resulting edited volume of papers (see Good [1989]).

8. Graduate students in environmental studies have been surprised in my anthropology of place seminar when I have asked them to identify their own (often uncritical) alignment with "environmentalism" as a situated ideology; their scientific and botanically weighted training often does not invite them to situate environmental studies within a sociocultural context. The graduate program was conceptualized with requirements in the social and interpretive courses, such as environmental ethics and third world development, to encourage students to understand Gill's claim about the inextricability of conceptions of nature with what he calls society.

9. A symbolic construction, the Dreaming is explained by Povinelli (1995: 509) as "the given condition of the human and natural world established in the ancestral past."

10. For a current history of environmental change on Kosciusko, see Dodson et al. (1994) who pay attention also to ecological variations in a single locale over time.

11. Such as diprotodons that vanished at least 35000 years ago.

12. For a brief and eloquent environmental history of European and Aboriginal management of Australia's lands, see Rolls (1994).

13. Griffiths (1991: 88) argues for the "broadening of our historical perception of landscape from isolated sites to whole cultural patterns." See also Ken Taylor (1992: 61) who reminds us that historical and social values inhere in the landscape; such associative values cannot be merely preserved in "isolated sites preserved as museum pieces" but must also be preserved as ongoing ways of living. Cultural heritage, as the "new banner" (Griffiths 1991: 101) runs the risk of ossification also.

14. See Johnson (1974) and Jameson (1987) for contrasting perspectives. See Dover (1994) and Frawley (1992) for perspectives from environmental history.

15. Frawley (1992) outlines the evolution of these distinctions in Australian environmentalism.

16. Similarly, historic sites often invite the English parkland image, flattening history and homogenizing diverse landscapes. See Egloff (1988) for a plea for the preservation of historic social landscapes that are linked to an Australian national identity, rather than from a derivatively high English tra-

dition; she uses Port Arthur in Tasmania as a positive illustration of "a blurred penal settlement with a turn of the century rural village overlay" (1988: 221) that enables us to witness a landscape's ongoing history, "a plethora of history" (1988: 224).

17. His "bushman," though, is not generic, but male (see Schaffer 1988). Cattlemen tend to use the term "country" rather than bush (or land) (Hodges 1993: 78).

18. White (1981: 102) continues the analysis linking city and bush to Kipling's contrast between metropolis and fringes of empire.

19. For a detailed comparative cultural analysis of an Australian culture of nationalism, see Kapferer (1988). Kapferer writes that "the nation for Australians is the exemplification of nature as the cosmically unifying principle" where suffering and conflict derive from going against the natural (1988: 17).

20. See also White 1981: 132, Schaffer 1988: 115, and Kapferer 1988, *passim.*

21. See Hughes's (1994) "Spirit of Bush Prevails over Hard Times." Hughes suggests that determination and an independent spirit passed down from the pioneers of Victoria's rugged high country is helping Corryong to survive.

22. For example, on one property where I conducted research the loss of the leases would mean a total reduction of sixty to seventy cattle out of a total of five hundred, two hundred of which are run on the lease to reduce pressure on non-leasehold property.

23. See Nathan (1993) for the judgement.

24. Similarly the centralizing hierarchy of the United States legal system "exalts national values over local ones" and national parks are mandated to manage "natural" resources at the expense of those community resources that have no formal status under law; these include historical structures, ongoing living traditions, and strong place attachment (Sax 1984: 506).

25. Gare provides a concise summary of the scale of this construction project (1992: 209). Water is passed through seven power stations to produce 5000 million kilowatt hours of electricity. It brought 800 kilometers of roads, 1500 kilometers of tracks, sixteen large dams, plus smaller ones, 145 kilometers of tunnels, two large pumping stations, over 80 kilometers of aqueducts, and hundreds of kilometers of high-tension power transmission lines. Gare notes that at the peak of construction in 1959 the Scheme's construction involved seven thousand persons. Four new townships were created just outside the Park, and one within.

26. In Australia's island state, the Tasmanian Traditional and Recreational Land User Federation affirms a cultural frontier tradition, asserts a strong

tie to the land, and works to mediate the tension between center and periphery (Cubit 1991). A diverse group, "they all had one thing in common, a concern that land use decisions by land managing agencies were affecting their lifestyles and cultural heritage"; they sought political engagement, a legislative watchdog role, involvement in community organizations, and a commitment to traditional use and recreation on public lands (Cubit 1991: 2). As Simon Cubit has noted, the World Heritage Area Management Plan for Tasmania has excluded European cultural landscapes from its understanding of landscapes and perpetuates the notion of wilderness as empty (1992).

27. Most recently the high country community has responded proactively to the scientific community in empirical terms working towards techniques for measuring and evaluating the sustainability of a high country operation. Central here is an initiative "which is farmer led," called Project F.A.R.M.E.R. (Farmer Analysis of Research, Management and Environmental Resources). Ecological monitoring through computer packages together with production and financial information on an individual property basis is central to Project F.A.R.M.E.R.

28. Widely circulated and displayed, the volume was also distributed to the schools.

REFERENCES

Alexander, Donald. 1990. "Bioregionalism: Science or Sensibility?" *Environmental Ethics* 12: 161–73.

Ansley, Bruce. 1994. "High Country Sell-out." *New Zealand Listener*, July 16–22: 18–25.

Ansley, Bruce. 1995. "Rolling Out the Red Carpet." *New Zealand Listener*, May 13–20: 18–23.

Badone, Ellen. 1992. "The Construction of National Identity in Brittany and Quebec." *American Ethnologist* 19: 806–17.

Batteau, Allen W. 1990. *The Invention of Appalachia*. Tucson: The University of Arizona Press.

Clark, E. 1992. "Alpine Grazing: a Tale of Two States." *Les Alpes Australiennes: Revue de Géographie Alpine* LXXX (2–3): 129–55.

Cohen, Anthony. 1982. "Belonging: The Experience of Culture." In Anthony Cohen, ed., *Belonging: Identity and Social Organisation in British Rural Cultures*. Manchester: Manchester University Press. 1–17.

Cubit, Simon. 1991. "Understanding Traditional Recreational Land Users." Paper written for the Legislative Council Select Committee on Public Land Usage.

Cubit, Simon. 1992. "Who Goes There!—Traditional Recreation and the World Heritage Area." *The Tasmanian Naturalist*, October: 10–13.

Dodson, J. R., T. De Salis, C. A. Myers, and A. J. Sharp. 1994. "A Thousand Years of Environmental Change and Human Impact in the Alpine Zone at Mt. Kosciusko, New South Wales. *Australian Geographer* 25(1): 77–87.

Dominy, Michèle D. 1993a. "'Lives Were Always, Here': The Inhabited Landscape of the New Zealand High Country." *Anthropological Forum* 6: 567–85.

———. 1993b. "Photojournalism, Anthropology and Ethnographic Authority." *Cultural Anthropology* 8: 317–37.

———. 1995. "White Settler Assertions of Native Status." *American Ethnologist* 22: 358–74.

Dovers, Stephen. 1994. "Australian Environmental History: Introduction, Review and Principles." In S. Dovers, ed., *Australian Environmental History: Essays and Cases*. Melbourne: Oxford University Press. 2–19.

Edgar, Grahame. 1969. "Report to the Honourable T. L. Lewis, M.L.A., Minister for Lands, on Investigations into Controlled Grazing and Longer Term Leases in the Kosciusko National Park." Unpublished Manuscript.

Egloff, Juliet. 1988. "Port Arthur: A Nineteenth Century Landscape, Part 2." *Landscape Australia* 3: 221–24.

Fairburn, Miles. 1989. *The Ideal Society and its Enemies: The Foundation of Modern New Zealand Society, 1850–1900*. Auckland: Auckland University Press.

Flannery, Timothy Fridtjof. 1994. *The Future Eaters: An Ecological History of the Australasian Lands and People*. Chatswood, NSW, Australia: Reed.

Frawley, Kevin. 1992. "A 'Green' Vision: The Evolution of Australian Environmentalism." In Kay Anderson and Fay Gale, eds., *Inventing Places: Studies in Cultural Geography*. Melbourne, VIC: Longman Cheshire Pty. Ltd. 215–34.

Gare, Neville. 1992. "The Snowy Mountains Scheme." *Les Alpes Australiennes: Revue de Géographie Alpine* LXXX(2–3): 201–25.

Gill, Nicholas. 1994. "The Cultural Politics of Resource Management: The Case of Bushfires in a Conservation Reserve." *Australian Geographical Studies* 32: 224–40.

Gomez-Pompa, Arturo, and Andrea Kaus. 1992. "Taming the Wilderness Myth." *BioScience* 42: 271–79.

Good, Roger, ed. 1989. *The Scientific Significance of the Australian Alps*. Canberra: Australian Alps National Parks Liaison Committee.

Good, Roger. 1992. *Kosciusko Heritage: The Conservation Significance of*

Kosciusko National Park. Hurstville, New South Wales: National Parks and Wildlife Service.

Graber, Linda H. 1976. *Wilderness as Sacred Space.* Washington D.C.: Association of American Geographers, Monograph Series, No. 8.

Grenier, Philippe. 1992. "Introduction." *Les Alpes Australiennes: Revue de Géographie Alpine* LXXX(2–3): 10–36.

Griffiths, T. 1991. "History and Natural History: Conservation Movements in Conflict?" In D. J. Mulvaney, ed., *The Humanities and the Australian Environment.* Occasional Paper No. 11. Australian Academy of Humanities. 87–109.

Hancock, W. K. 1972. *Discovering Monaro: A Study of Man's Impact on his Environment.* Cambridge: Cambridge University Press.

Handler, Richard. 1994. "Romancing the Low: Anthropology vis-à-vis Cultural Studies vis-à-vis Popular Culture." *Polar: Political and Legal Anthropology Review* 17(2): 1–6.

Helms, R. 1893. "Report on the Grazing Leases of the Mount Kosciusko Plateau." *New South Wales Agricultural Gazette* 4: 530–31.

Hepworth, John. 1987. "The Dancing Valley of the Mountain Horsemen." In Bryan Jameson's *Movement at the Station: The Revolt of the Mountain Cattlemen.* Sydney: William Collins Pty Ltd. 133–41.

Hodges, S. 1992. "Interpreting the Australian Alps." *Les Alpes Australiennes: Revue de Géographie Alpine* LXXX(2–3): 97–126.

———. 1993. "A Sense of Place." In Don Garden, ed., *Created Landscapes: Historians and the Environment.* Carlton, Victoria: The History Institute. 73–88.

Hughes, Gary. 1994. "Spirit of the Bush Prevails Over Hard Times." *The Age,* May 30: 1.

International NGO Consultation on the Mountain Agenda, 1995, Third Annual Report (advanced text) on Agenda 21, Chapter 13, Sustainable Mountain Development, to the United Nations Commission on Sustainable Development, April.

Jameson, Bryan. 1987. *Movement at the Station: The Revolt of the Mountain Cattlemen.* Sydney: William Collins Pty Ltd.

Johnson, Dick. 1974. *The Alps at the Crossroads.* Melbourne: Victorian National Parks Association.

Kapferer, Bruce. 1988. *Legends of People, Myths of State: Violence, Intolerance, and Political Culture in Sri Lanka and Australia.* Washington D.C.: Smithsonian Institution Press.

King, H. W. H. 1959. "Transhumant Grazing in the Snow Belt of New South Wales." *The Australian Geographer* 8(4): 129–40.

Levanthes, Louise E. and David Robert Austen. 1985. "The Land Where the Murray Flows." *National Geographic* 168 (2 [August]): 252–78.

Levine, Lawrence. 1988. *Highbrow/Lowbrow: The Emergence of Cultural Hierarchy in America*. Cambridge: Harvard University Press.

Lines, William J. 1991. *Taming the Great South Land: A History of the Conquest of Nature in Australia*. Berkeley: University of California Press.

Mayor, Federico. 1995. Official Opening by the Director-General UNESCO, to the workshop on World Heritage Convention and Cultural Landscapes, Australia ICOMOS (International Council on Monuments and Sites), Thursday, April 27, Sydney Opera House, Sydney.

Mulvaney, John. 1992. "The Alpine Cultural Heritage in Perspective." In Babette Scougall, ed., *Cultural Heritage of the Australian Alps*. Canberra: Australian Alps Liaison Committee. 9–17.

Nathan, Judge. 1993. "Tom Groggin Station Judgment." *Voice of the Mountains: Journal of the Mountain Cattlemen's Association of Victoria* 16: 61–64.

National Parks and Wildlife Service. 1988. *Kosciusko National Park Plan of Managment*. Second edition. Sydney: National Parks and Wildlife Service of New South Wales.

Parsons, James J. 1985. "Views and Opinions: On 'Bioregionalism' and 'Watershed Consciousness.'" *The Professional Geographer* 37(1): 1–6.

Povinelli, Elizabeth A. 1995. "Do Rocks Listen? The Cultural Politics of Apprehending Australian Aboriginal Labor." *American Anthropologist* 97: 505–18.

Pyne, Stephen. 1991. *Burning Bush: A Fire History of Australia*. Sydney: Allen and Unwin.

Rolls, Eric. 1994. "More a New Planet than a New Continent." In S. Dovers, ed., *Australian Environmental History: Essays and Cases*. Melbourne: Oxford University Press. 22–36.

Rose, Deborah Bird. 1995. "Nourishing Terrains of Aboriginal Australia." Paper presented to a workshop on Indigenous Cultural Landscapes, Australia ICOMOS, at the Australian Heritage Commission, Canberra, February 21.

Sax, Joseph L. 1984. "Do Communities Have Rights? The National Parks as a Laboratory of New Ideas." *University of Pittsburgh Law Review* 45: 499–511.

Schaffer, Kay. 1988. *Women and the Bush: Forces of Desire in the Australian Cultural Tradition*. Cambridge: Cambridge University Press.

Strathern, Marilyn. 1982. "The Village as an Idea: Constructs of Village-ness in Elmdon, Essex." In Anthony Cohen, ed., *Belonging: Identity and Social*

Organisation in British Rural Cultures. Manchester: Manchester University Press. 247–77.

Taussig, Michael. 1992. *The Nervous System*. New York: Routledge.

Taylor, Ken. 1992. "Cultural Values in Natural Areas." In Babette Scougall, ed., *Cultural Heritage of the Australian Alps*. Canberra: Australian Alps Liaison Committee. 55–66.

Ward, Russel. 1993. *The Australian Legend*. Melbourne: Oxford University Press, 1958.

White, Richard. 1981. *Inventing Australia: Images and Identity 1688–1980*. St. Leonards, Australia: Allen & Unwin.

———. 1991. *"It's Your Misfortune and None of My Own": A History of the American West*. Norman: University of Oklahoma Press.

Worster, Donald. 1992. *Under Western Skies: Nature and History in the American West*. New York: Oxford University Press.

CONTRIBUTORS

Barbara Ching is Assistant Professor of English at The University of Memphis. She has published several articles on the construction of cultural hierarchies and is writing a book on hard country music for Oxford University Press.

Gerald W. Creed is Assistant Professor of Anthropology at Hunter College and the Graduate School of the City University of New York. He has conducted extensive fieldwork in rural Bulgaria spanning the communist and postcommunist eras. His book on agrarian change in a Bulgarian village will be published by Pennsylvania State University Press in 1997.

Michèle D. Dominy is Professor of Anthropology at Bard College. She has been conducting fieldwork in New Zealand's South Island since 1986 and is currently preparing a monograph on cultural identity and spatiality among high country sheep station families there.

Marc Edelman is Associate Professor of Anthropology at Hunter College and the Graduate School of the City University of New York. He is the author of *Siete décadas de relaciones soviético-latinoamericanas* (Mexico: Centro Latinoamericano de Estudios Estratégicos, 1987) and *The Logic of the Latifundio: The Large Estates of Northwestern Costa Rica since the Late Nineteenth Century* (Stanford University Press, 1992).

Aaron A. Fox is Assistant Professor of Anthropology at the University of Washington and a professional country musician. He has published several articles on country music, and his forthcoming book is an ethnographic study of language, music, and emotion in a small Texas town.

Beatrice Guenther is Assistant Professor of French and German at the College of William and Mary. She has published on Jovette Marchessault's and Michèle Lalonde's plays. Her book, entitled *The Poetics of Death: The Short Prose of Kleist and Balzac* will be published by the State University of New York Press in 1996.

Aisha Khan is Assistant Professor in the Department of Africana Studies and the Department of Anthropology at SUNY at Stony Brook. She is co-editor of *Women Anthropologists: A Biographical Dictionary* (1988). Her research focuses on social inequality and identity construction in the Caribbean. She is currently preparing her book manuscript, *Purity, Piety, and Power: Ideology and Identity in the Indo-Caribbean*, for publication.

Susan H. Lees is Professor of Anthropology at Hunter College of the City University of New York. She specializes in ecological and economic anthropology and has published extensively on power relations in irrigated agriculture. She has engaged in field research in Mexico, Peru, Brazil, and Israel.

William J. Maxwell is Assistant Professor of English and an affiliate of the Unit for Criticism and Interpretive Theory at the University of Illinois, Urbana-Champaign. He has published on multiculturalism in the university, the subterranean ties between proletarian literature and the Harlem Renaissance, and the difficult marriage of rap music and postmodern theory.

David Maynard is currently writing a book on the politics of cultural identity in Brittany. His research interests also include forms of domination and resistance in late capitalist societies, ethnoregionalist political movements in Western Europe, and the political economy of the inner city in the United States.

Elizabeth A. Sheehan teaches anthropology at American University. She has published articles on the public role of intellectuals and universities in Ireland as well as an article on Victorian clitoridectomy. She is currently working on a study of women and violence in the Catholic Church.

INDEX